I0795659

POSTCARD HISTORY SERIES

Greater Rochester

A CENTURY OF PROGRESS

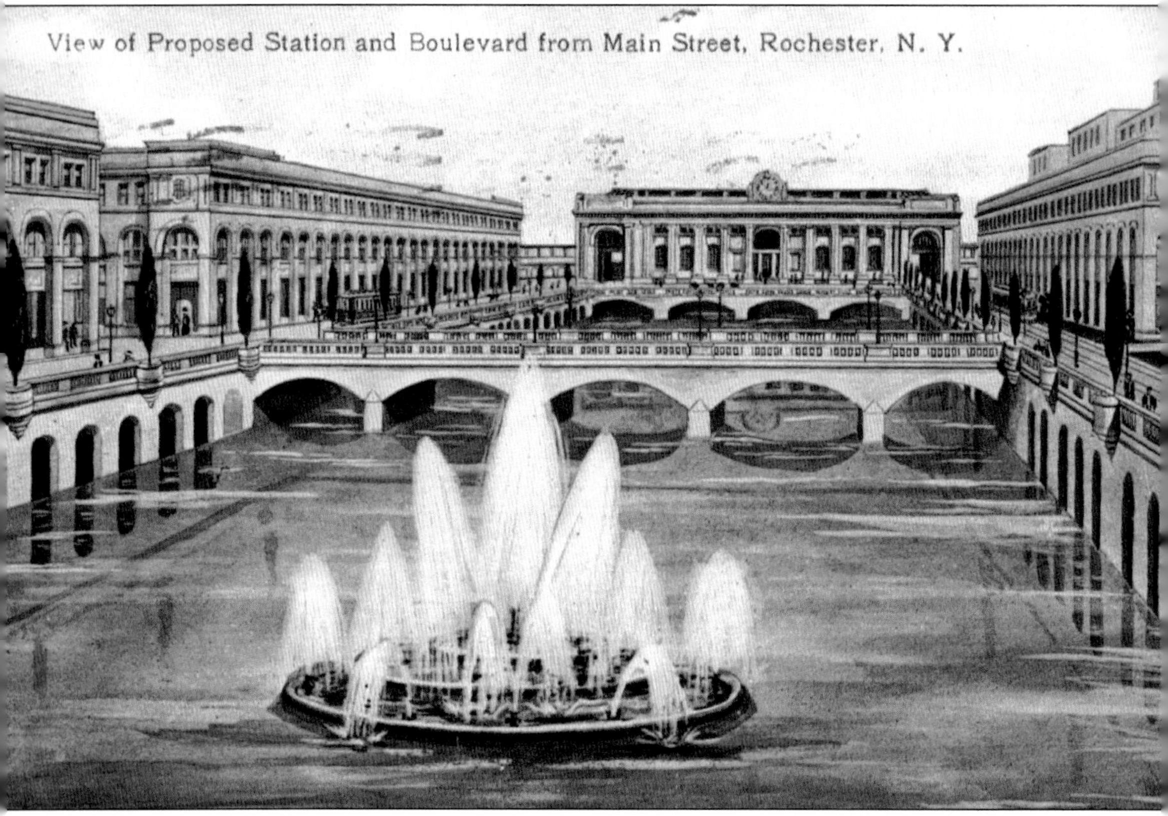

Bold civic visions of things to come were a favorite subject for postcards. This proposed boulevard, encompassing the Main Street Bridge with a substantial railroad station in the distance, never came to pass. Architects were fascinated with the neoclassical influences of the Chicago World's Fair, which may explain the excessive use of arches depicted in this postcard sent in 1911.

POSTCARD HISTORY SERIES

Greater Rochester

A CENTURY OF PROGRESS

Michael Leavy

ARCADIA PUBLISHING

ISBN 978-0-7385-1143-6

Published by Arcadia Publishing
Charleston, South Carolina

Printed in the United States of America

Library of Congress Catalog Card Number: 2002111905

For all general information contact Arcadia Publishing at:
Telephone 843-853-2070
Fax 843-853-0044
E-mail sales@arcadiapublishing.com
For customer service and orders:
Toll-Free 1-888-313-2665

Visit us on the Internet at www.arcadiapublishing.com

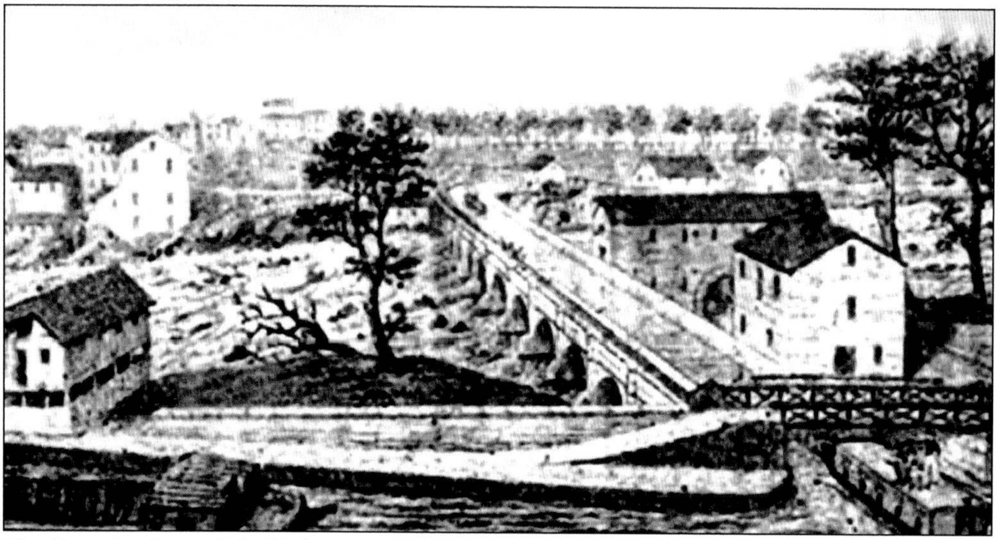

The Erie Canal wended whichever way the political winds blew. By grabbing it from other towns that fought for its right of way, Rochester's founders unleashed the industrial revolution upon their budding town in the broadest forms. The energy and potential is evident in this early etching of the first aqueduct to cross the Genesee River at Rochester. Built in 1823 of sandstone, it quickly began to leak and crumble. Rochesterians, barely out of their rustic pioneer days, quickly built a new one so sturdy it would later support a subway system and platform to carry Broad Street. Passengers gliding over the new aqueduct would gaze at the crumbling arches of its predecessor, a romantic ruin that showed nothing could slow the progress of this "Young Lion of the West."

Contents

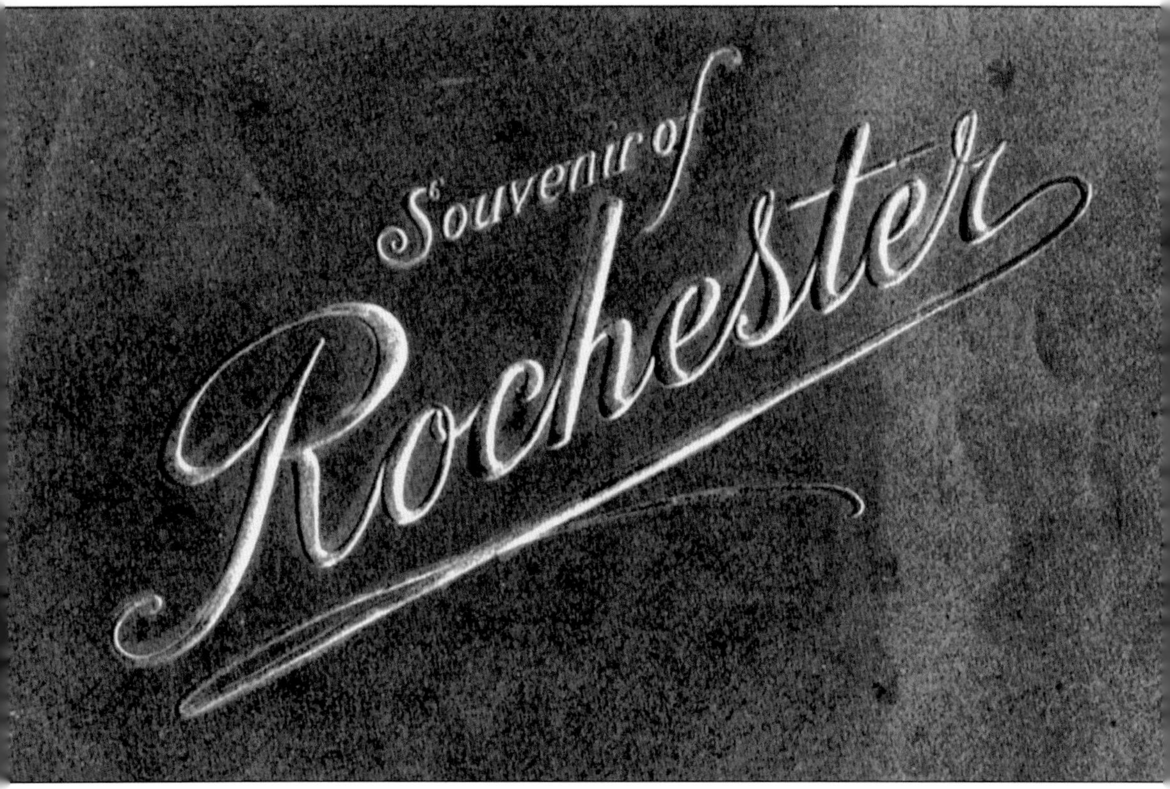

Amazing civic accomplishments came to Rochester one after the other. Professionals were brought in to record them in souvenir forms to lure businesses and institutions to this growing city by the falls. Using adjustable lenses that kept a building's perspective straight, photographers took stunning photographs of the city's glittering architectural delights. Photographers had the power to actually close off a street and empty it of people and vehicles so their images would be uncluttered. Pictured is the cover of a *c.* 1900 souvenir booklet. The booklet's original images, used for postcards (many of which are included here), have not been published in over a century.

Introduction

Once, during casual conversation, an associate pulled a piece of film from his wallet. Flexing it between my fingers, I aimed it at the light. The associate told me it was an end cut off a roll of film that went on the first moon landing. As I handed it back, I saw that his words had raised goose bumps on my arm. He added that he was involved in Kodak's Apollo project and was the first man to see the images of the moon as they emerged during processing.

His words made me realize, as never before, just how important photography is to Rochester. It is to Rochesterians what baseball is to Cooperstown and beer is to Milwaukee. There is something in the water that makes us not simply glance at photographs the way others might but to quietly study them. Subconsciously, the play of light and dark in images makes us moody.

We are creatures of a wonderful indoctrination brought on by our being the "Image Center of the World." Ever since artists and chemists began sprinkling treated salts and starches on emulsion-smeared plates in hopes they would record light, we have been at the forefront of photographic evolution. Whether developing systems to peer into space or plumb the depths of the oceans—or recording chemical electrical flickerings deep inside the human body as if in search of a soul—Rochester has pioneered imaging technologies that have not only improved our lives but also made our imaginations a kind of film ready to record the wonders of our existence.

In our quest for knowledge, we can usually believe what we see. We can record the activity of subatomic energy, watch the random bumpings of genes when some ancient pull in the blood rouses them and sends them on a course that might show us ways to stave off heartache. By looking deep in the universe we actually look back in time, absorbing the vivid colors of stars that died millions of years ago and whose light only reaches us now. It is a good heritage, this imaging culture that sometimes lets us take for granted the stream of silver screen stars that come to Rochester, their Mecca, for awards. Among them have been Katherine Hepburn, Gregory Peck, and Jimmy Stewart. The possibilities of our imaging technologies are endless. They allow us, as Shakespeare's decrepit King Lear cried, ". . .to take upon us the mystery of things as if we were God's spies!"

In light of all this, to regard the postcard as lowly, pedestrian, or inane would be to ignore a rapidly growing sentiment that they are an irresistible slice of Americana. Is the postcard an art form? It certainly used artists like photographers, printers, colorists, engravers, lithographers, illustrators, and even poets. Sadly, many of those who created these little snapshots of our culture did not leave us their names.

To array a fistful of postcards on a table is to set the pageant of history in motion. The history buff has a chatty informer in them. Beyond the artwork and photography, the scribbled messages, often from homesick travelers, let us look into America's heart.

European postcards date back to the 1840s. In 1873, the United States Congress gladly authorized use here. Correspondence could now be sent from the east coast to the west coast for only a penny. It is no wonder postcards became the overwhelming source of communication, worldwide, for generations. Photographers cleaned off their lenses, artists unraveled their rolls of brushes, printers fine-tuned their presses, and across America small wire racks filled with glittering postcards were prominently placed on sale counters.

To the camera-wielding citizens of Greater Rochester, there was nothing ordinary about postcards. Even small surrounding communities like Lima, New York, would produce hundreds of cards. In doing so, they provided us a pictorial history of 19th century small town life. Rochester institutions imported the best photographers to capture and then project to the world the community's accomplishments and matters of civic pride. Proprietors and manufacturers, from bankers to buggy makers, had cards made to advertise their business. Many were satisfied to have the card simply make it across the city, or even into the next neighborhood, as a form of cheap advertising. A range of these postcards, many unique and not published in over a century, are presented here.

Enjoy the nostalgia; the charm and quaintness. But keep a keen eye. Some photographers, while recording their immediate present, captured images that allow us to walk back through 10 million years of evolution.

One

Souvenir

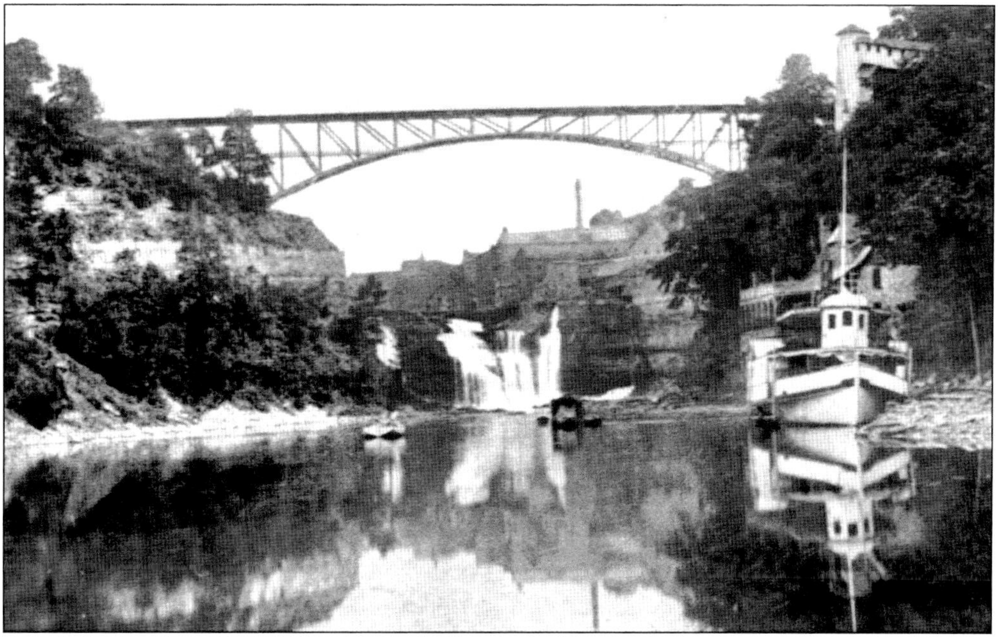

A blend of the scenic and industrial are captured in this 1898 *Souvenir of Rochester* view printed by the Royal Arcanum. A steamboat plies the Genesee at the base of the lower falls, which marked the southern end of river navigation from Lake Ontario. At the upper right is an elevator that lowered guests to the landing, and Glen House visible behind the steamboat. The Driving Park Bridge, a marvel for its time, followed earlier wood and iron spans that either deteriorated or collapsed. Carthage, an early rival to Rochesterville, hoped to make this spot the milling and shipping center for upstate New York. Note the mills around the falls. The collapse of their wooden bridge and routing of the Erie Canal to the south ended their challenge.

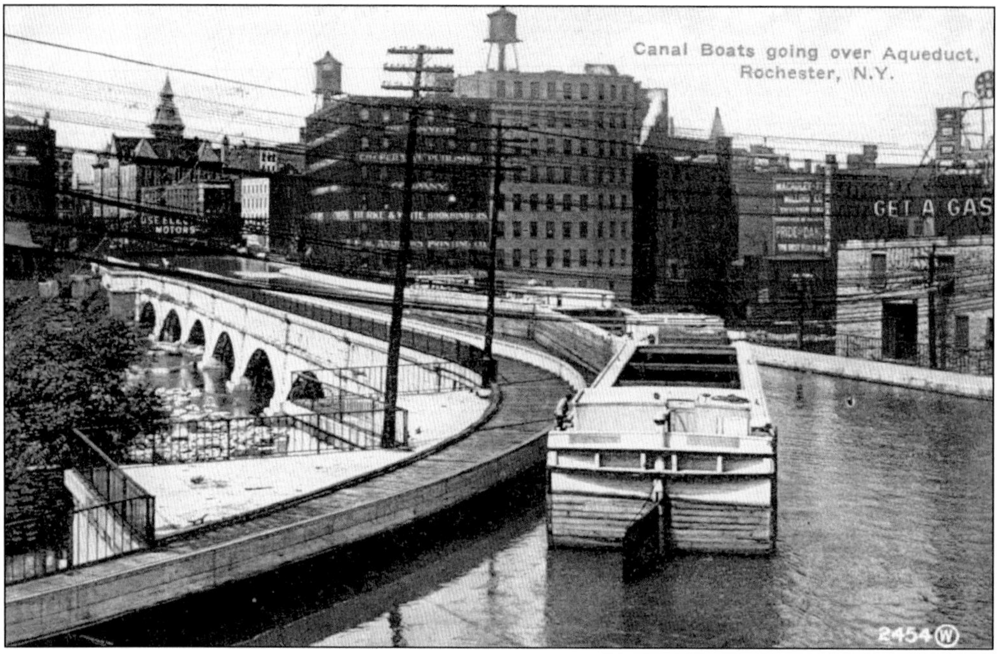

Postmarked May 2, 1913, this hand-colored view of a barge crossing the aqueduct captures the intense industrialization that formed around the canal and river. The quaint folklore surrounding the Erie tends to ignore that it was also a slow-moving sewer, a convenient dump for everything from dead cats, human, and animal waste, to broken furniture. When its current was finally increased to a measly three miles an hour, it only meant it brought disease and stench, along with its needed commerce, that much faster.

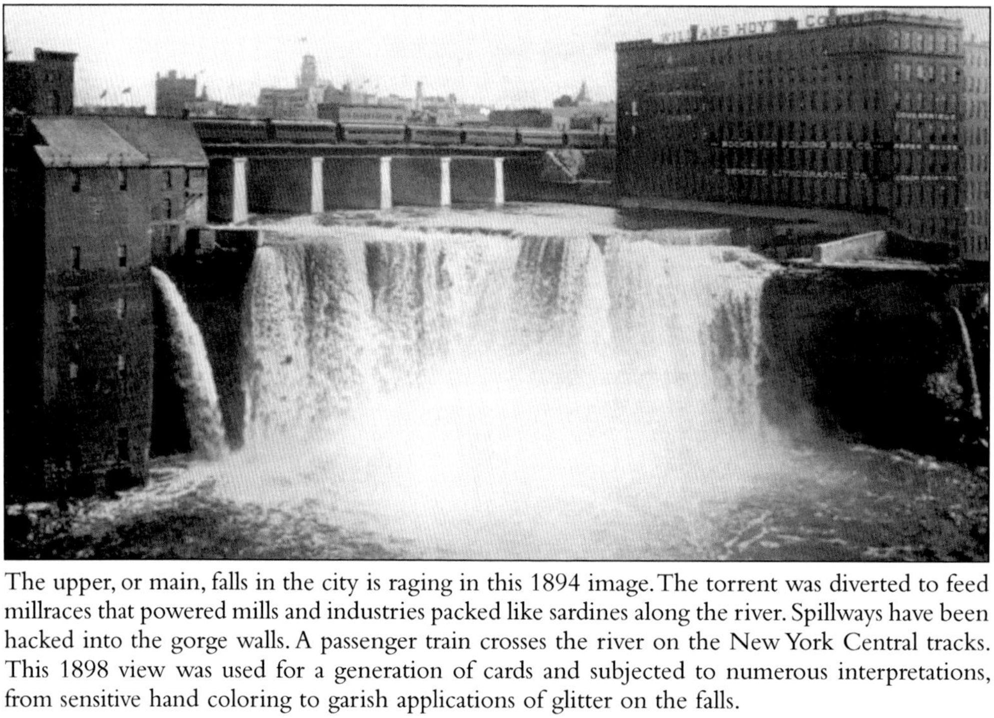

The upper, or main, falls in the city is raging in this 1894 image. The torrent was diverted to feed millraces that powered mills and industries packed like sardines along the river. Spillways have been hacked into the gorge walls. A passenger train crosses the river on the New York Central tracks. This 1898 view was used for a generation of cards and subjected to numerous interpretations, from sensitive hand coloring to garish applications of glitter on the falls.

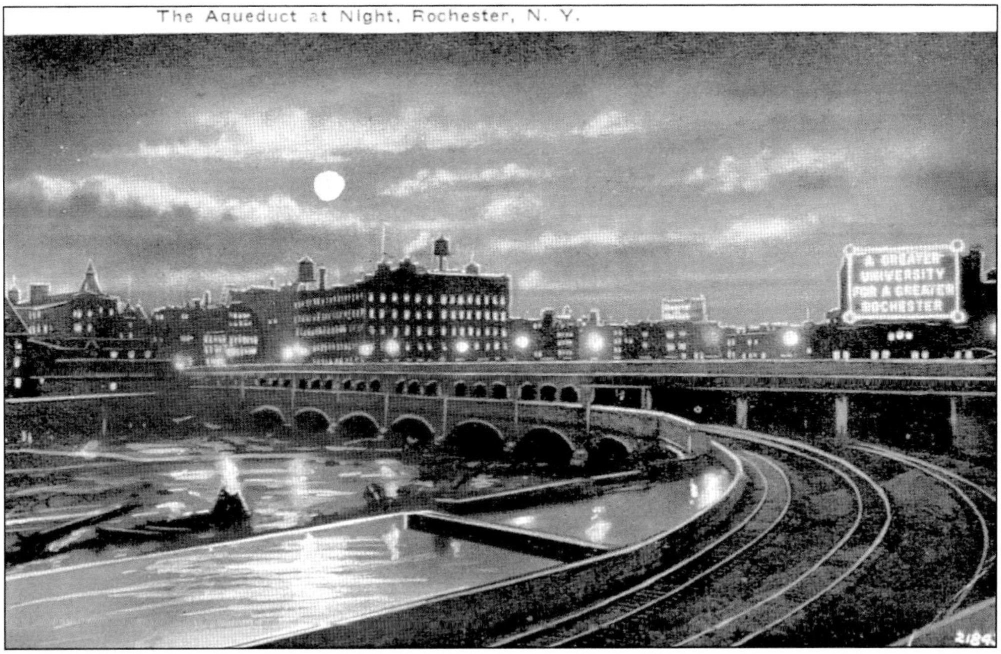

The city shimmers in this moody night-scape offered by Scrantoms, a local retailer. The massive 1842 aqueduct now supports a subway and an upper platform that carries Broad Street over the river. The canal that brought prosperity by cutting shipping costs up to 90 percent has been rerouted around the city. The aqueduct was called "towering" when the city was level with the river. Industrialization has brought the level of the city up well over 60 feet.

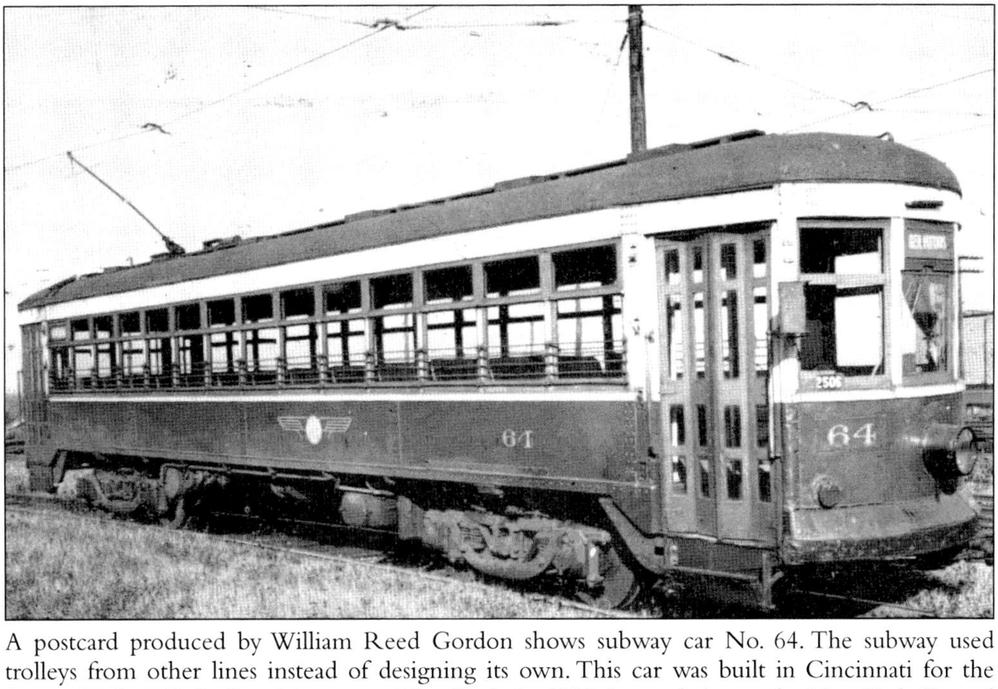

A postcard produced by William Reed Gordon shows subway car No. 64. The subway used trolleys from other lines instead of designing its own. This car was built in Cincinnati for the Rome-Little Falls Railroad in upstate New York. In 1938, it traveled over the New York Central to Rochester to begin subway service.

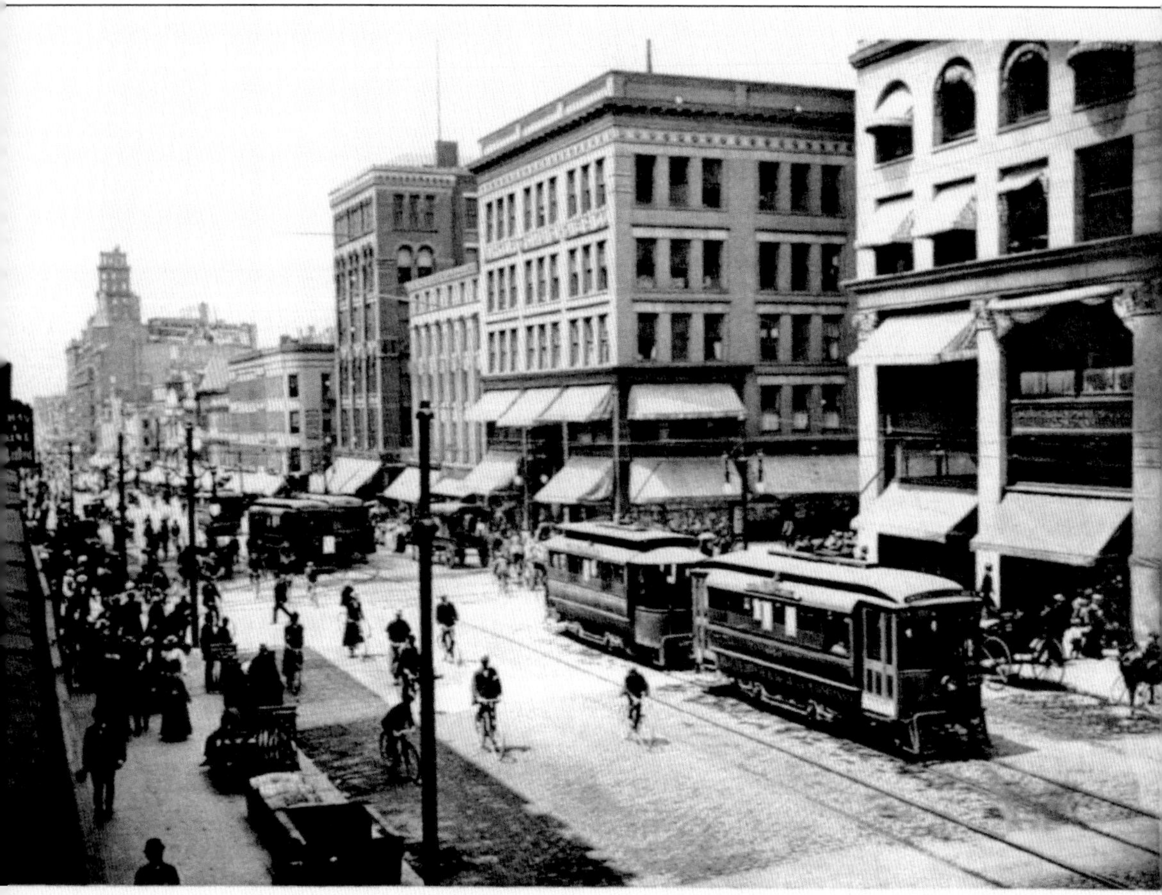

MAIN STREET, EAST, FROM ST. PAUL STREET

This noted city view, published in 1900 by the L.H. Nelson Company for the *c.* 1900 *Souvenir of Rochester* shows Main Street looking west from St. Paul before automobiles. The image was used years after the automobile arrived because of its sense of order and building facades that gave artists large areas to apply their colors.

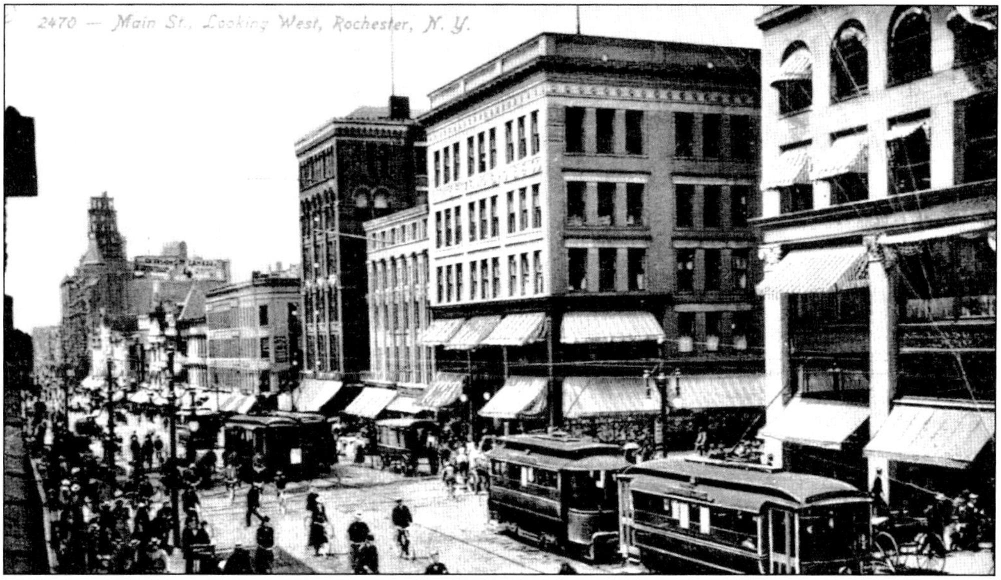

A hand-colored rendering of the adjacent image mailed in 1906 was tastefully produced in Germany. Pains were taken to not obliterate the fine details of the original. An azure-colored sky and brightly striped awnings make a pleasing background for the trolleys that underwent varied color schemes from card to card. The German artist skillfully removed the post just left of center and seamlessly filled in behind it.

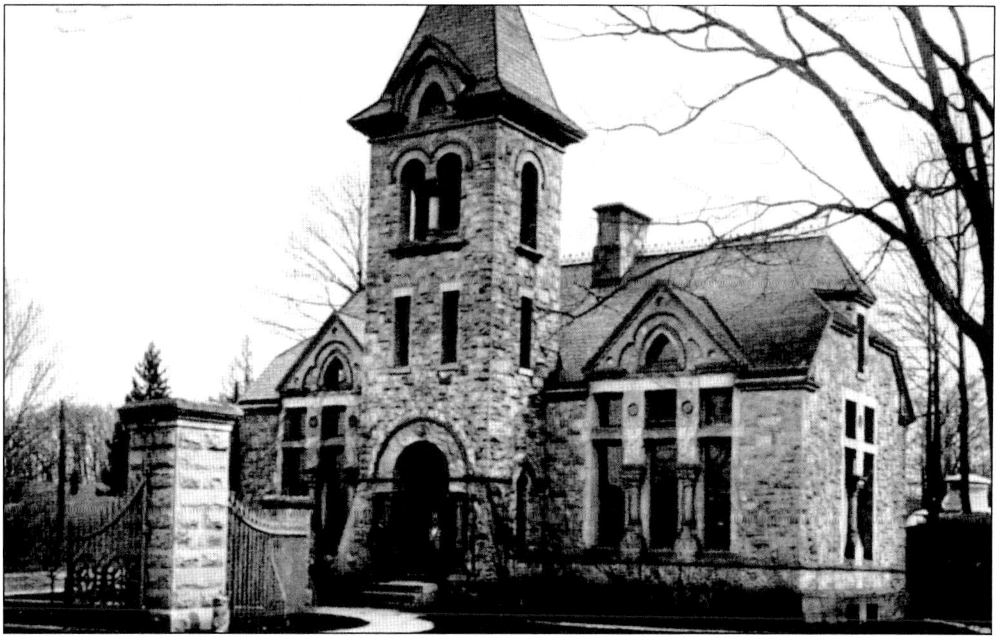

Rochester's parks and cemeteries were important civic enterprises that often gained international recognition. Mount Hope Cemetery, dedicated in 1838, was one of them. It continues to be visited for its statuary and landscaping, as well as its famous buried, among them Susan B. Anthony and Frederick Douglass. This did not stop some artists from altering the appearance of this original 1898 "Entrance to Mount Hope Cemetery" view. The cut stone was sometimes colored brick red. Color sells and the dignity of the gray stone must have seemed too drab to get attention.

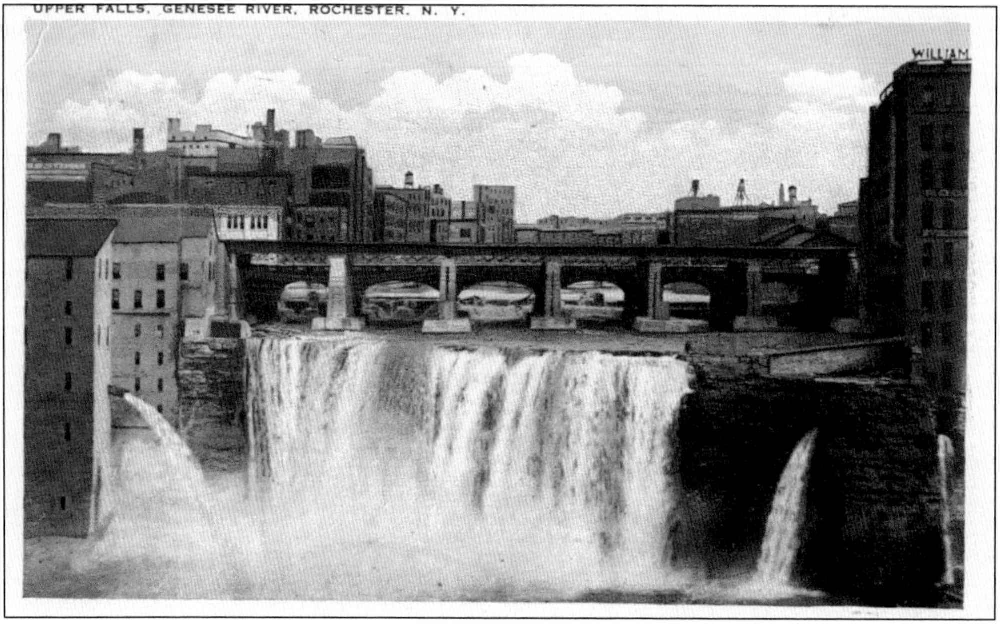

The upper falls of the mighty Genesee is spanned by the New York Central tracks. This is a white-border era card dating to World War I.

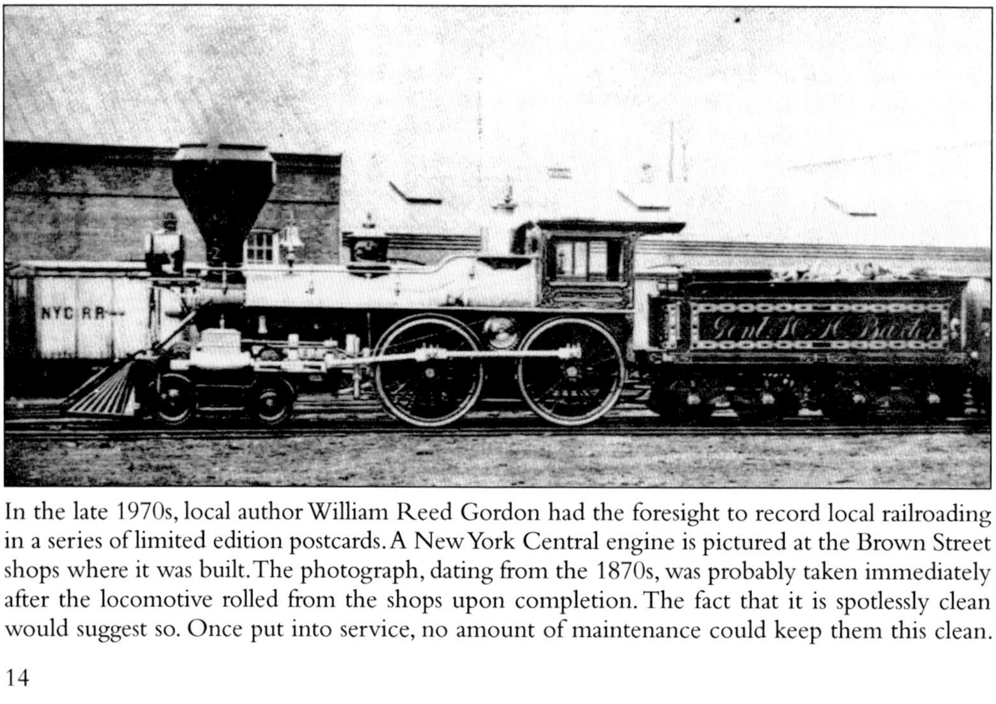

In the late 1970s, local author William Reed Gordon had the foresight to record local railroading in a series of limited edition postcards. A New York Central engine is pictured at the Brown Street shops where it was built. The photograph, dating from the 1870s, was probably taken immediately after the locomotive rolled from the shops upon completion. The fact that it is spotlessly clean would suggest so. Once put into service, no amount of maintenance could keep them this clean.

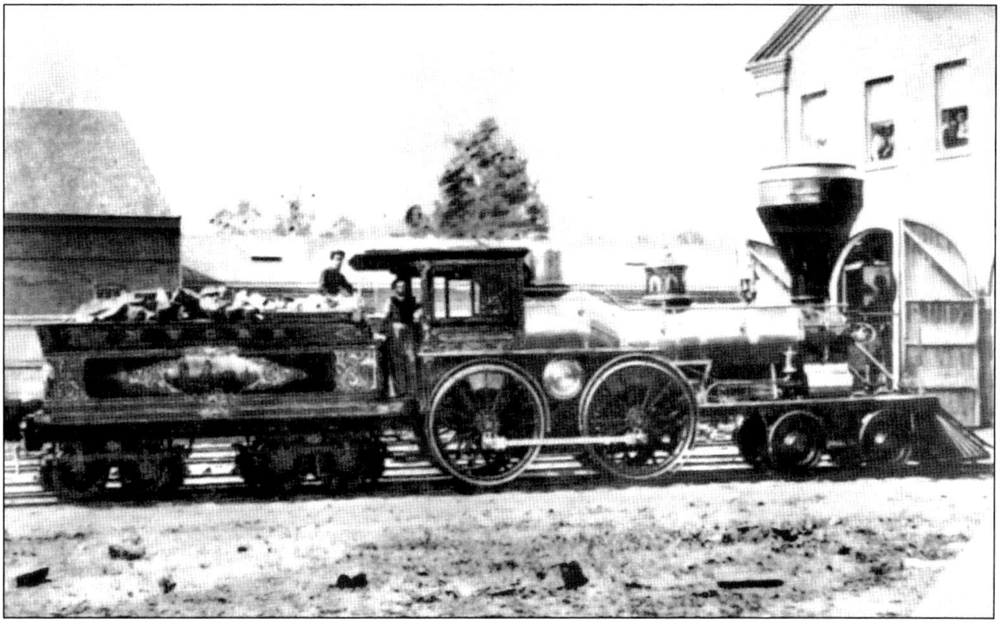

The engine in this Gordon postcard was also built *c.* 1870 at the Rochester Brown Street shops. It is a dazzling example of expert machining and artistry. Brightly painted in red, green, and gold and with hand painted frescos on the tender and headlamp, it was a moving work of art. The boiler, clad in Russian iron, had a shimmering blue cast. Further adornments included polished brass fittings and ornate ironwork.

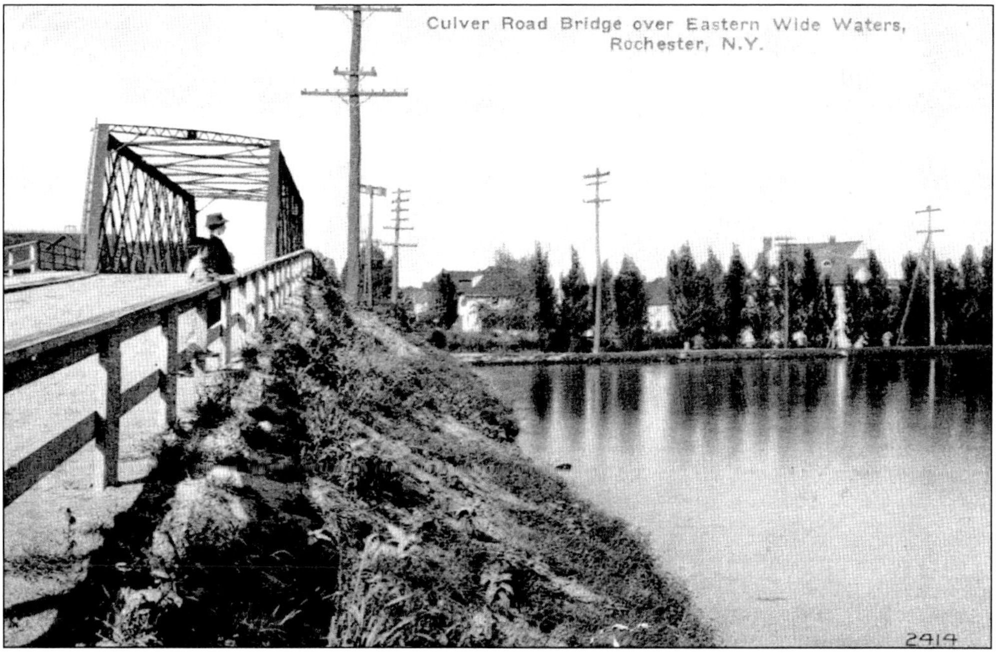

An example of how cards were an inexpensive form of communication is evident in this one sent from Chili, New York, to Thorndale Terrace on the city's west side. They were perhaps 15 miles apart. This restful *c.* 1910 view of the Culver Road Bridge is pictured where it crosses over the Eastern Wide Waters of the Erie Canal in Rochester.

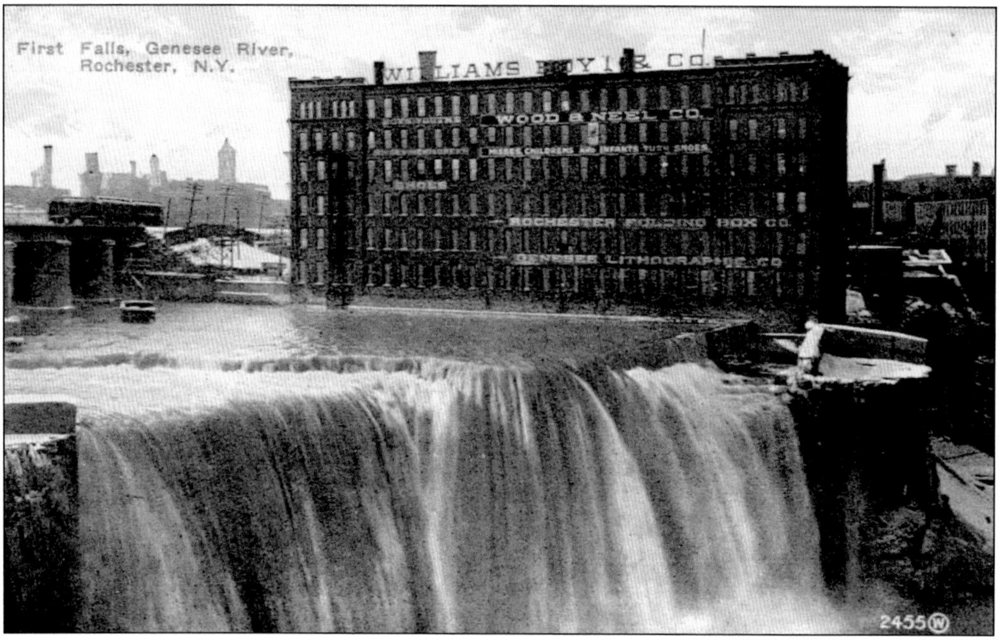

Among the companies housed in the massive brick Williams, Hoyt and Company building were Genesee Lithographic Company, Rochester Folding Box Company, and shoemaker Wood and Neel. This sublime view of the Upper Falls is to the west.

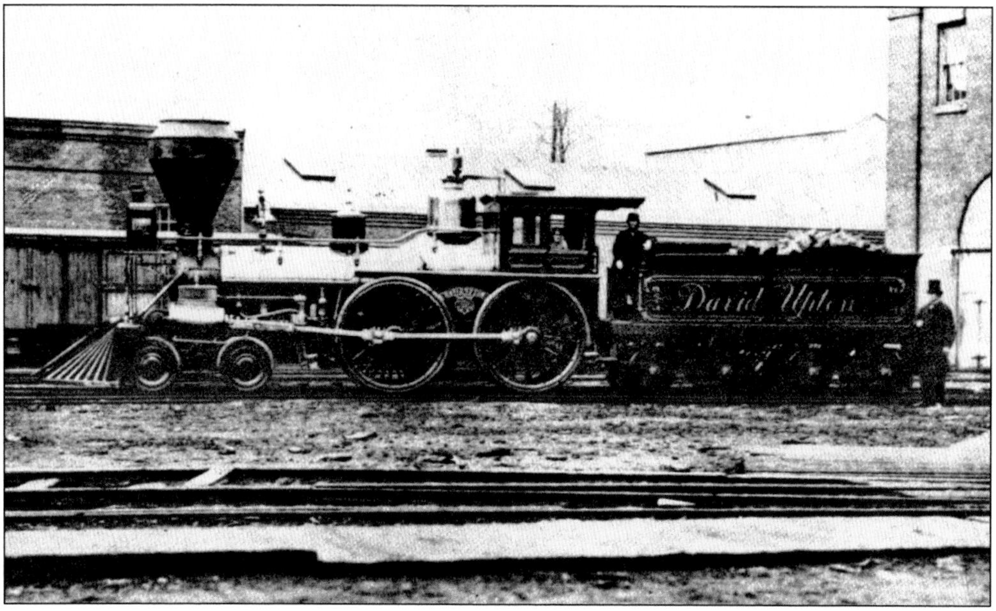

The David Upton 4-4-0 locomotive gets its moment in front of the camera in this *c.* 1870 photograph taken at the Brown Street facilities. Few photographs of early Rochester railroading survive. This engine is a wood burner. Note the large balloon smokestack and wood piled in the tender. Engines were slowly being converted to coal fuel. This is a Gordon postcard.

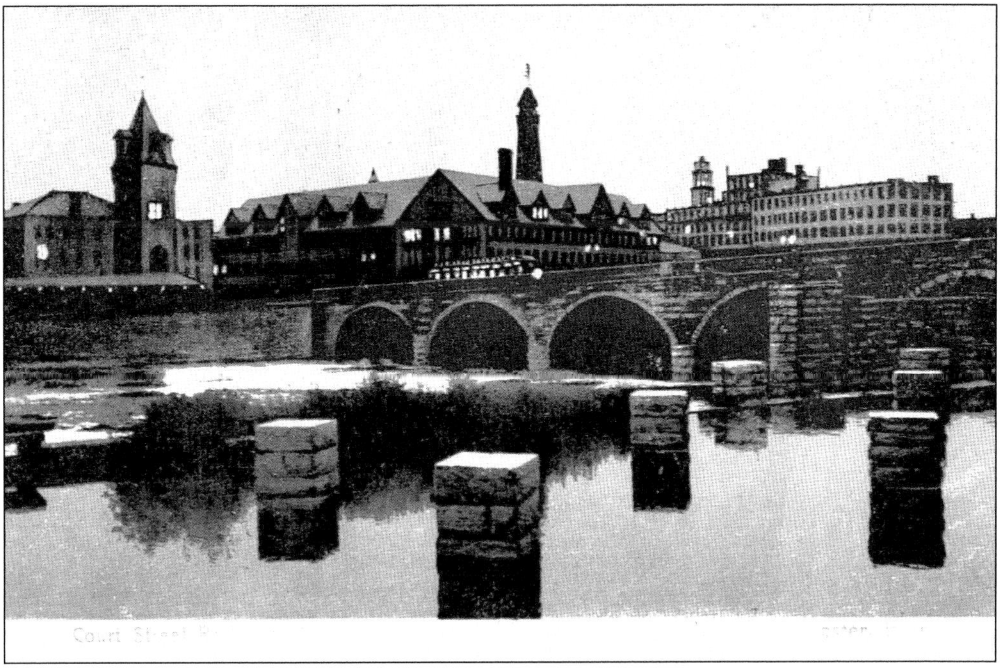

A view of the Court Street Bridge, with the Kimball Tobacco Company illuminated beyond it, shows the skill of a German artist to apply transparent layers of color to turn a daylight exposure into a night scene. The card is postmarked November 5, 1906. It was published by the Rochester News Company and was printed in Dresden, Germany.

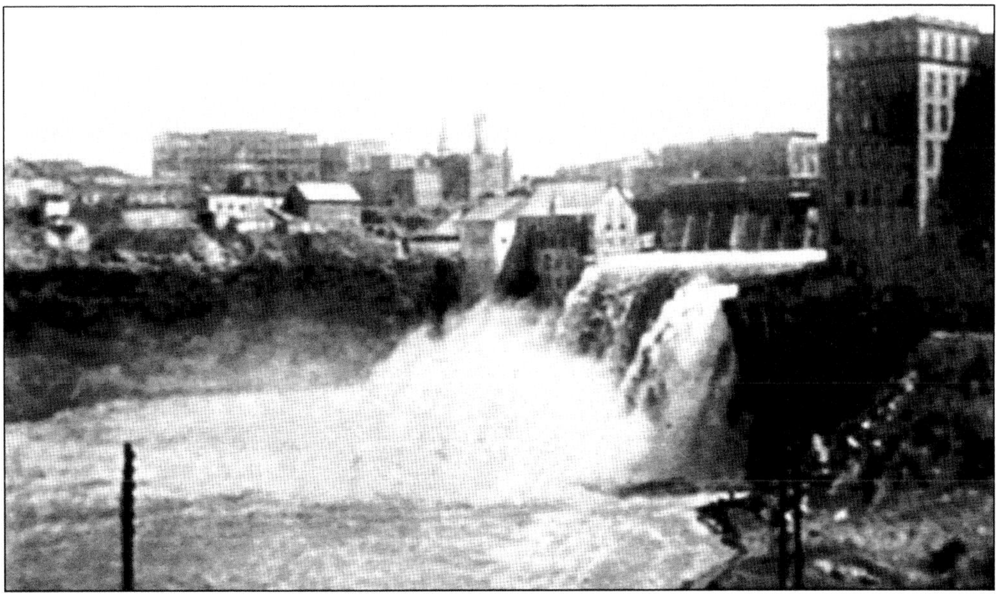

An 1898 souvenir view of the upper falls looking east is grittier and gives a more realistic view of what the area looked like. Beyond those squat mills were rough neighborhoods, illness, pollution, and hard times aplenty in spite of the city's growing prosperity.

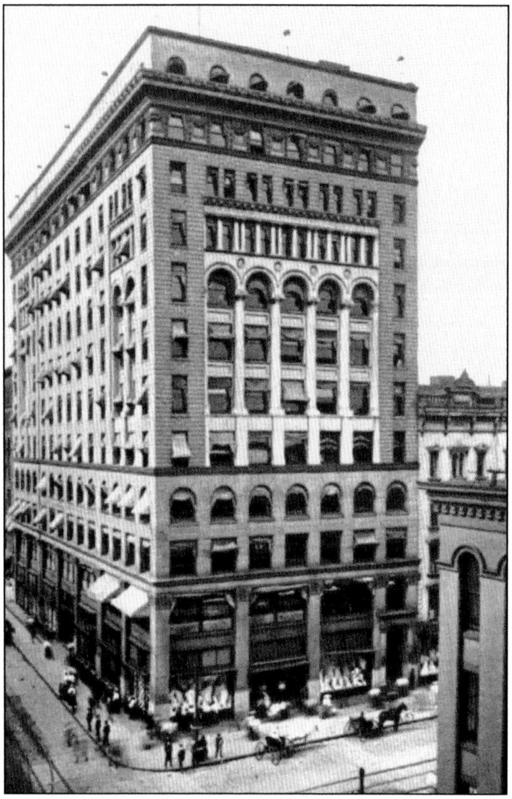

The Granite Building on East Main Street was one of the first to employ a steel frame. The 11-story, granite-clad structure survived a devastating fire and remains in use today. It housed Sibley, Lindsay and Curr, the dominant retailer in western New York with burgeoning retail and wholesale divisions. The owners boasted of 195,841 square feet or 4.5 acres of retail space.

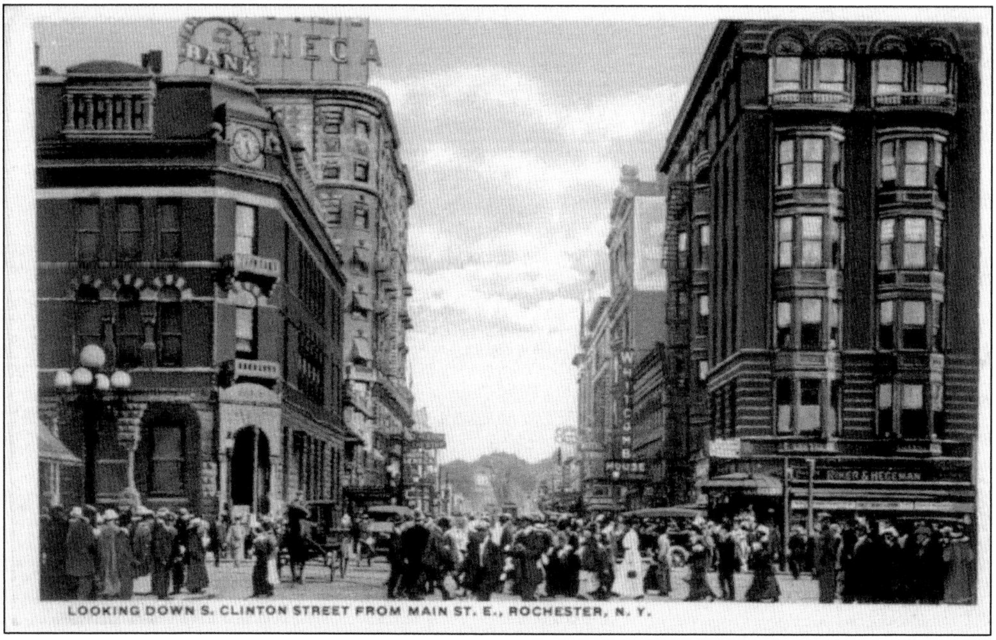

The intersection of East Main and South Clinton is bustling with activity. A multi-globe streetlight adorns the corner on the left.

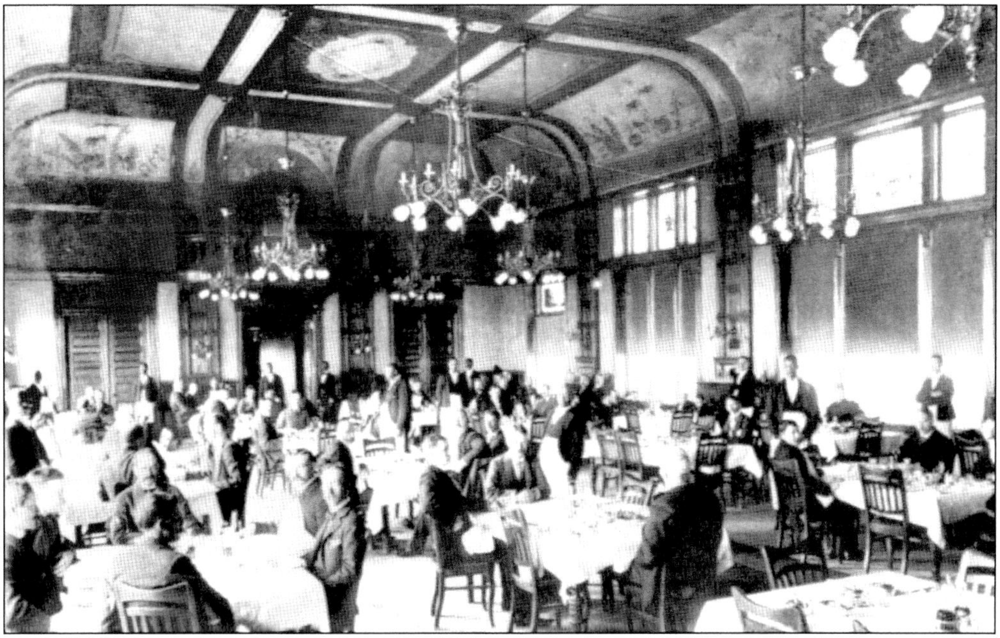

A look of unbridled prosperity fills the tearoom-restaurant in the Granite Building. In this souvenir view, frescoed ceilings and gas chandeliers capture the Victorian elegance of the Gay Nineties. It was a gathering place for local businessmen. This group seems content and ready to push themselves away from their tables, satisfied with their meals and with their own well being.

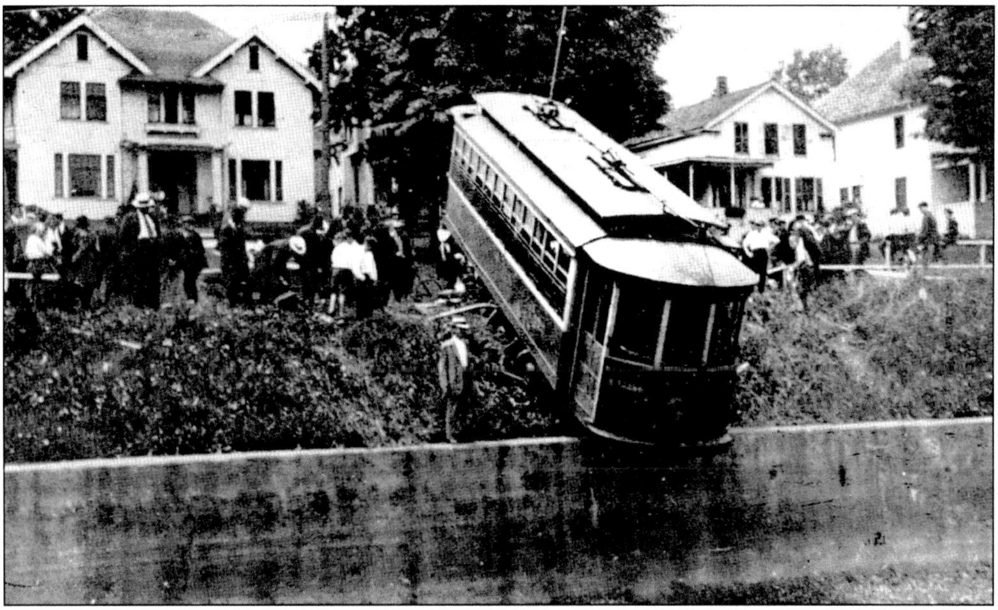

It was a close call for car No. 32 when it derailed along the Erie Canal in 1917. The car would be sent to a Utica line during World War I. This is a William Gordon postcard.

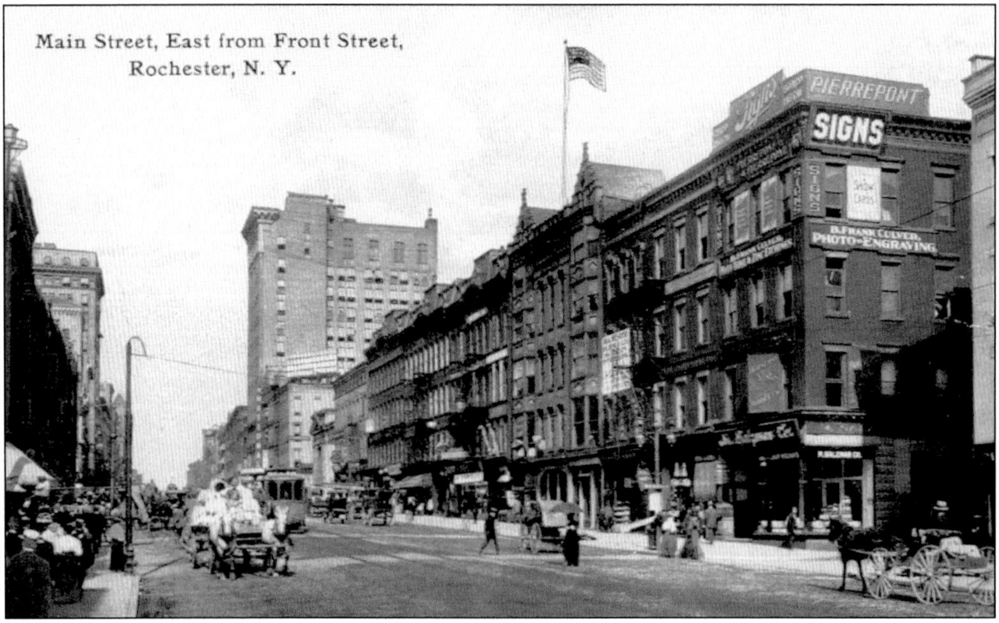

Here is a view looking east up Main Street from Front Street. This row of buildings actually traversed the river along Main Street Bridge. They were unsightly, rickety affairs from the back. Tenants had no qualms about using the river for a dump.

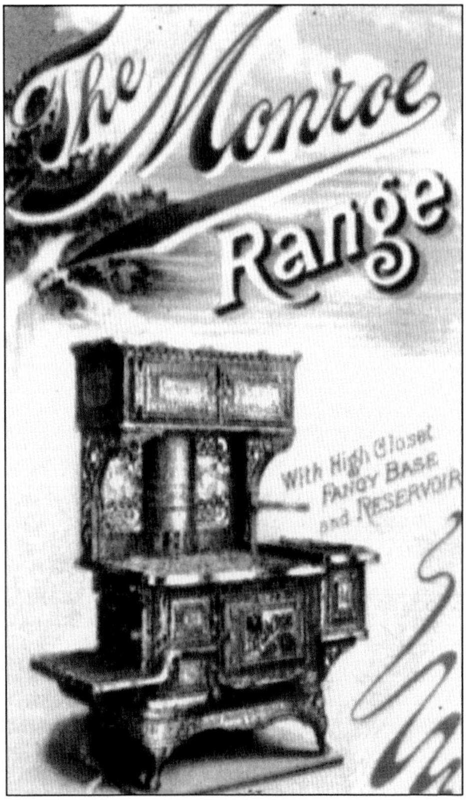

Colorful advertisement cards were popular after the Civil War. This one, produced by Rochester's Co-Operative Foundry sings the praises of the Monroe Range. The wood-burning stove has elaborate cast iron detailing and polished nickel trim. The size and weight of these stoves required delivery in sections to be later bolted together once inside the kitchen. They would sometimes provide heat for the entire house. Proud owners made sure they kept their stoves polished.

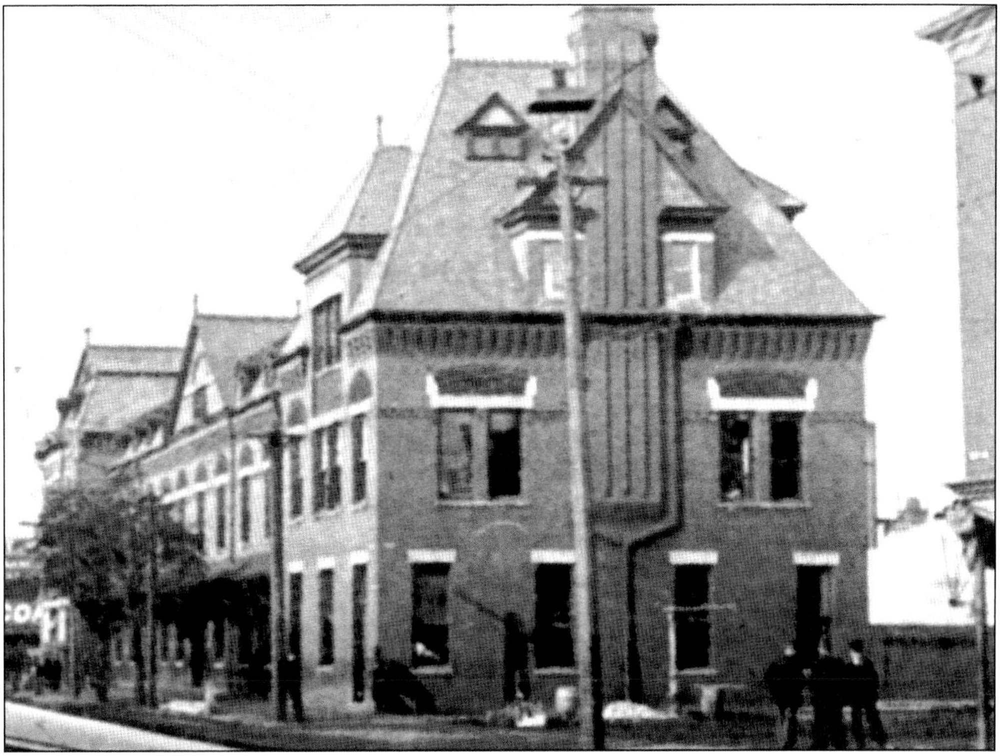

The Buffalo, Rochester, and Pittsburgh Railroad prided itself on how well it maintained its equipment and facilities. Their West Main Street and Oak Street depot was originally the Pitkim Hotel near the basin, where the Erie and Genesee Valley canals joined, and not far from Susan B. Anthony's house. Diminished passenger travel on canals, due to faster train travel, left many early inns abandoned. This BR&P landmark would later house Nick Tahous restaurant—home of the world famous "Garbage Plate."

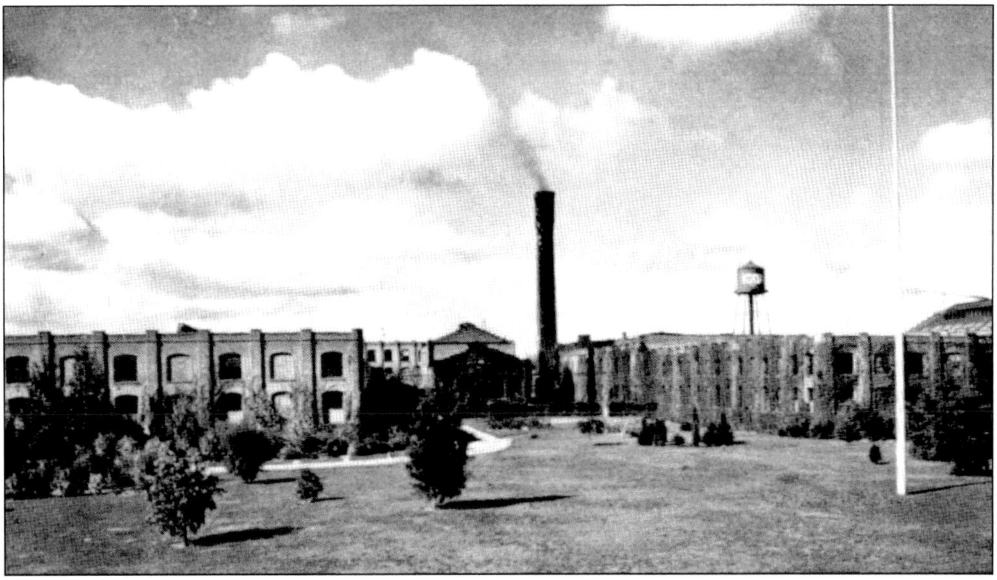

A turn-of-the-century view of Kodak Park from *Souvenir of Rochester.*

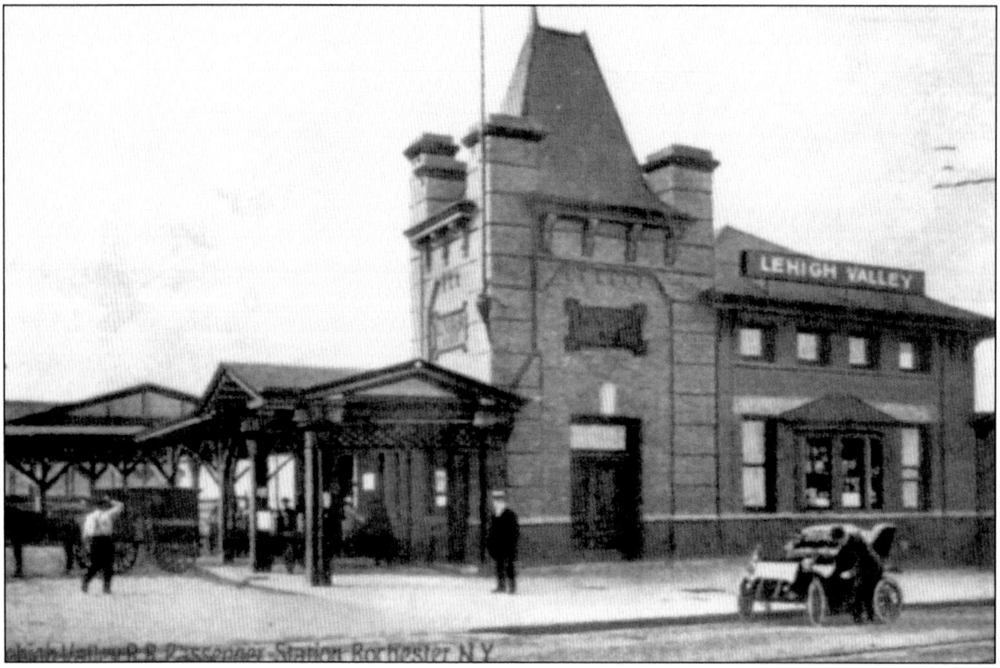

The approaches to the handsome Lehigh Valley station were built on girders over the river at Court Street. On the opposite side of the river stood the Erie Railroad station.

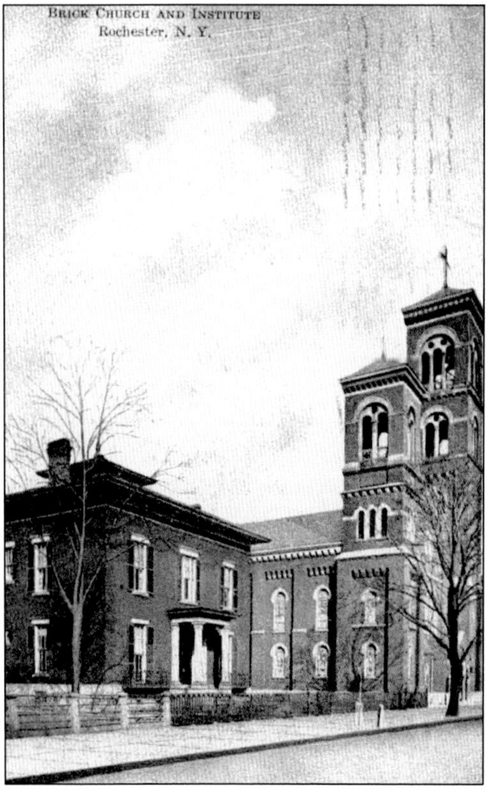

This is an August 1911 view of the Brick Church and Institute. The Rochester congregation dates back to mid-1820s.

The Soldiers and Sailors Monument in Washington Square was dedicated on May 30, 1892. Pres. Benjamin Harrison gave a speech to the 10,000 citizens who marched in a two-mile parade to the site. People sometimes think it curious that Abraham Lincoln was put atop a monument in Washington Square. This card was printed in Frankfort, Germany, and is colored in subtle hues.

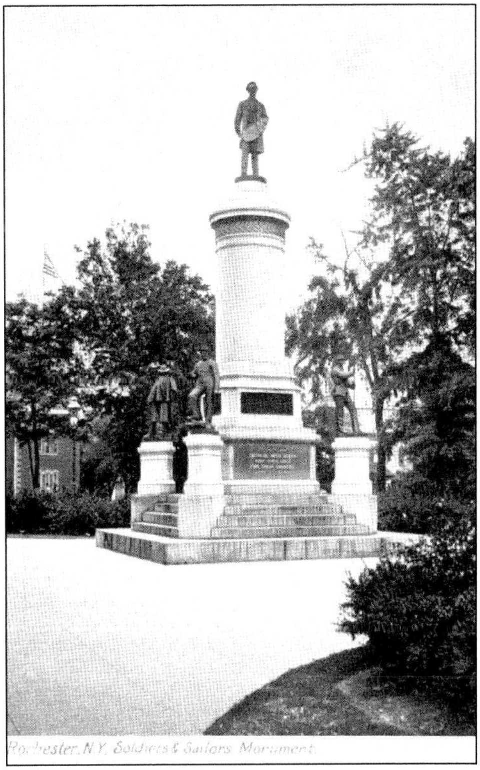

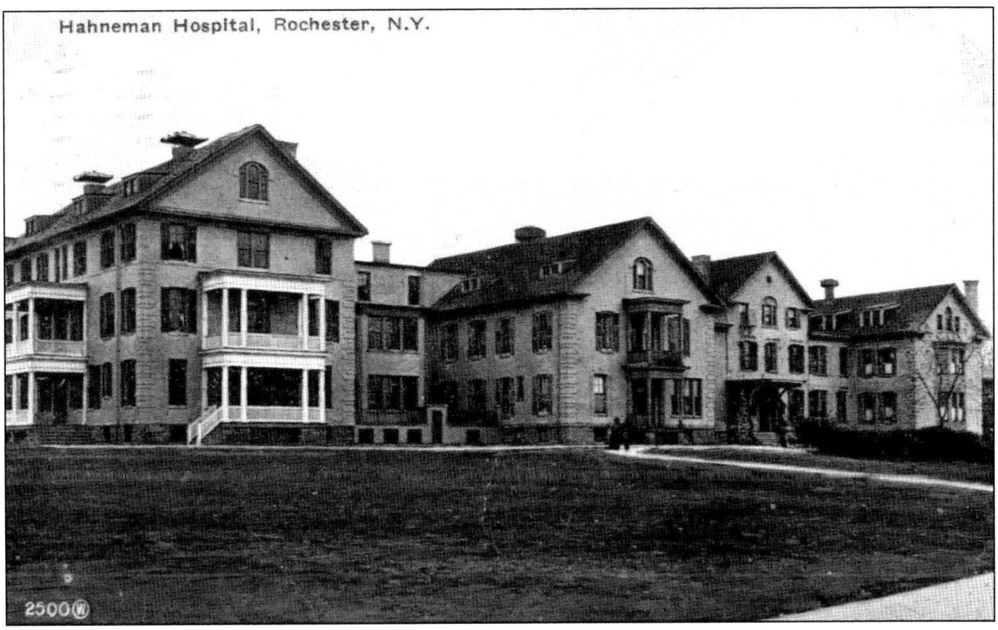

In 1912, a girl writes her cousin, "momma got home (from here) Monday feeling much better than when she went. She only intended to stay a week but she had to stay longer." The Hahneman Hospital opened, in 1889, in the former home of Judge Henry Selden on Rockingham Street. It would later become Highland Hospital. In the 1820s, the poor were cared for at municipal locations like pesthouses or the Monroe County Poorhouse on South Avenue.

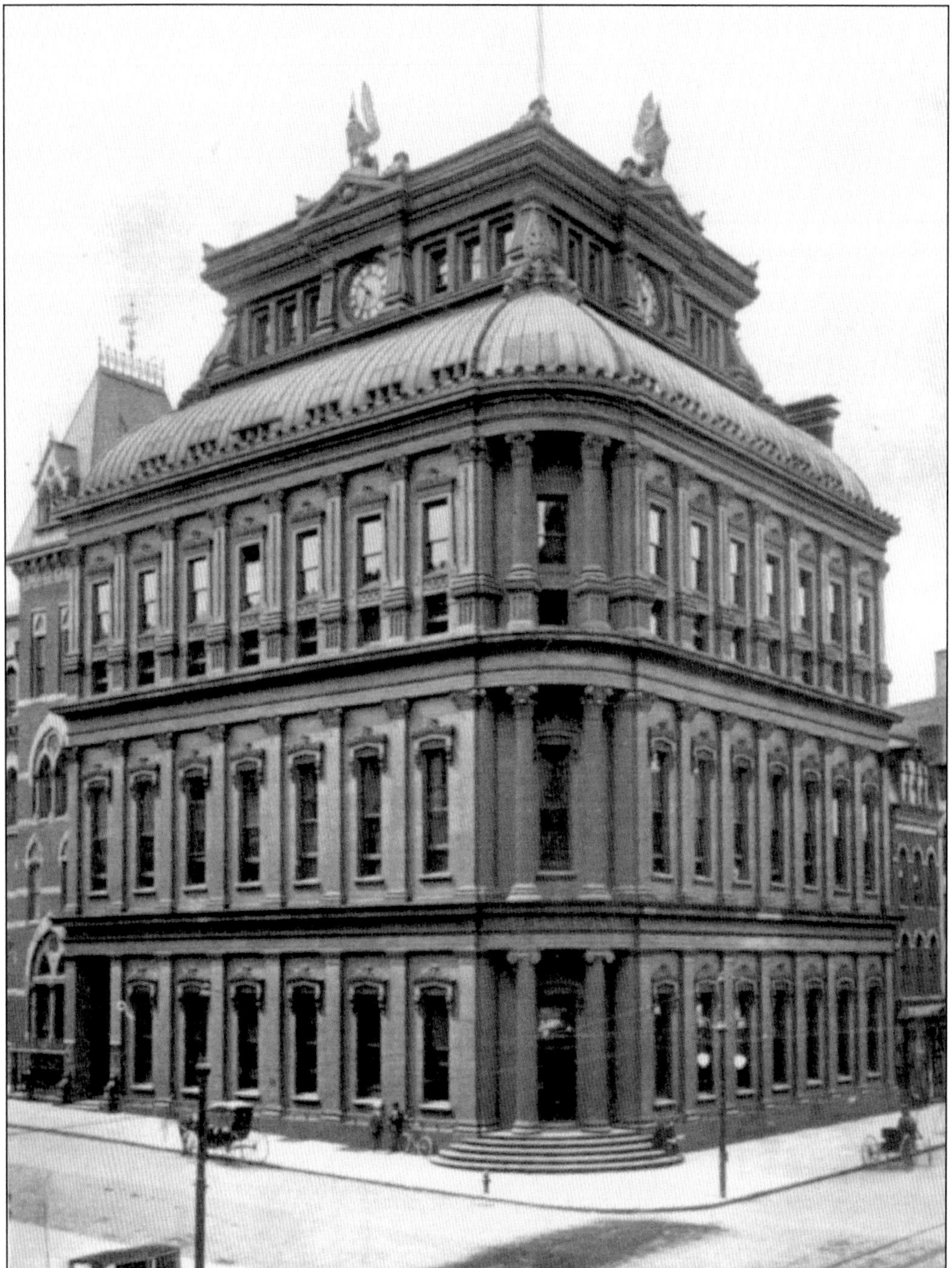

Rochester Savings Bank built the original part of this stunning structure in the 1840s and gradually enlarged it. Located on the southeast corner of West Main and South Fitzhugh Streets it is both breathtaking and sedate, projecting a quiet dignity over the usually bustling intersection. George Eastman worked here as an office clerk during the day and then traveled to his State Street office to assemble dry plates for resident photographers. This photograph is from the *c.* 1898 *Souvenir of Rochester.*

An artist has brought a level of warmth to Rochester Savings Bank. Using the original, a colorful winter sky has been added and the stone façade has been dyed red to suggest it is built of brick instead of stone. The ability to change it so dramatically while making it as appealing as the original photograph says something about the artist's skills.

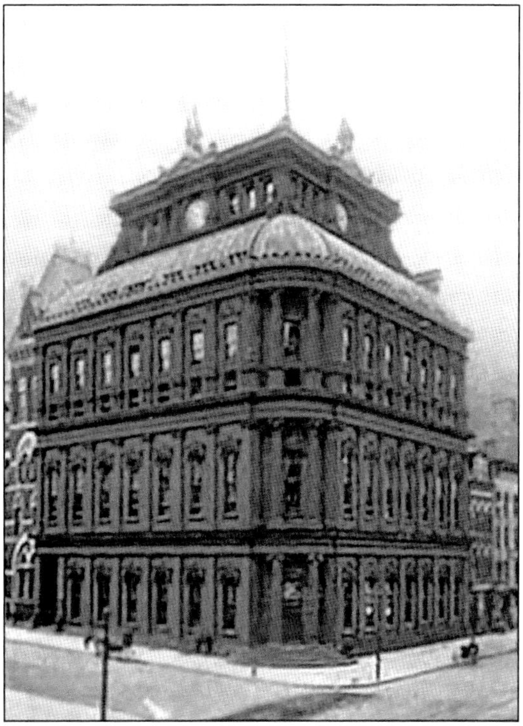

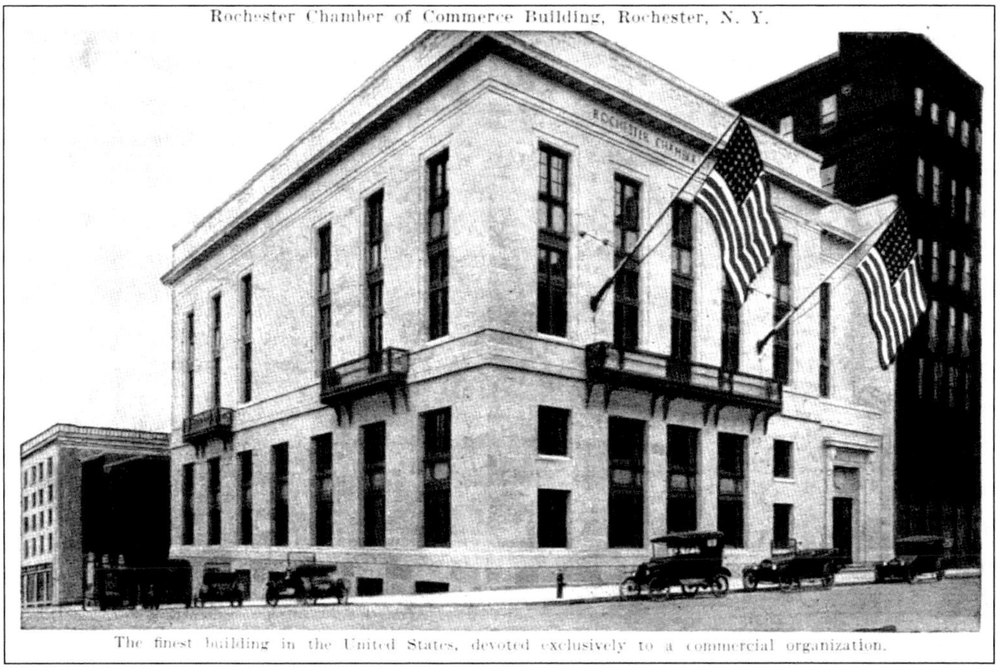

Located on St. Paul Street, the Rochester Area Chamber of Commerce was established in 1887. The postcard claims it is the "finest building in the United States devoted exclusively to a commercial organization."

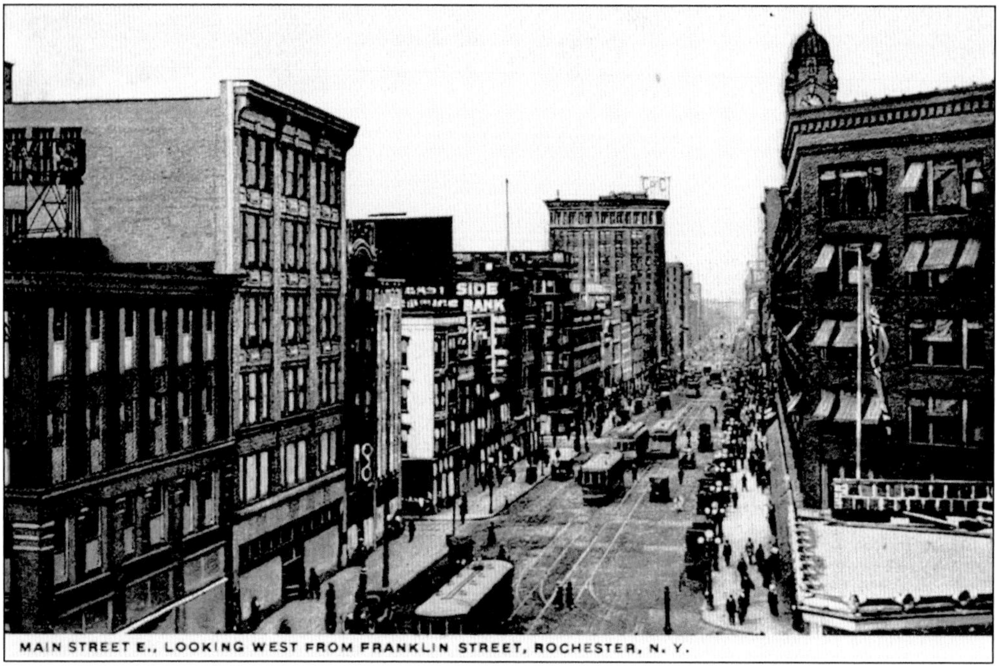

Trolleys still rule the stone streets in this lofty view looking west from Franklin Street. On the right is Sibley's grand new location. The architect may have been put off by the Victorian-era frilliness of the Powers Building and therefore made his creation solid and bold.

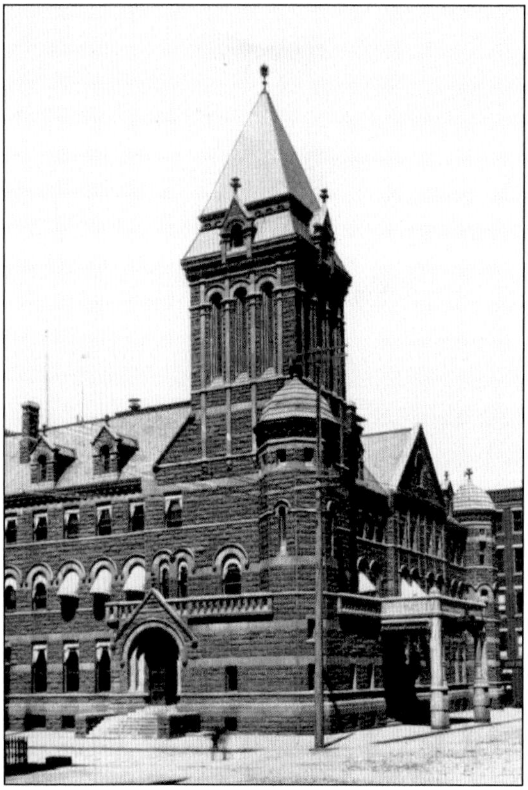

The "Old Federal Building," as it was often called, was the government building and post office on North Fitzhugh Street and Church Street. Construction on the fortress-like structure began in 1884 and finished in 1891. It fell into disrepair and was resurrected in 1978 as Rochester's new city hall. In spite of its brooding bulkiness, the neo-Romanesque masterpiece was a triumph for its local designer Harvey Ellis and represented a high point in civic grandeur.

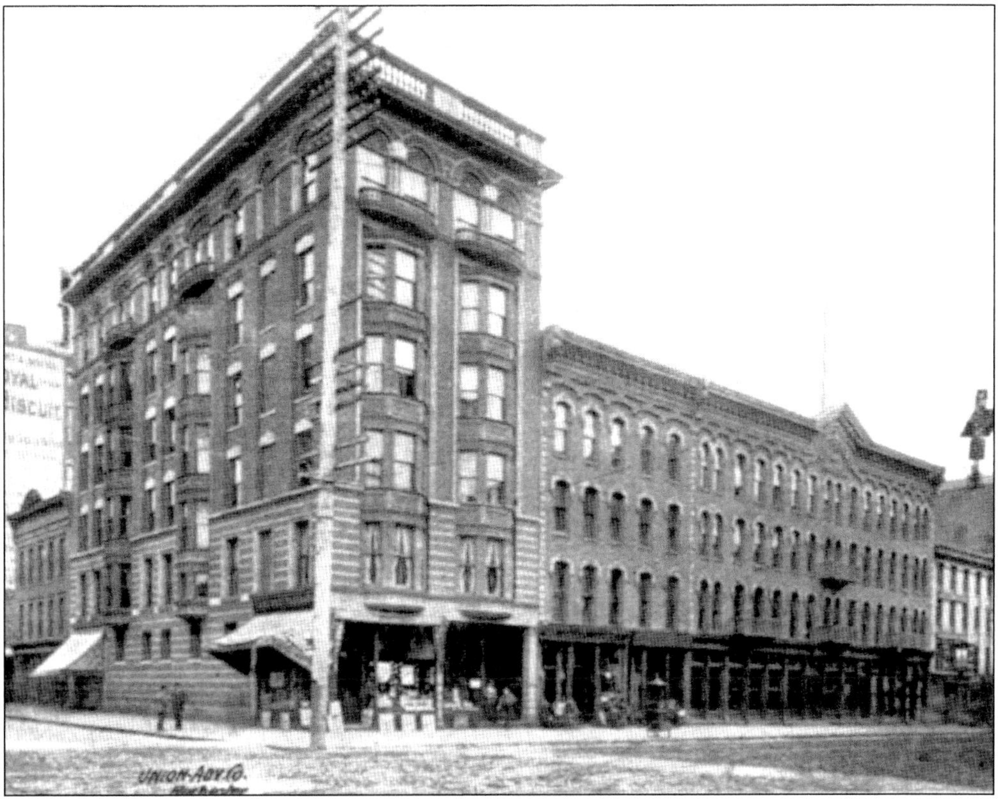

The Union Advertising Company produced this advertisement card for the Whitcomb House on East Main Street. The hotel provided rooms that were "Large and Airy, Supplied with Bath heated by Steam. Lighted by electricity."

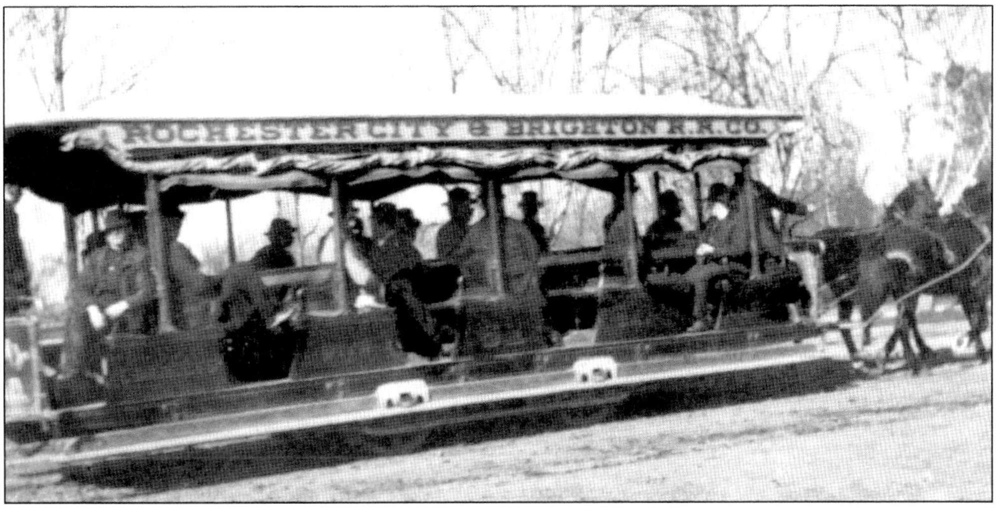

A 10-bench open car drawn by a matched team brings passengers to destinations along the Rochester City and Brighton Railroad Company. The line opened in 1862 and serviced Lake Avenue, Exchange Street, and Mount Hope Avenue with connections at Portland and Bay for trains to Sea Breeze. In this Gordon postcard, we can see rolled up awnings along the car that were lowered when it rained.

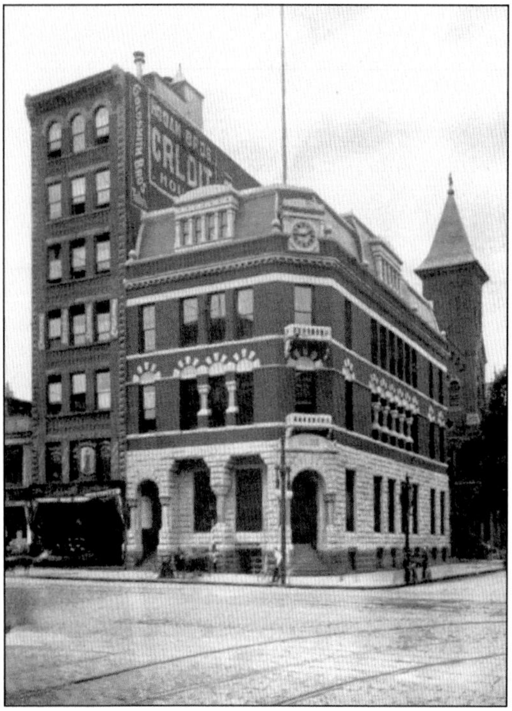

East Side Savings Bank on the corner of Main Street East and South Clinton appears rather quiet. The photographer may have chosen a Sunday when the intersection was clear. The tower behind it is the Universalist church. There are no electric trolleys yet. The tracks are for horse cars. The stone streets are "macadamized." The city had a stone yard where unemployed men could break stone for new streets rather than accept charity.

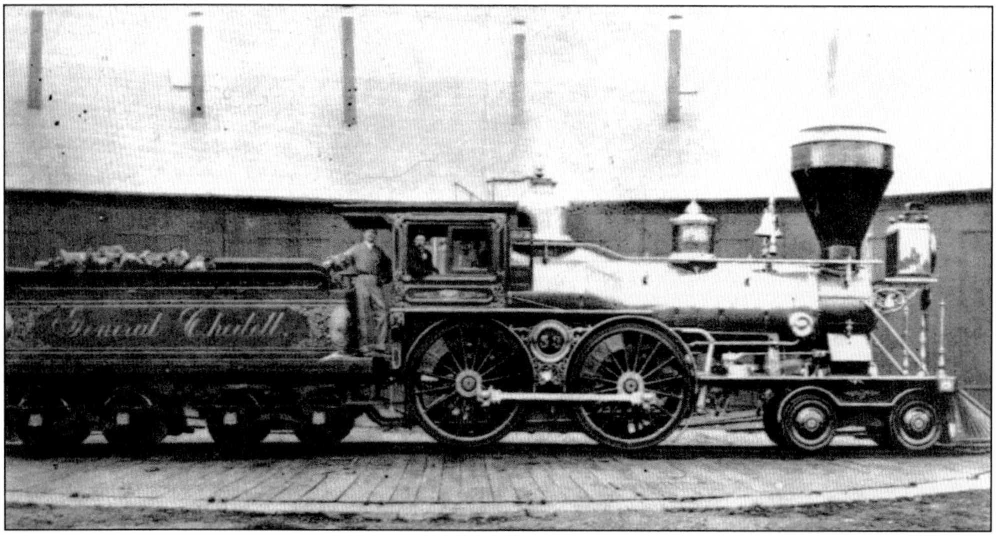

This brightly colored New York Central engine, the General Chadhill, is a wood-burning, balloon-stacked beauty. In this William Gordon postcard, the engine is posed on a wooden turntable, a round platform used to swing equipment around to change direction. Behind it is the roundhouse where engines were serviced. It was something to see a steam engine like this in motion. Imagine the wheels of the brightly-colored engine revolving, the drive rods and valve assemblies all moving uniformly while the bell clangs, the whistle gives a few short toots and a cloud of steamy smoke raises from the stack.

Among the masterpieces architect Andrew J. Warner created for the city was city hall, completed in 1875. The Erie Canal ran behind it.

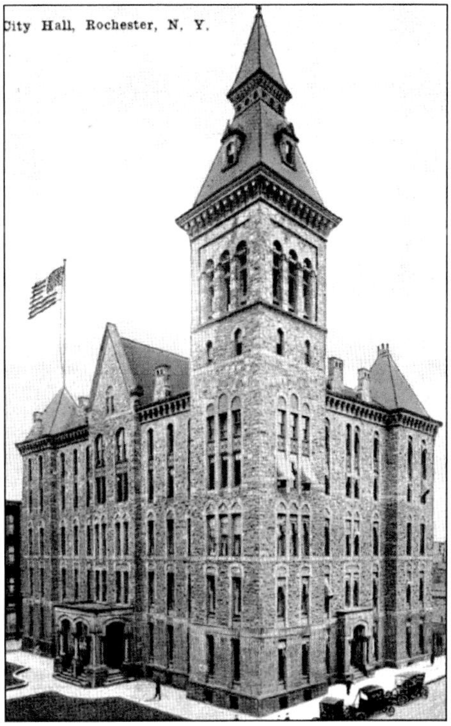

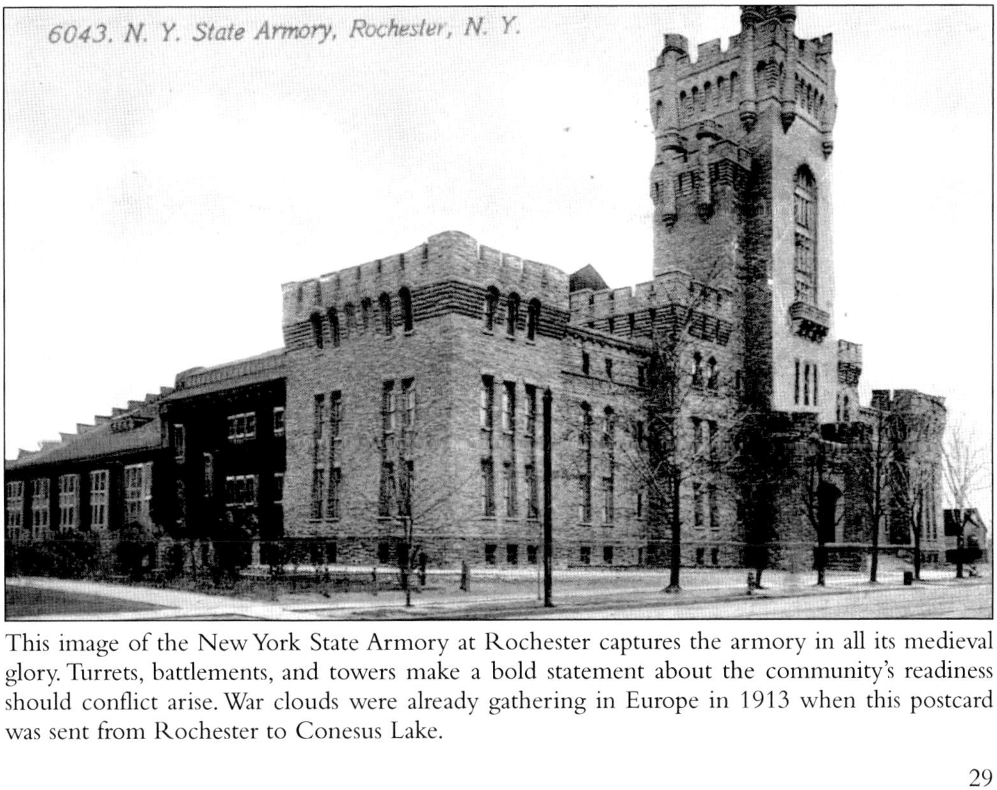

This image of the New York State Armory at Rochester captures the armory in all its medieval glory. Turrets, battlements, and towers make a bold statement about the community's readiness should conflict arise. War clouds were already gathering in Europe in 1913 when this postcard was sent from Rochester to Conesus Lake.

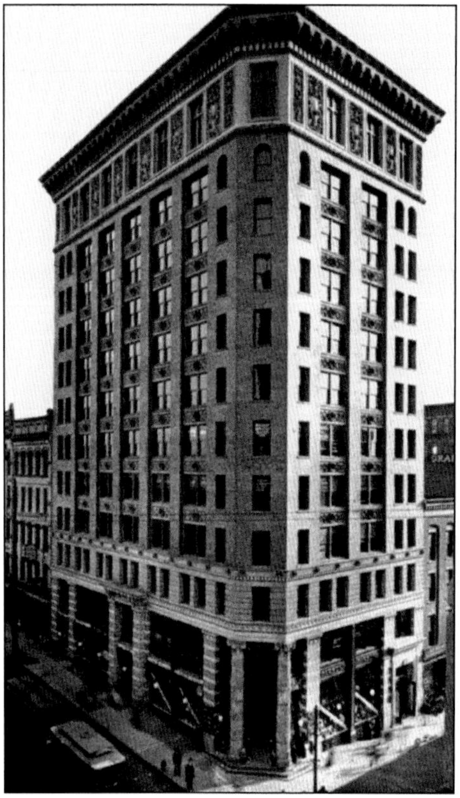

Built in 1894 as the Keeler and Kimball building, this impressive 12-story building was also the chamber of commerce. The large band of intricate panels around the top, together with the elaborate overhang, was meant to give the "skyscraper" the look of a single column. On November 9, 1980, carefully placed charges brought the structure down in a few minutes. This original souvenir photograph was used for numerous cards.

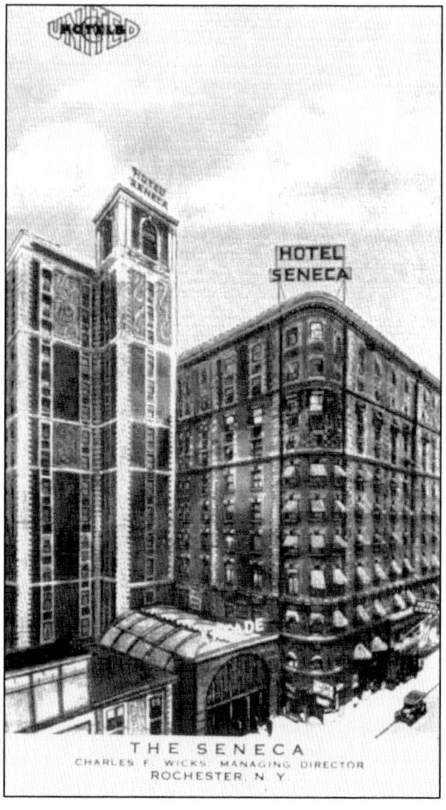

With its completed annex and arcade, the Hotel Seneca increased its accommodations to 550 rooms.

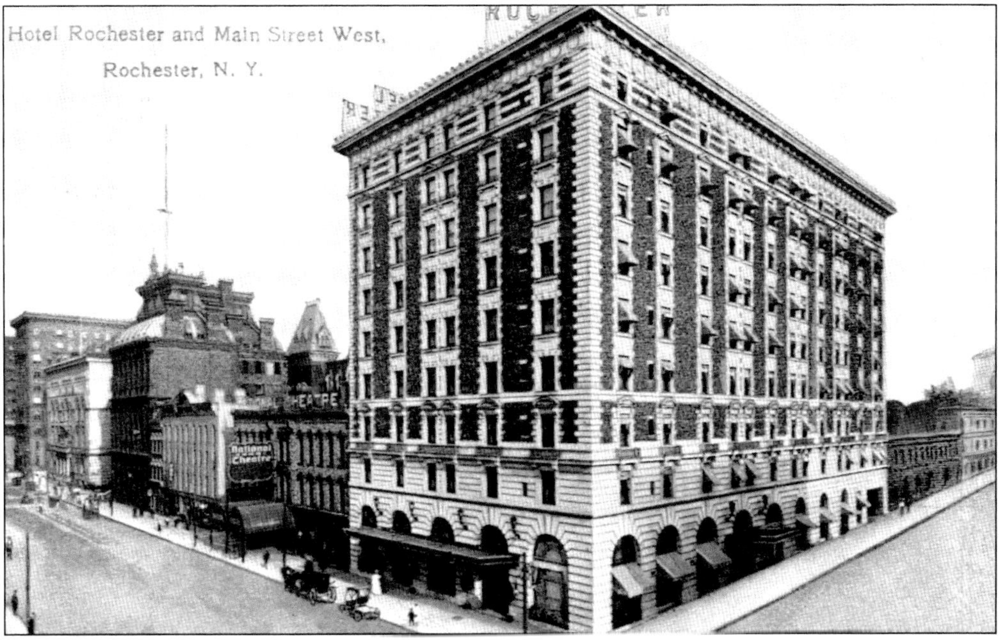

The Hotel Rochester, built *c.* 1907, formerly the National Hotel, adds a touch of Europe to the southeast corner of West Main Street and Plymouth Avenue. It was built at a time when architects were insecure about a distinct American approach to architecture and opted for traditional European influences. The hotel would fit as nicely into a Paris street corner as any in America. The Crystal Dining Room was a favorite evening stop. Shortly after that destructive rampage called urban renewal, this lovely façade was humiliated by a fake blue brick cladding.

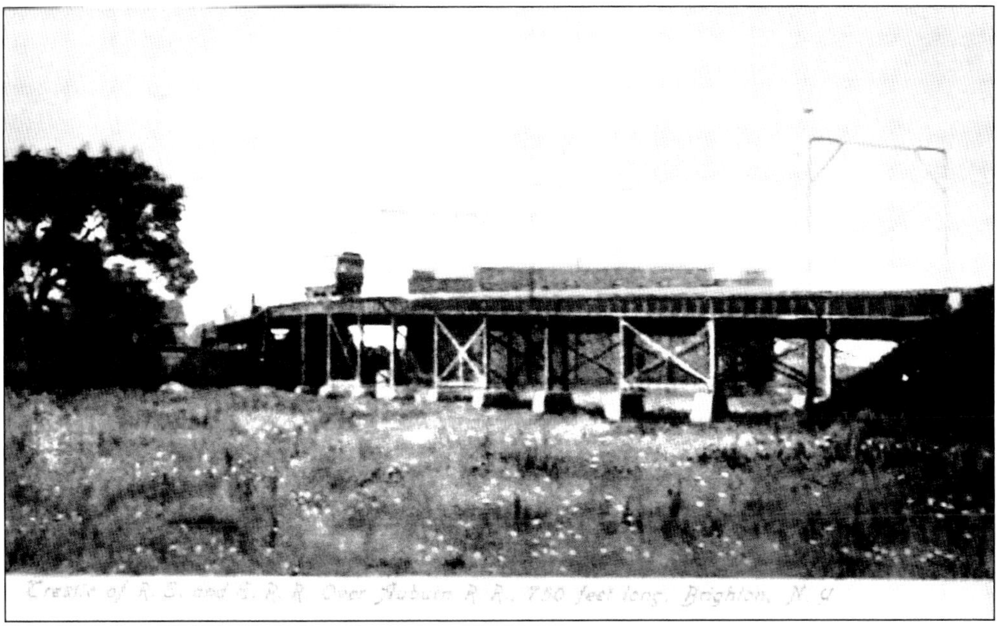

An interurban cruises lightly over the 750-foot long Rochester, Syracuse, and Erie trestle in Brighton. The line had many unique features, among them a dual track overhead wiring system. It also had compact stations that were attractive and well maintained.

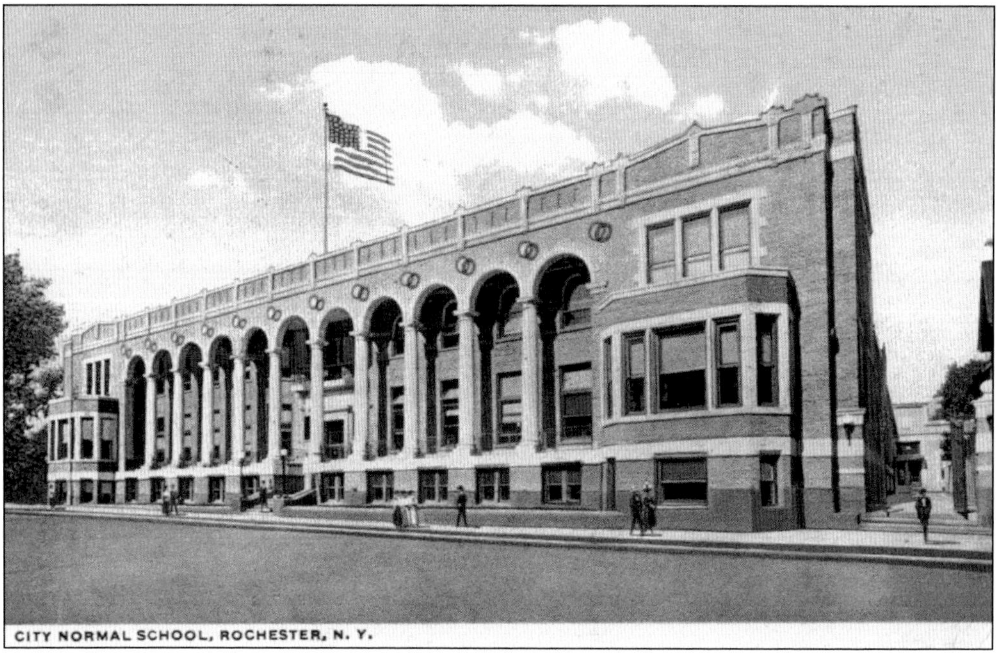

In this white-border era card, Old Glory flutters proudly over the Romanesque arches of the City Normal School.

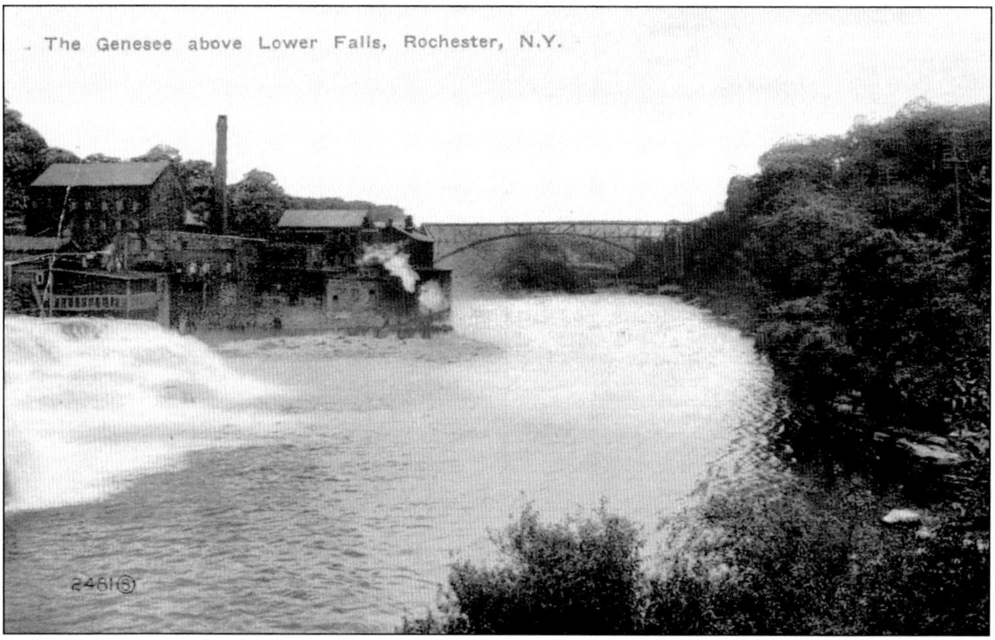

The Driving Park Bridge is visible in the center of this northward view of the Genesee just before it plunges over the Lower Falls. To the right is the Middle Falls, a lesser cascade that powered the mills, substations, and factories pictured beyond the falls. The area was full of interesting millraces, mill canals, spillways, towlines, and power grids. This card was sent in June of 1919.

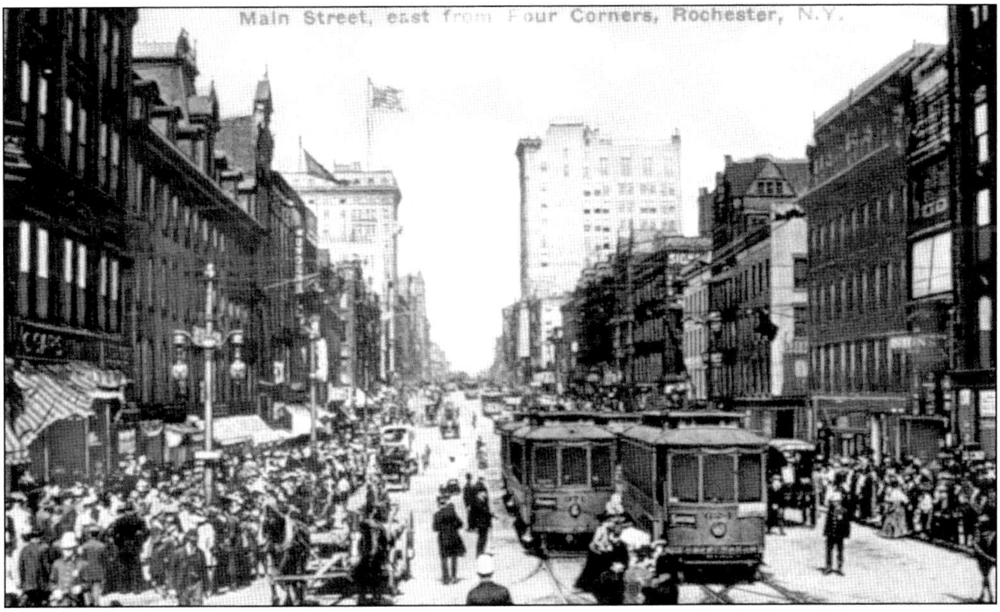

Horse drawn trolleys are but a mere memory now with the arrival of electrified cars, after the turn of the last century. In this view looking east, a small armada of the handsome new cars is gathered at the Four Corners waiting to take passengers in any direction they desired. Note the fine track work embedded in the stone street.

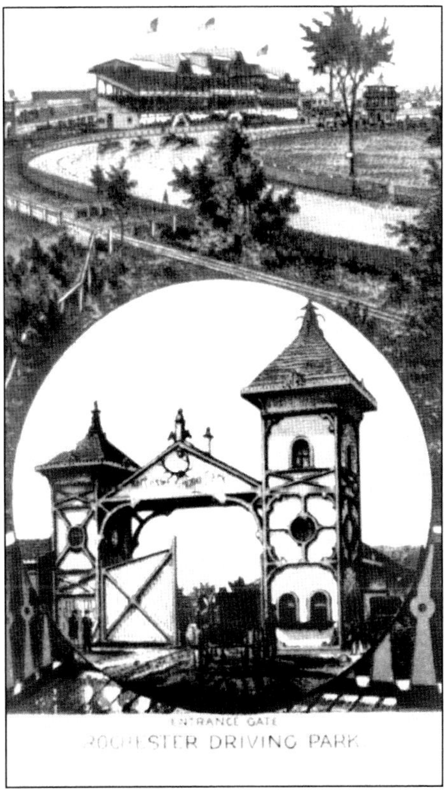

Steady growth and prosperity turned people's minds to recreation. There were 100 pleasures to be had in the city or at the many resorts springing up along Lake Ontario and its secluded bays. The city was filled with natural attractions that brought steamboat and rail excursions from across the country and Canada to view the falls. Rochesterians, however, sought other diversions, one being a trolley ride to the Driving Park for a day of horse betting.

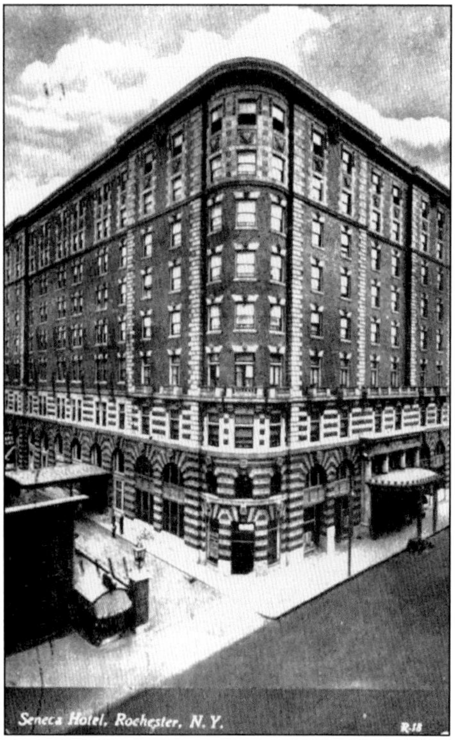

The stately Seneca fills a corner in the heart of downtown with an air of importance. The annex, with its covered arcade, has not been built yet.

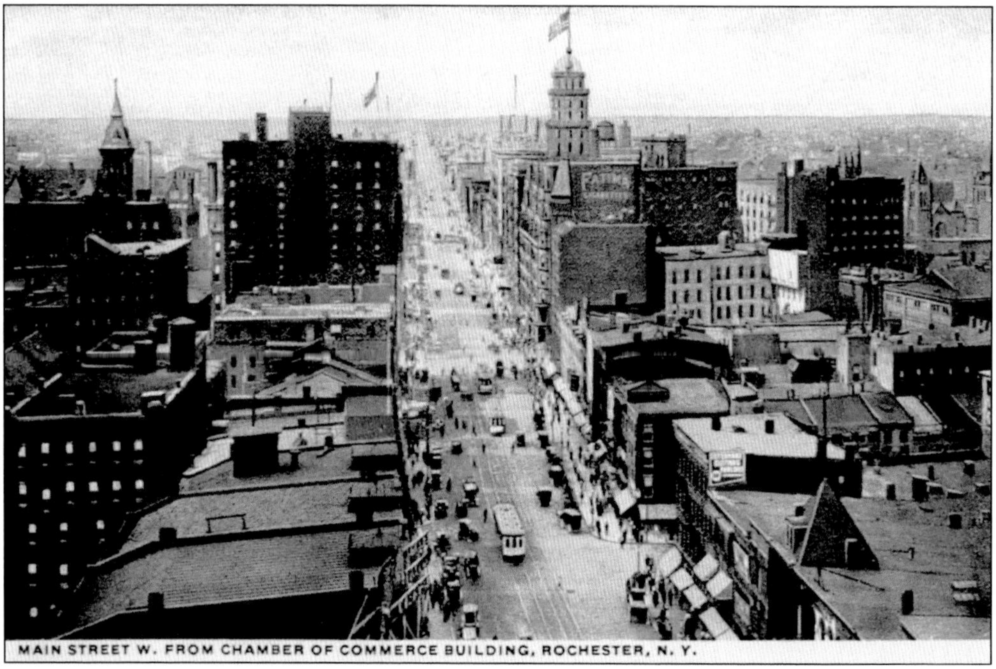

What may appear to us as a mishmash of tarred rooftops was probably considered thrilling in its day. This view taken from the top of the chamber of commerce not only provided a lofty view but also showed how the old commerce blocks that grew around the river and canal during the early boomtown days of Rochesterville were slowly being replaced with skyscrapers.

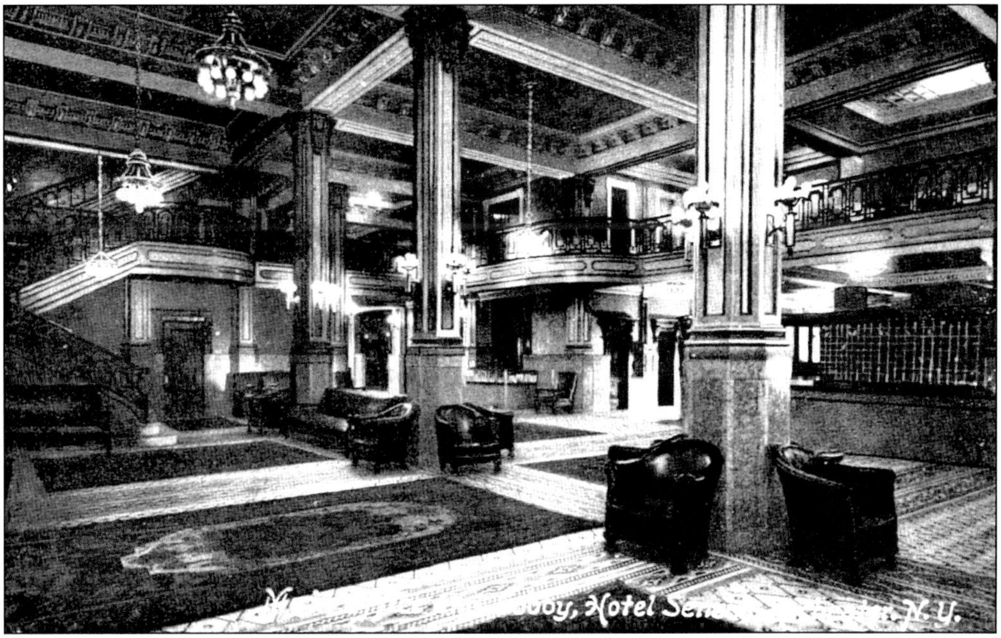

The richly appointed details of the Seneca's lobby glow in an incandescence only achievable by the greatest lithographers of the day—the Germans. Everyone from the wealthiest proprietor to the poorest buggy maker, who had to count his pennies to have a card made, sought their craftsmanship. This card, published in Germany, is an example of their patience and artistry. During World War I trade ceased and card production came to America. It took us a generation to duplicate their skills.

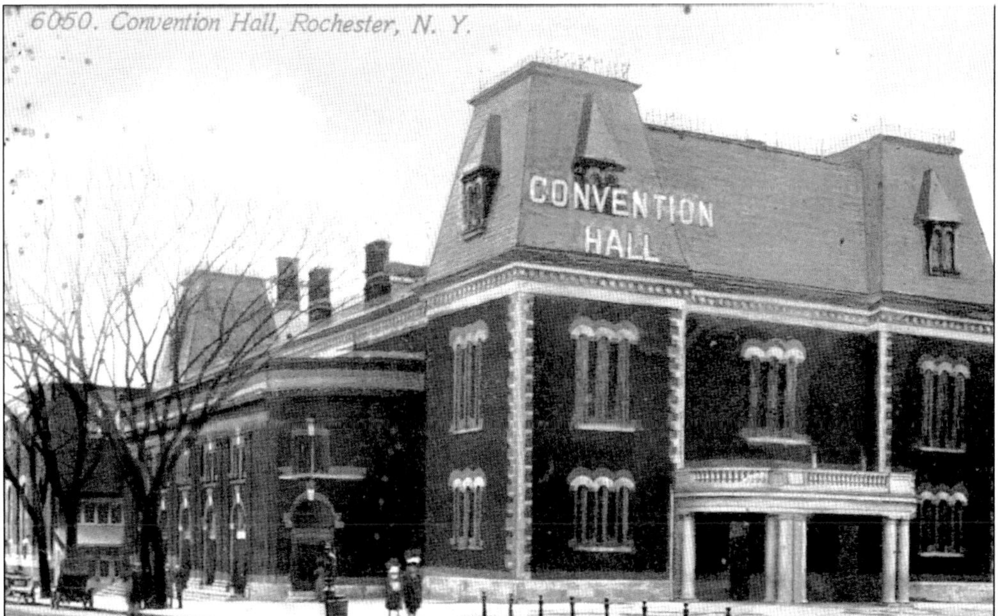

This sturdy structure has worn many hats since its construction in 1868. It was built as a New York State armory and then became the convention center pictured here. Additionally, it has served as a concert hall, office building, and the current home of GEVA Theater.

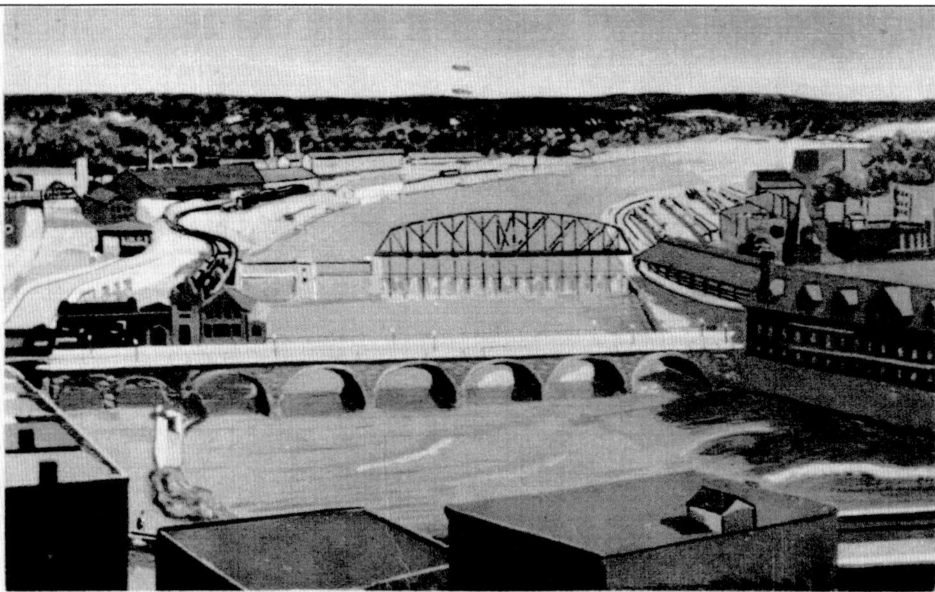

Court Street Bridge and the Barge Canal Terminal from Chamber of Commerce, Rochester, N. Y. — 20

Sent in 1948, this card is amateurish in its coloring and obliterates many details. Nonetheless, it tells us a lot. The Court Street Bridge is flanked on the east by the Lehigh Valley Station and on the west by the Erie Station. The Barge Canal terminal is just beyond it, the Genesee River having become part of the Erie Canal at the turn of the 20th century. The girder bridge spans the joint New York State and Rochester Gas & Electric dam project that used water to generate electricity.

BROAD STREET AND COURT STREET BRIDGES AND N. Y. STATE BARGE CANAL TERMINAL, ROCHESTER, N. Y.

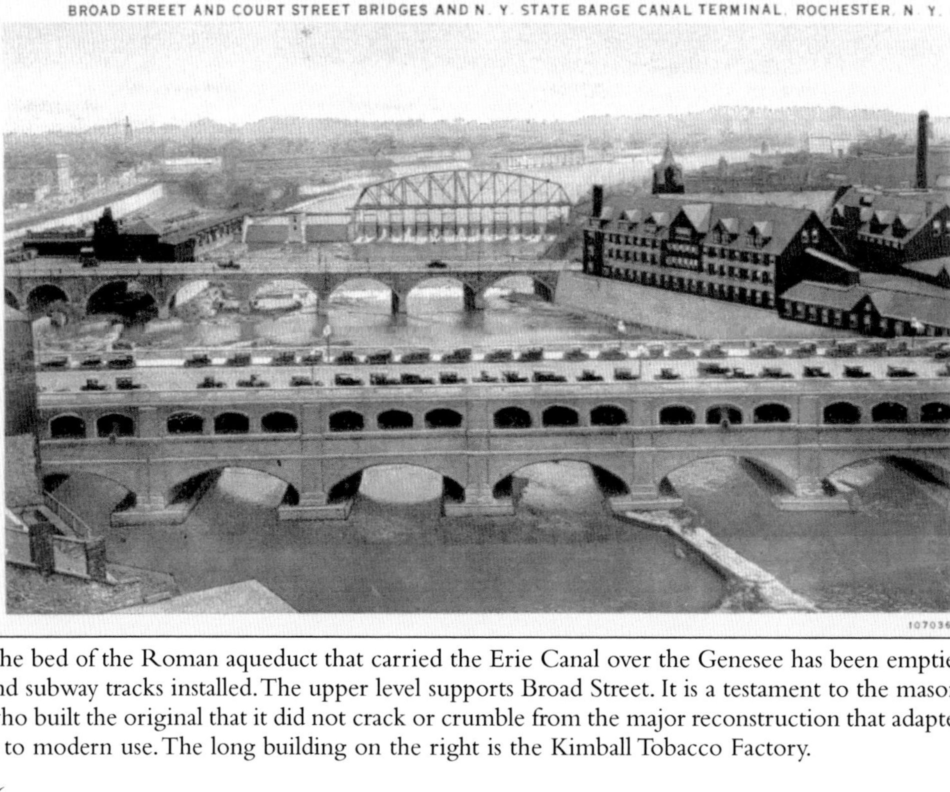

107036

The bed of the Roman aqueduct that carried the Erie Canal over the Genesee has been emptied and subway tracks installed. The upper level supports Broad Street. It is a testament to the masons who built the original that it did not crack or crumble from the major reconstruction that adapted it to modern use. The long building on the right is the Kimball Tobacco Factory.

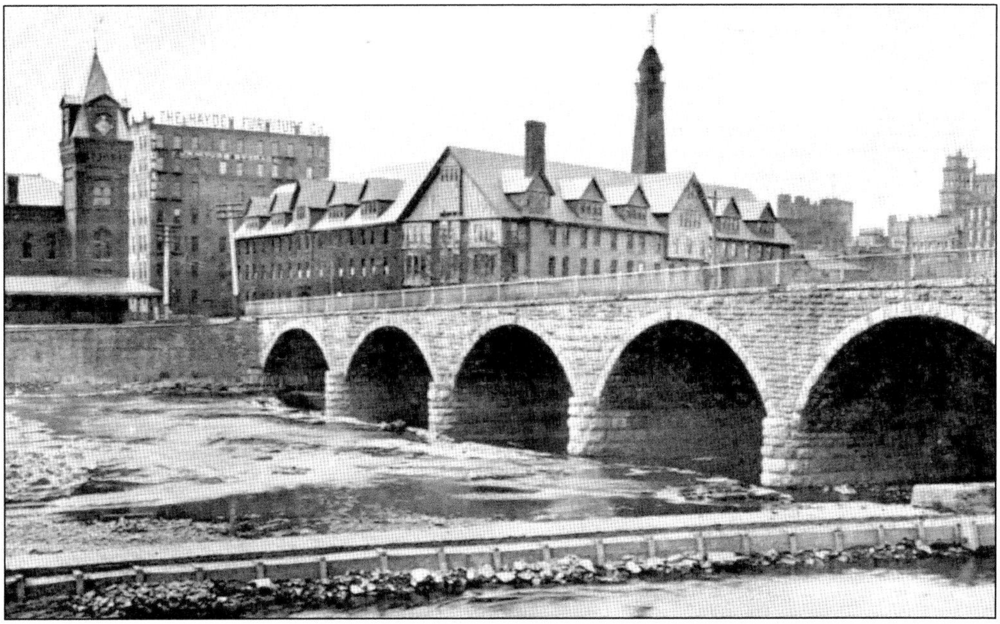

Court Street Bridge, completed in 1893, was not far from the fording place used by the Senecas. This stone arch bridge replaced several predecessors, included a bowstring truss bridge that got twisted like a pretzel in 1887 when a windstorm sent parts of two spans and a tangle of telegraph and telephone wires and poles into the river torrent. Kimball Tobacco Factory is beyond the bridge. The statue of Mercury can be seen atop a tower.

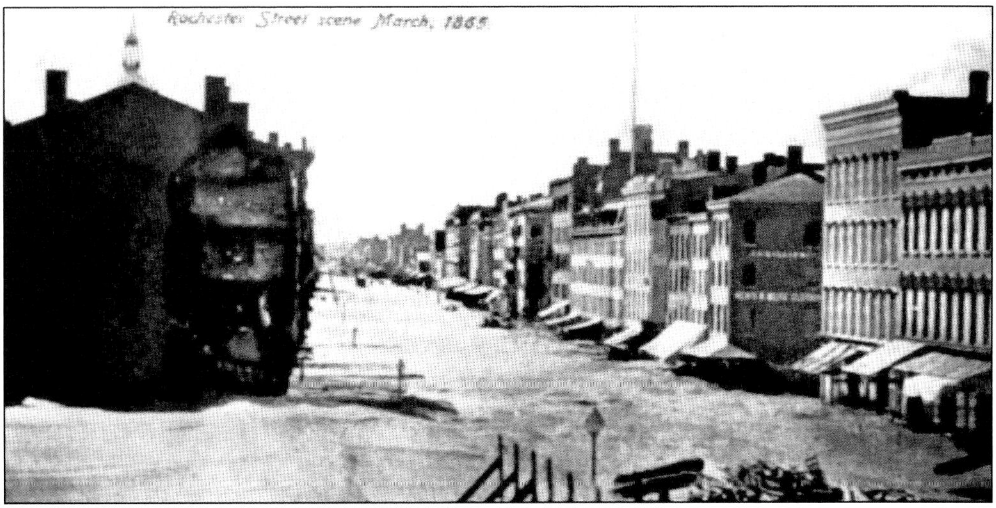

The mighty Genesee sometimes resisted its confinement through the heart of the city. Prolonged rains resulting in swelling streams, torrential runoffs, and spring thaws brought fits of anxiety to proprietors around the river. The most devastating flood came in 1865 when the river overflowed its banks in downtown, flooding the city from Four Corners to St. Paul Street. Efforts to reduce flooding included deepening the riverbed through the city and construction of a flood control dam at Mount Morris.

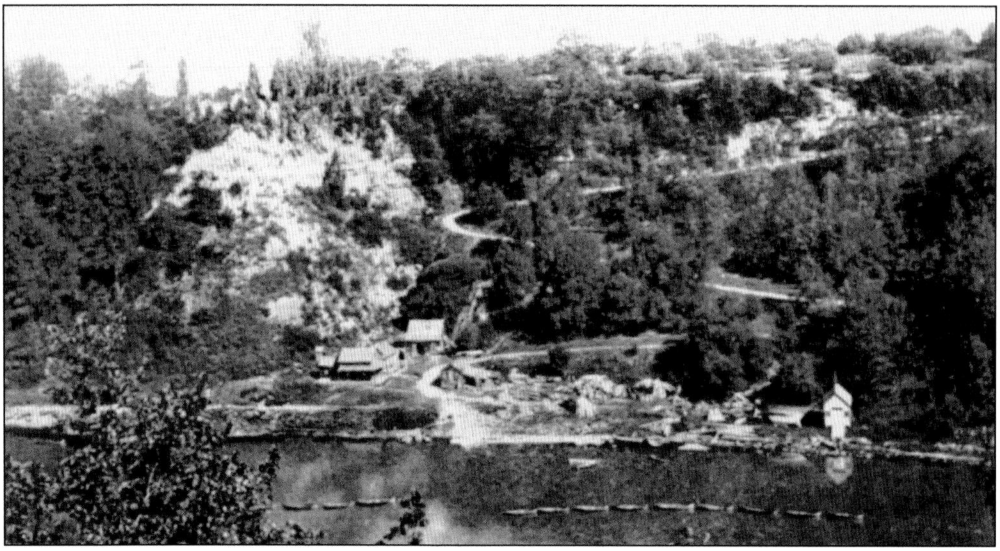

Brewers Dock was just north of the Lower Falls. It marked a shipping point where first schooners and then steamers plied the Genesee from Lake Ontario. Some thought Brewers referred to the many breweries along the top of the gorge but it actually referred to a businessman. Carthage, a rival to Rochester, had up to five steamers a week dock here. The Rochester Canal and Railroad Company built a three-mile line from the aqueduct at South Water Street to here. A team of horses pulled the stagecoach-like cars. Amazingly, the cars were then lowered and raised down the gorge using gravity. While one was lowered the other ascended.

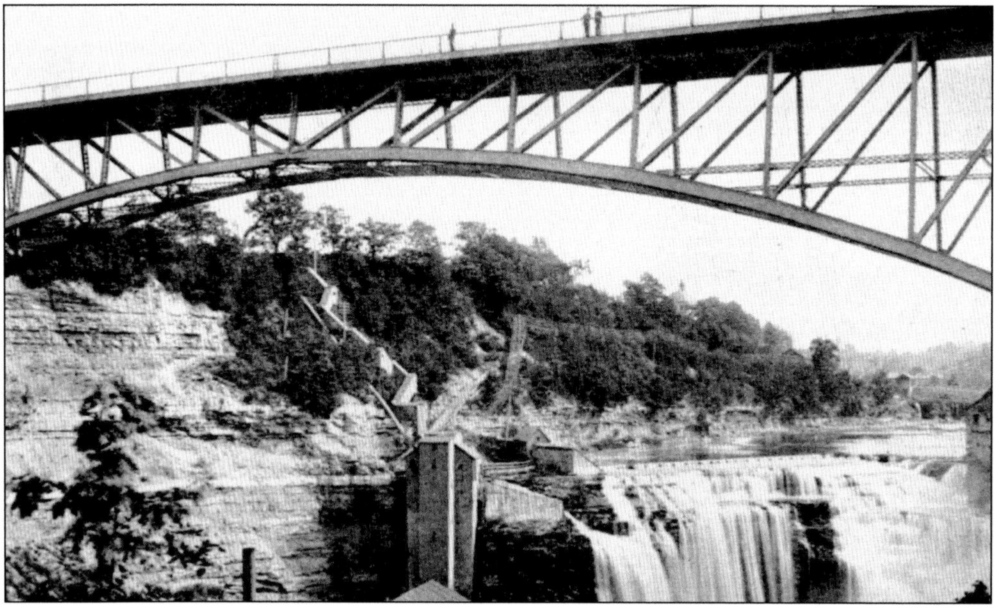

A bold view beneath the Driving Park Bridge, taken in the 1890s, shows a cluster of mills and related facilities around the Lower Falls. An enclosed stairway, leading from the summit of the gorge makes a steep and twisting descent to a small road. Variously colored bands of rock descend the gorge wall horizontally. Pioneers believed they were painted by an earlier race. They are actually different layers of limestone that, like rings on a tree, leave a visual record of the tens of thousands of years of river erosion.

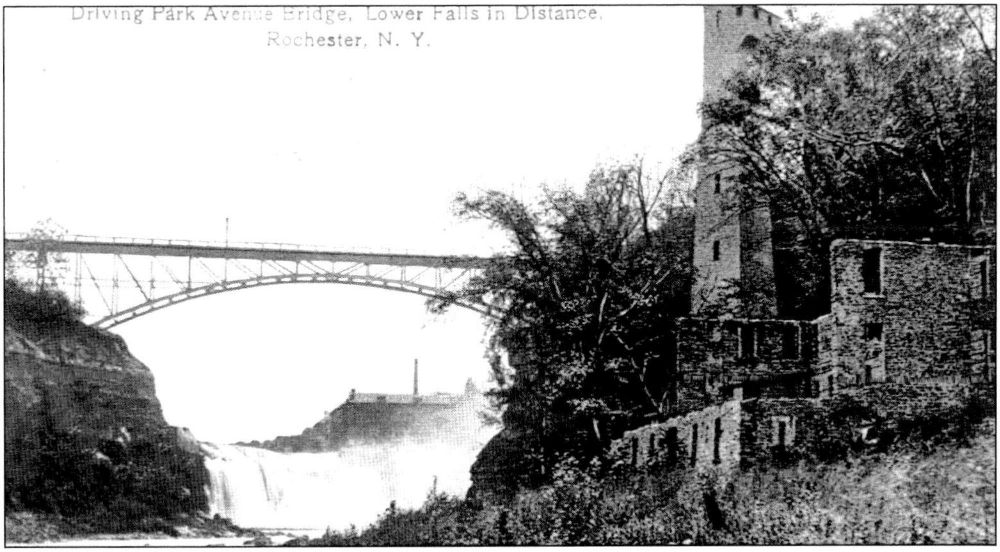

The ruins of the Glen House that burned in 1894 and the elevator tower that lowered guests from a platform in Maplewood Park sit forlornly to the side in this *c.* 1909 image of the Lower Falls. Huck Finn and Tom Sawyer would have been at home here. There were steamboats, river rats, mills, and even a large cave where they could preside over their gang of would-be pirates. Attempts to make this area a vacation center failed when trolley lines were put up on nearby Lake Avenue. This area was ignored in favor of the more exciting Ontario Beach Park.

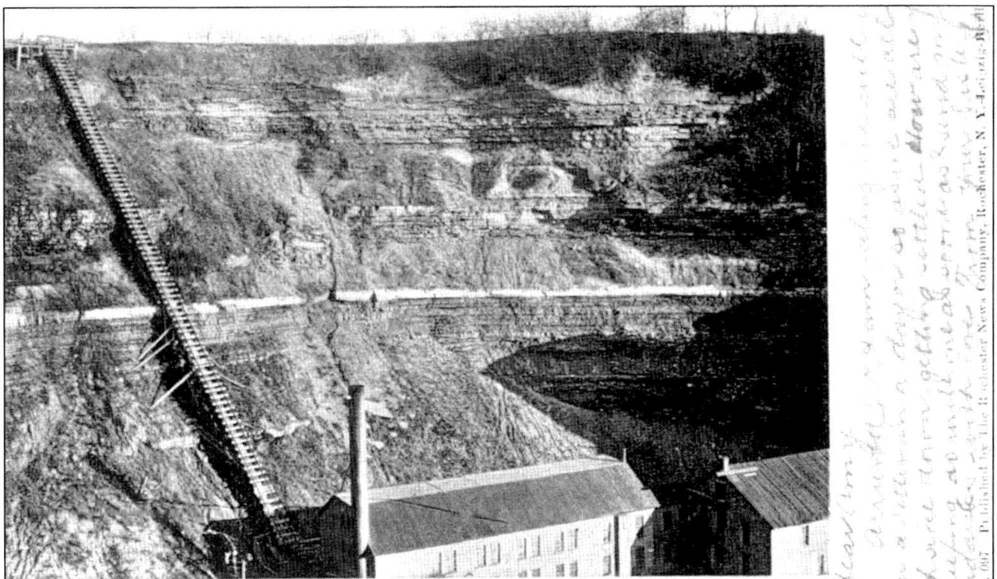

The bands of layered limestone, which were exposed as the river cut its way down through, are slightly more visible in this unusual photograph. The inclined track was used for raising and lowering supplies and is probably not unlike the parallel set of tracks used by the Carthage Railroad in 1831. Thrill seekers used the railroad as much as passengers because of the spectacular ride along the summit. When leaving the station by the aqueduct, the driver would blow his bugle to warn that his train was about to cross Main Street. He could not blow it on Sundays, though, because loud noises were illegal.

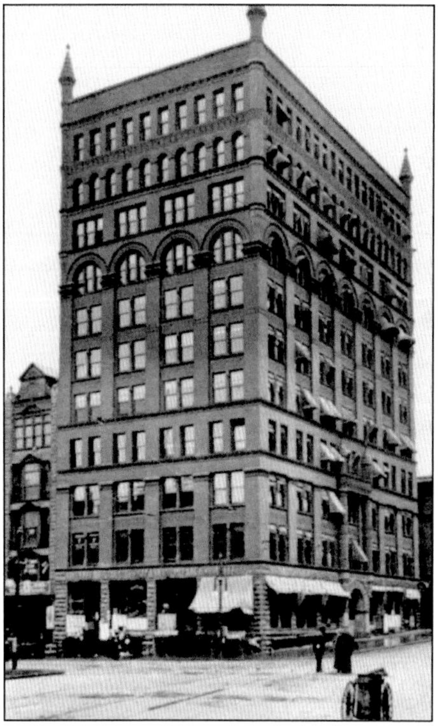

This original turn-of-the-century view of the Wilder Building underwent several interpretations in successive postcards. The 11-story "skyscraper" was kitty-corner from Daniel Powers's fanciful Powers Block at the Four Corners. A kind of competition developed in which Powers added floors and a tower so he could lay claim to the tallest structure in the city. The advent of hydraulic elevators allowed for increasingly taller buildings.

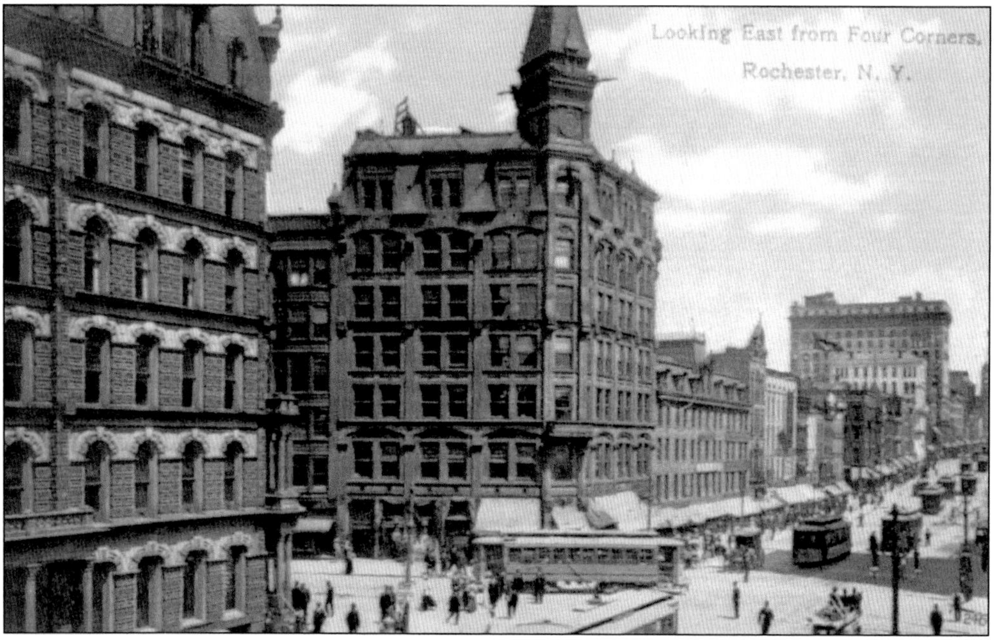

The Elwood Building fills the center of this postcard. Its Victorian tower had defiant dragon-like heads glaring out over the Four Corners. To the left is the Powers Building, a cast-iron and concrete building that was painted brick red in this card. The view east gives little indication of what was once Main Street Hill because newer construction gradually leveled it off. Additional horses were kept nearby to help horse cars up the hill. There was a round turntable embedded in the intersection of the Four Corners where the cars could be turned around.

In this *c.* 1909 German printed version of the original, the sky has been highlighted and the trolley on the right has been dyed a deep yellow. The artist painstakingly colored each window of the bold Richardsonian-styled skyscraper in pale blue to enliven the scene.

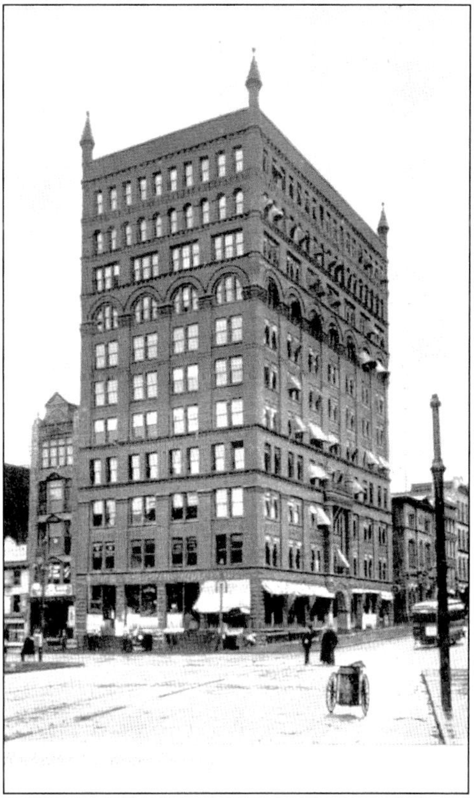

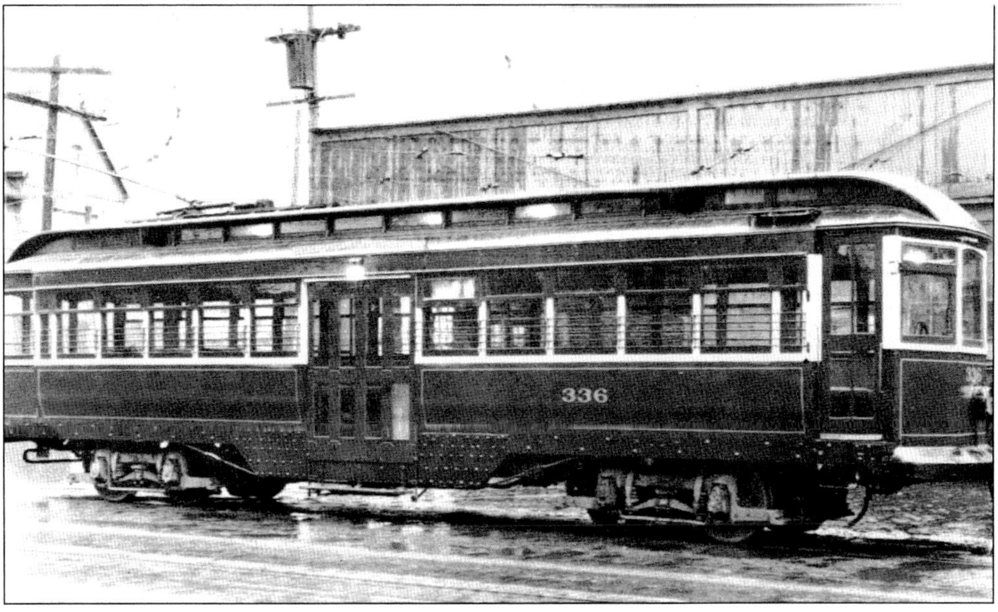

A car for the new subway has arrived at the St. Paul Street shops from Utica. It traveled the tracks of the Rochester, Syracuse, and Erie line to get here. In this William Gordon postcard, the subway car has not yet been appointed with a headlamp on its roof—something it would need in the dimly lit subway tunnel under the city.

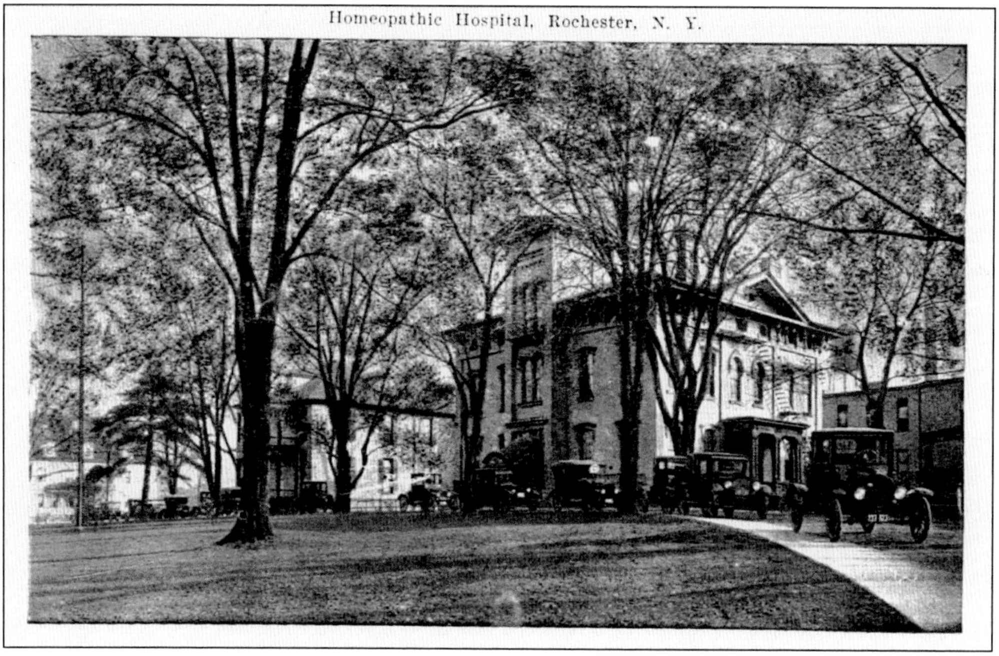

The Rochester Homeopathic Hospital opened in 1887 and would later become Genesee Hospital.

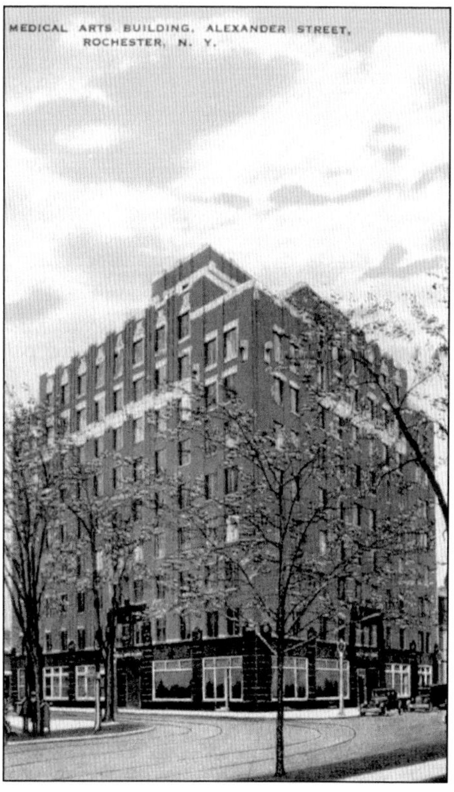

Built in the art-deco style, the Medical Arts Building on Alexander Street now houses offices for numerous professionals. The street level is clad in striking art-deco designs cast into black panels. The upper stories are actually not red brick as represented in this card but, rather, a light stone color.

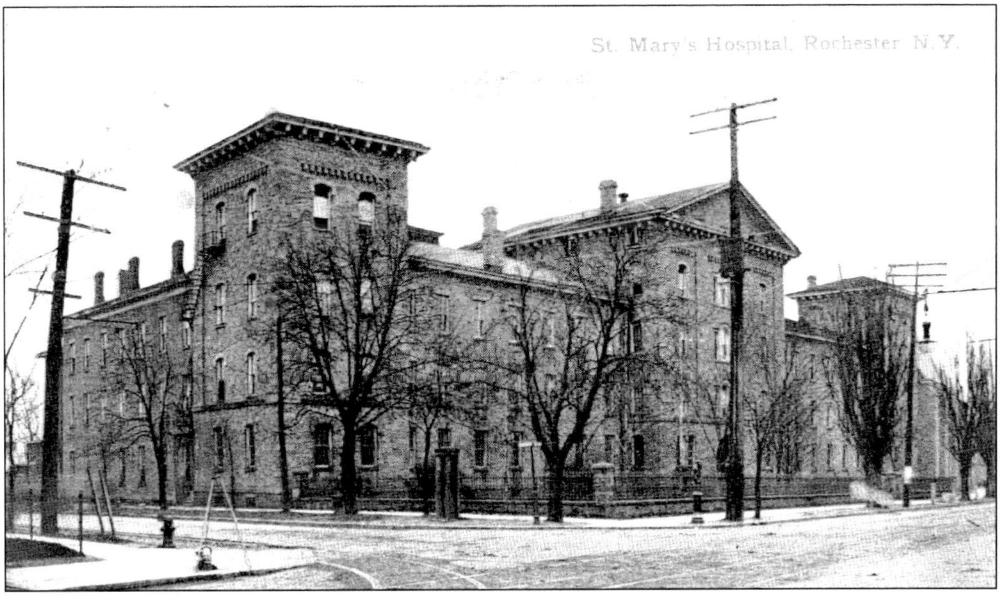

An order of Sisters established the foundation for St. Mary's Hospital in two horse stalls in 1857 where they did their earthly best to tend the endless stream of Civil War wounded that came up from the depots in wagons and ambulances. This new Saint Mary's Hospital was erected west of the city at Bull's Head. The Sisters brought fresh produce for patients from their Chili farm.

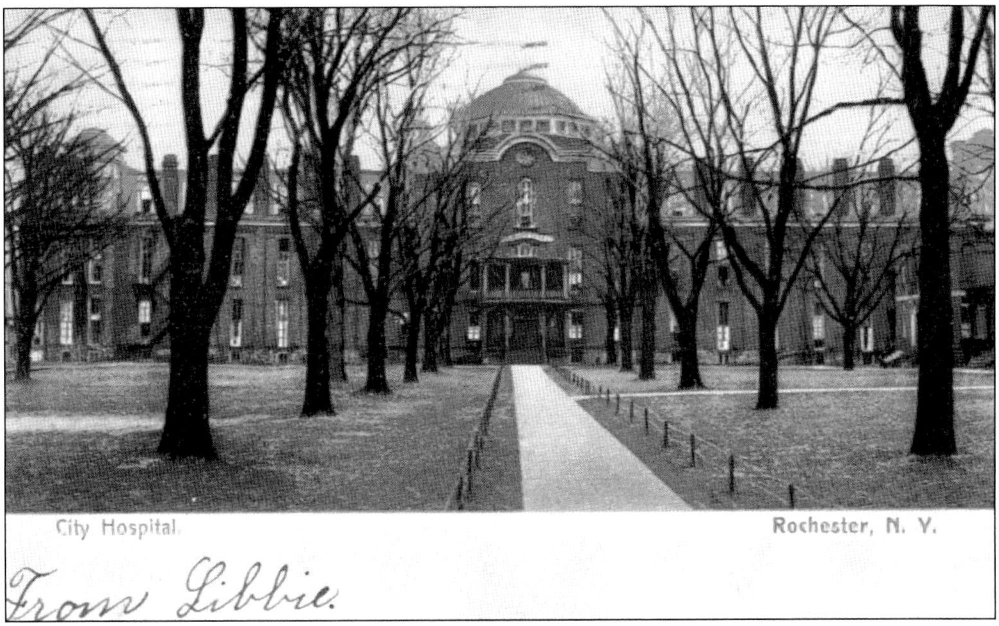

The City Hospital opened in 1864 on Buffalo Street (West Main). It later became Rochester General. Immigration by canal, stagecoach, and railroad brought contagious diseases to the city at alarming rates—so much so that they overwhelmed the city's capacity to deal with them, especially during outbreaks. Typhoid, smallpox, cholera, and influenza outbreaks required quarantines of populations usually outside the city. In small towns, the best way a family could protect itself during a smallpox outbreak was to hole itself up inside their house for several weeks and make no contact with neighbors until the disease blew through.

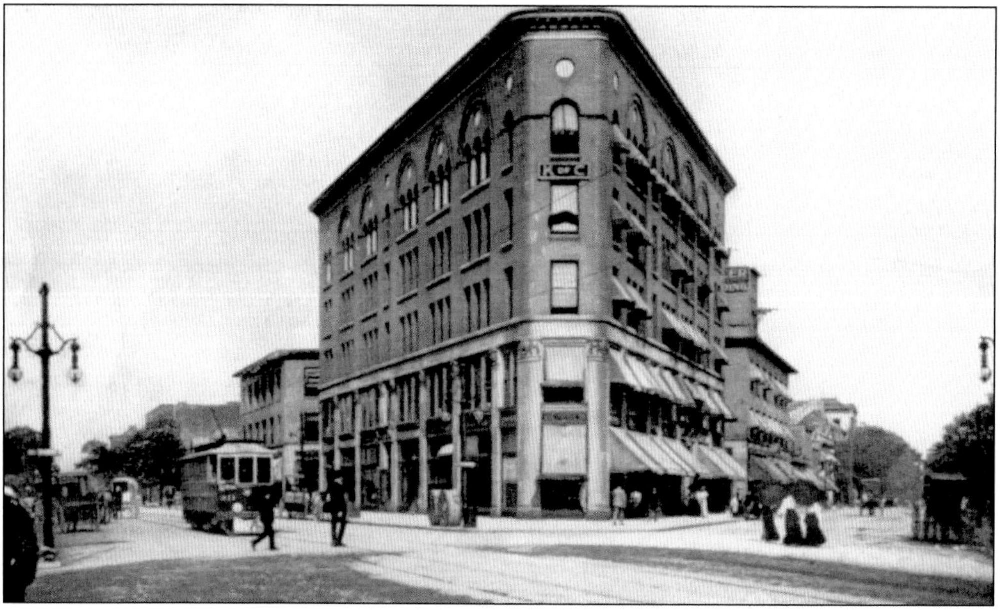

The Triangle Building dignifies the corner of East Main Street and East Avenue in a *c.* 1900 original souvenir photograph. Wealthy Rochesterians came down East Avenue from their mansions first in elegant carriages and then in expensive automobiles. Their drivers would park conspicuously in front of high-end stores and wait while their rich employers shopped. Local retailers pampered these prominent citizens whom they called the "carriage trade."

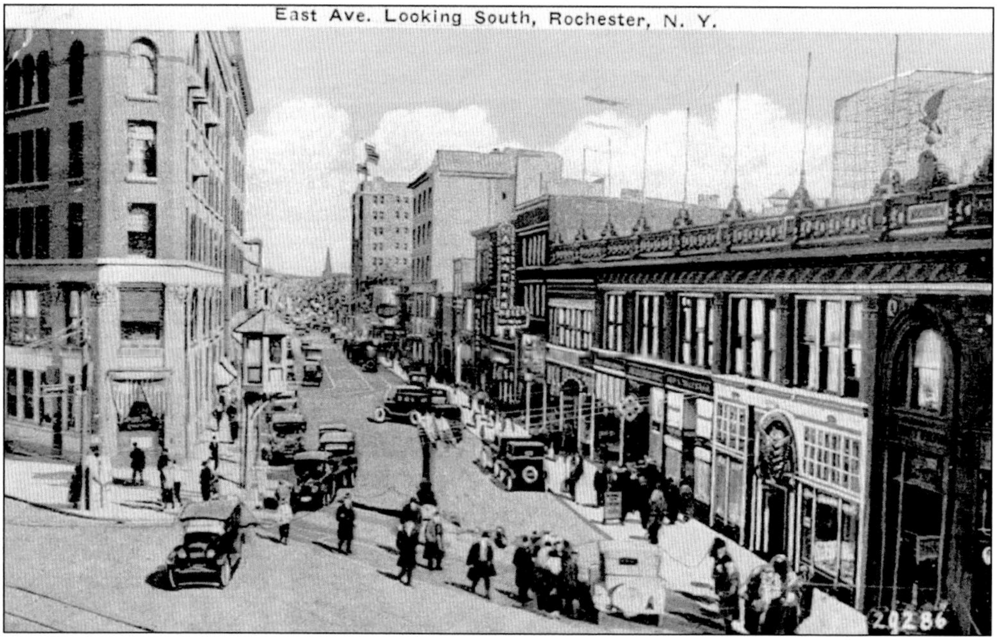

A Scrantoms postcard, *c.* 1928, captures an active business day at the intersection of East Main Street and East Avenue. A traffic tower has been erected in front of the Triangle Building on the left to regulate increasing automobile traffic. The Liberty Building across the street has a few classical architectural features along its top and even poles for colorful displays of flags and pennants during celebrations. The Manhattan Restaurant is just up along that block.

An original turn-of-the-century photograph from the *Souvenir of Rochester* booklet captures activity at the four corners. The Elwood building is on the right; the Powers Building is across the street on the left.

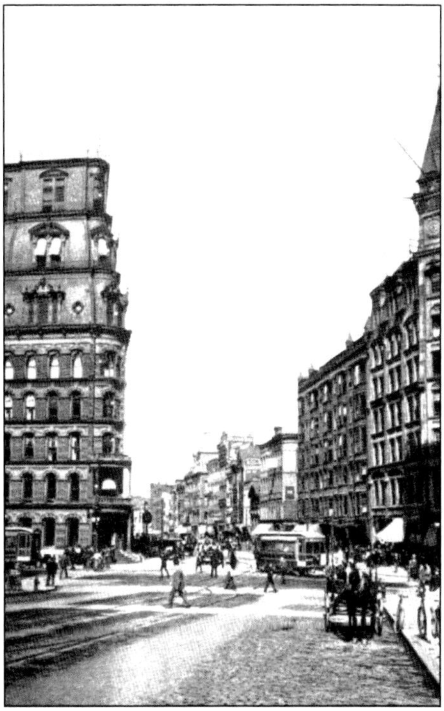

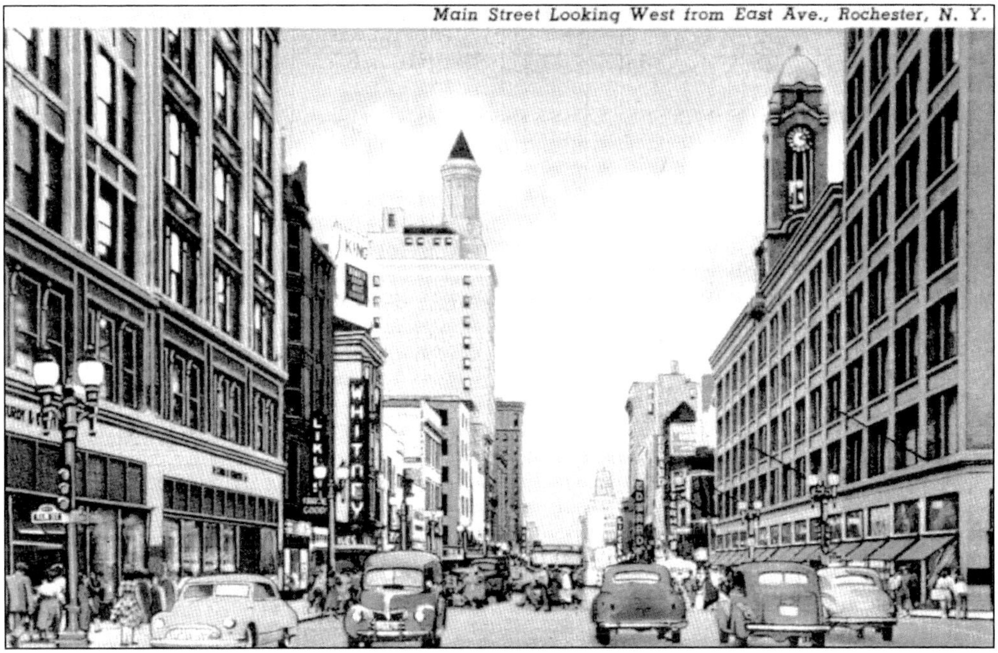

Bloated automobiles of the 1940s and 1950s fill Main Street in this card dated 1954. Sibleys, the retail giant of the region, is on the right. Rival department store McCurdy's is across the street. The two faced off for decades, but it was a common assumption that together they established the retail district for the city and therefore needed each other. The trolleys are gone from the modern city, replaced by busses. Even the subway has gasped its last breath, as cars are now the dominant form of travel.

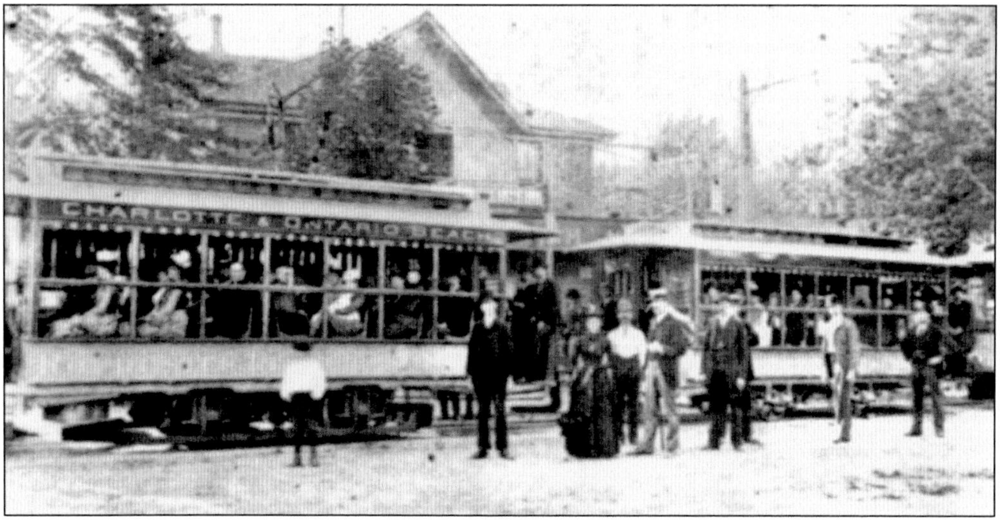

Charlotte and Ontario Beach trolleys and a trailer car are packed with families anxious for a day or two of recreation and excitement at Ontario Beach Park. The cars are in front of the Beach House on Lake Avenue.

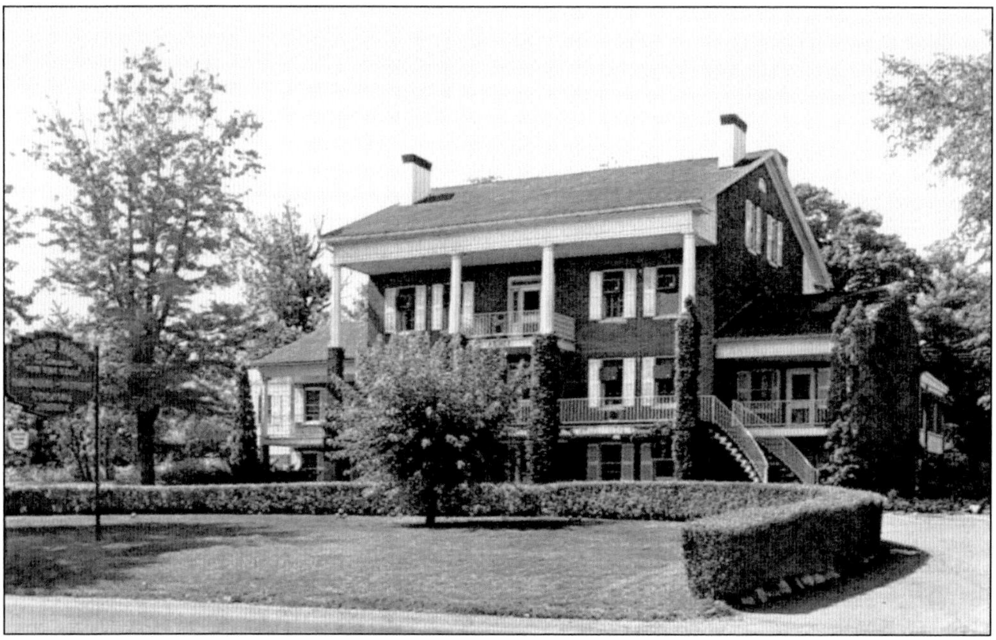

The Spring House Restaurant on Monroe Avenue was built as a canal inn beside the Erie Canal in 1822. The canal prism is still behind it and there is a set of locks just up the road behind Pittsford Plaza. Although there were mineral springs nearby, the Spring House gets its name from its upper-floor ballroom that "springs" from a double set of joists.

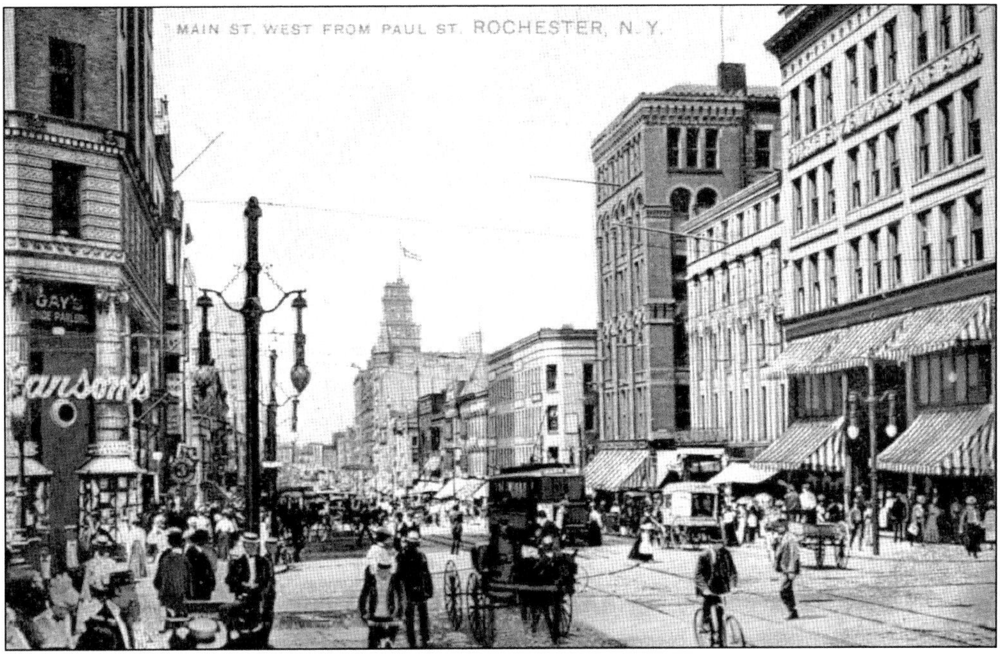

A 1907 image of Main Street looking west from St. Paul was taken when bikes, buggies, trolleys, and good-old foot power were the means by which city folk got around. There are no clattering tin lizzies yet to spook the horses and set the trolley conductors to cursing.

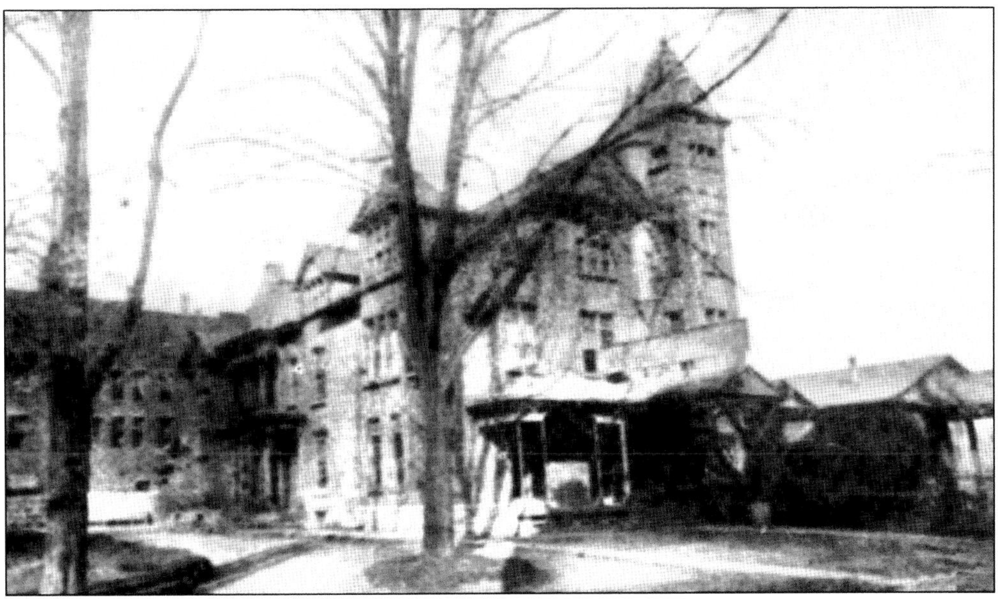

The Rome, Watertown, and Ogdensburg depot was located along the river north of downtown on State Street.

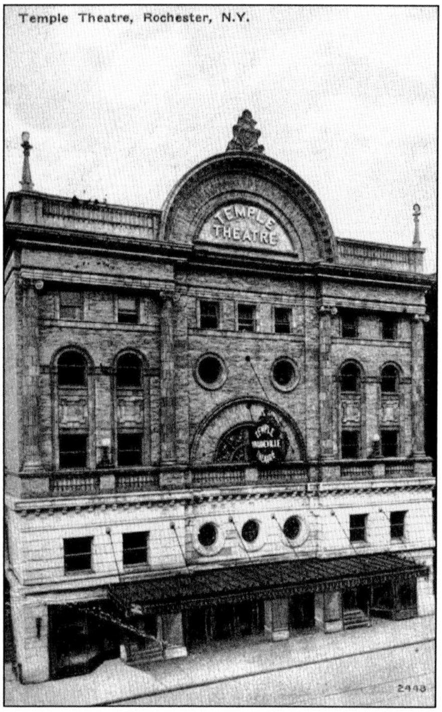

Most city neighborhoods eventually had their own theaters, but the real palaces were downtown. The Temple Theater on South Clinton as well as the RKO Palace, Regent, Lyceum, and Loews Rochester were among the grander houses that offered patrons vaudevilles, movies, and other entertainments. To step through their doors was to enter the world of the exotic. With soaring ceilings and staircases modeled after those in Italian villas that descended into piazzas, even the poorest soul was made to feel aristocratic when coming down from the balcony.

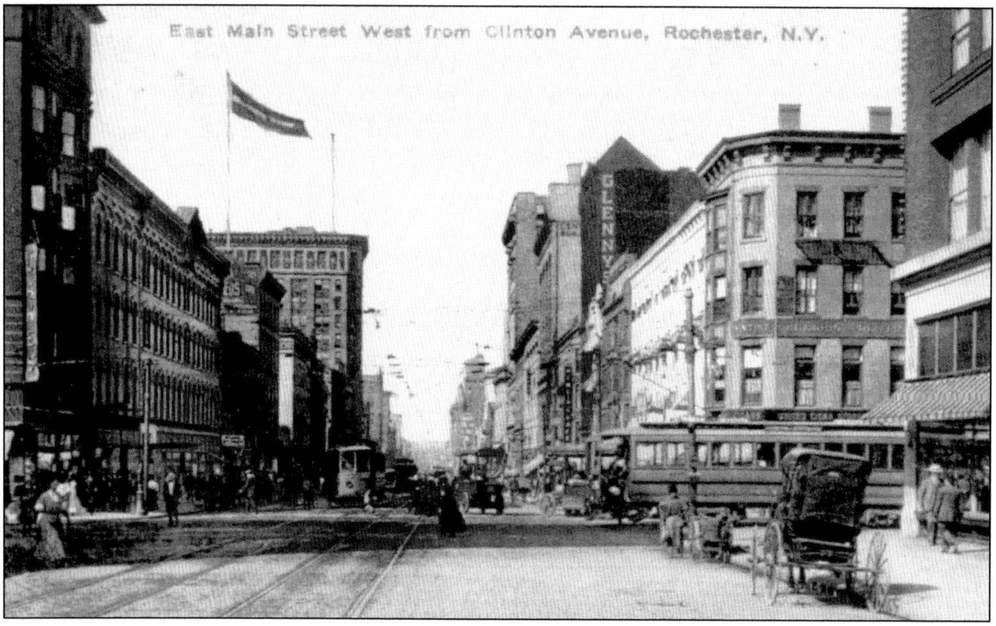

A trolley heads north after having just passed through the Main and Clinton intersection. This is a *c.* 1913 view, and already there were rumblings about getting these cars off the main roads. The overhead wiring was unsightly and the tracks needed constant repair, which caused back ups. The cars were dangerous when they made turns because the ends swung out over the tracks. They often caught a car fender or, worse yet, a pedestrian or horse. The Erie Canal also was considered a relic, and people wanted it out of the city because it stank and its confounded lift bridges were always jamming up causing long delays.

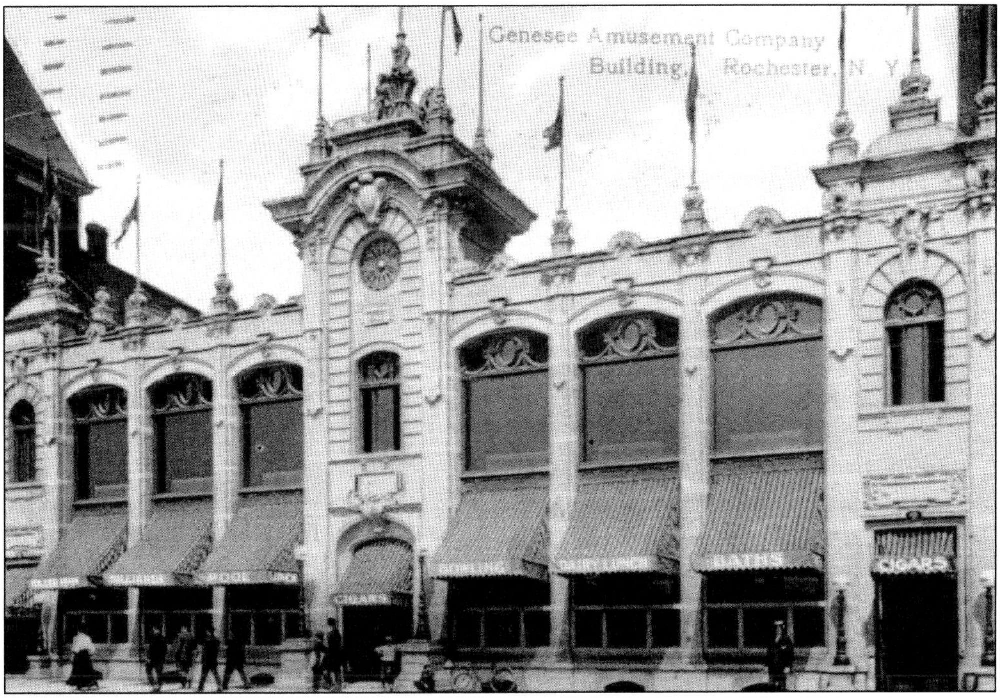

Passengers arriving on the Erie Canal, Erie Railroad, or Lehigh Valley were welcomed at the nearby Genesee Amusement Company. Visitors could refresh themselves with numerous indulgences, including swimming, baths, billiards, roller skating, and bowling. After a meal they could get a good cigar or ice cream.

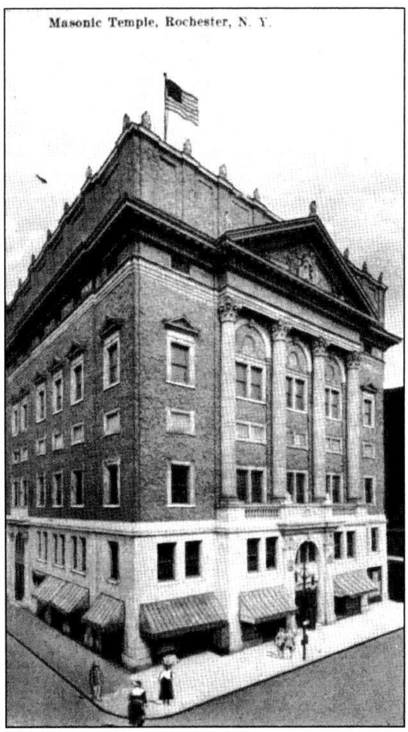

There had been some big changes when this postcard of the Masonic Temple was mailed in 1922. For example, prohibition was in effect, causing more harm than good as it gave rise to organized crime. Women finally won the right to vote in 1920. The Erie Canal was being rerouted around the southern part of the city, and the massive civic undertaking of building a subway and an elevated platform to carry Broad Street over the river was about to get underway.

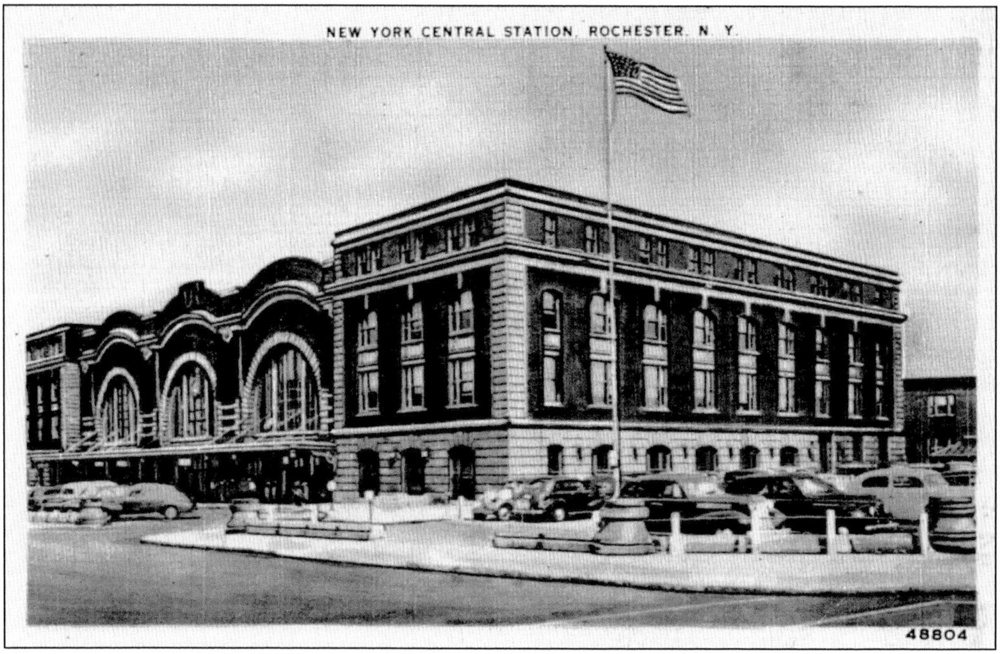

The New York Central Station opened on Central Avenue in 1913. It was a masterful creation by local architect Claude Bragdon. Large and graceful, its beauty resided in its simplicity. Many considered it one of the New York Central's 10 most beautiful stations.

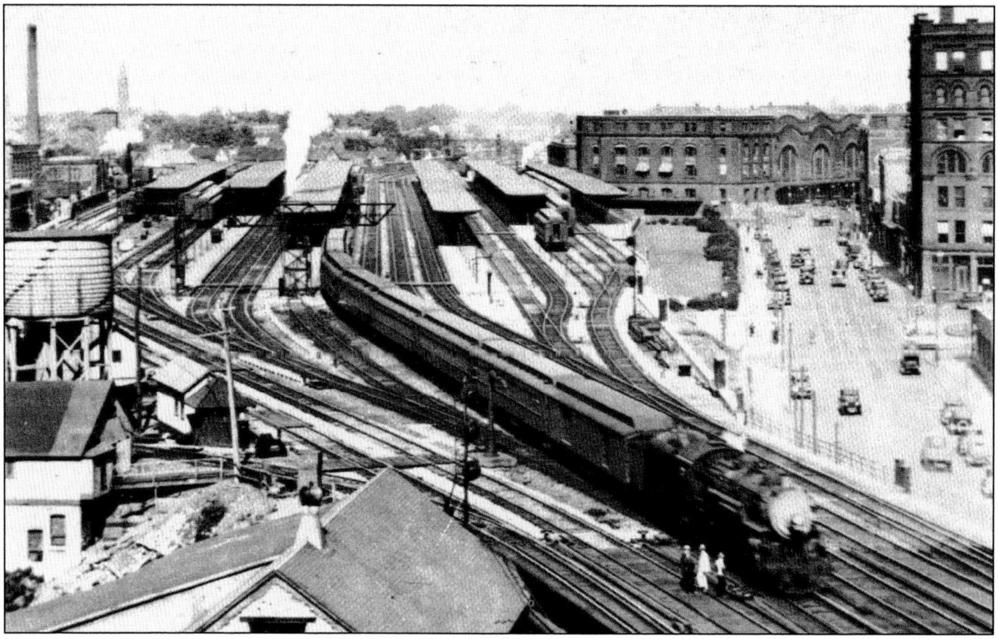

In this William Gordon postcard, 16 tracks are required to serve the New York City facility that was arrayed between the river and Central Avenue. The photograph was taken in 1917. The Claude Bragdon–designed station is visible upper right. Before the call of "all aboard!," the steam engines had to take on water and coal, food went to the elegant dining cars, and a few squirts of oil were applied to the engine's drive rods for good measure.

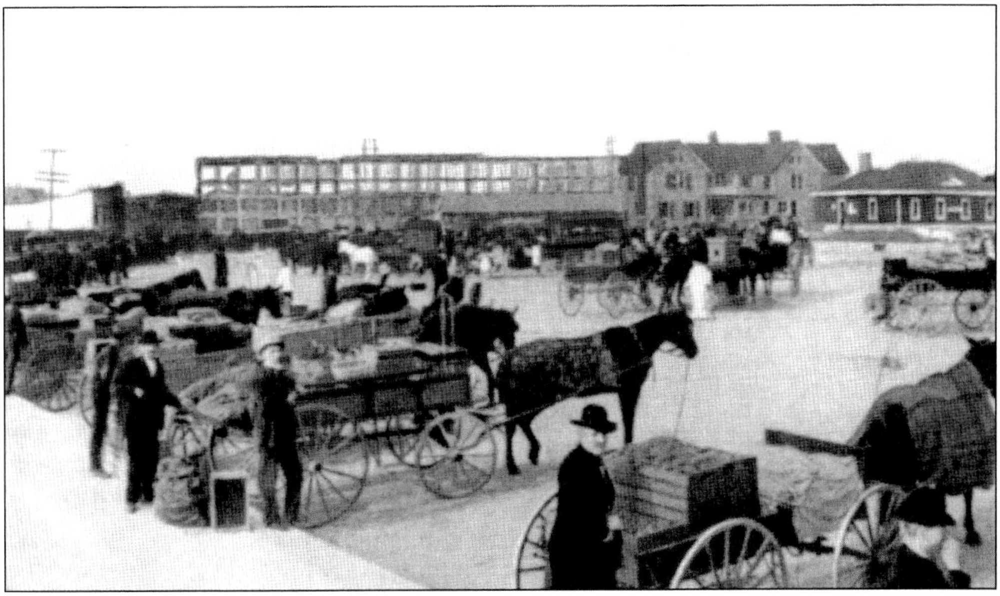

The public market near Central Avenue is pictured here as it looked at the beginning of the 20th century. It has always been a bustling place filled with hawkers shouting down the competition. For variety, good prices, and lots of character, there was no better place to spend a Saturday.

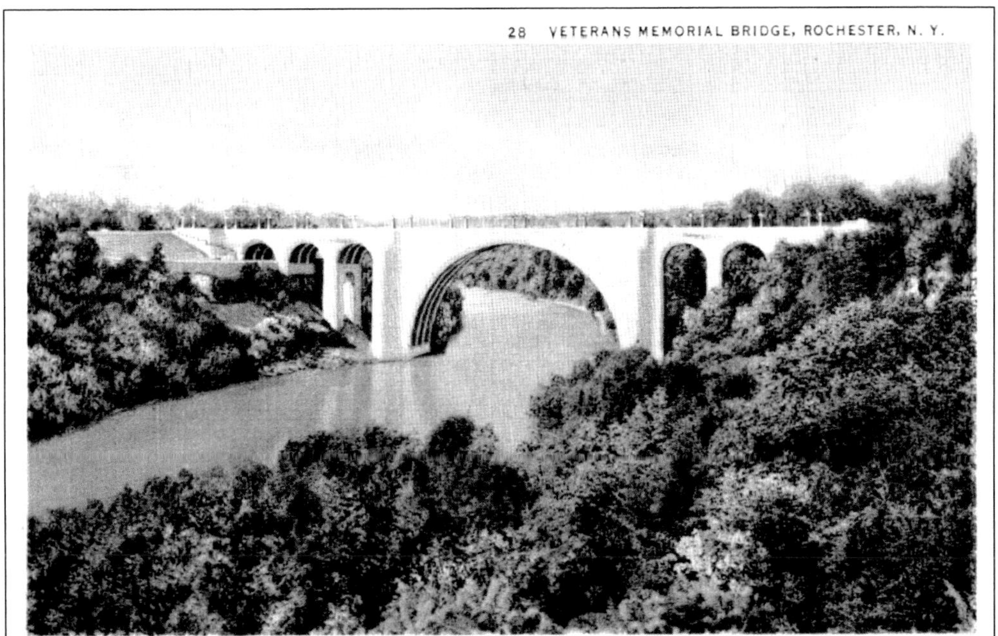

Postmarked April 1938, this postcard shows a bold view of the Veterans Memorial Bridge. It was another massive civil undertaking carried out nearly a century after the stone arches of the Erie Canal aqueduct were built across the Genesee.

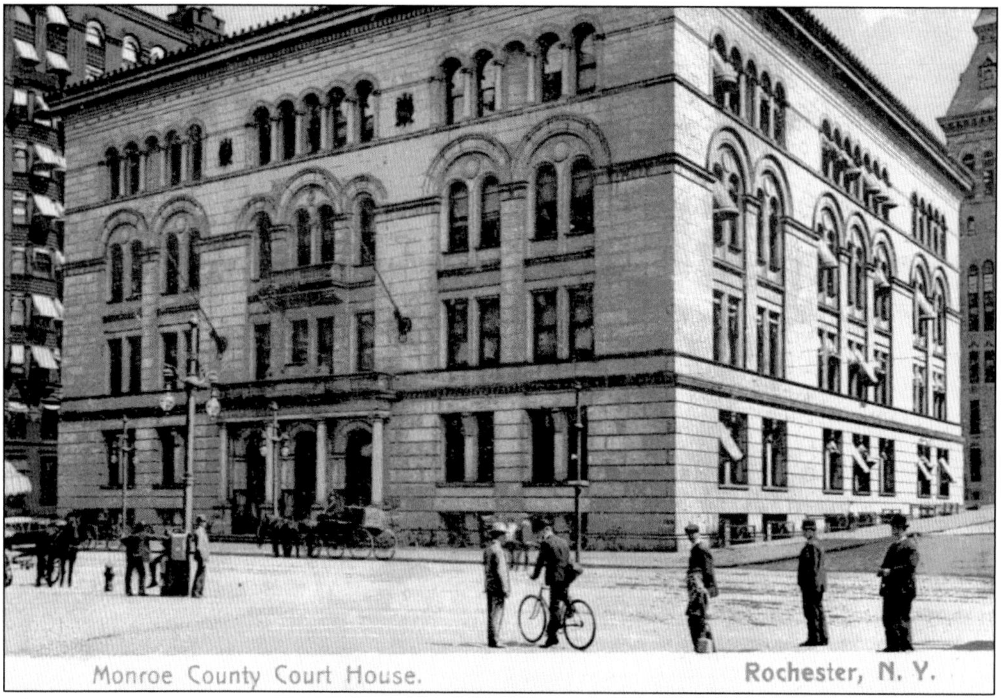

The Monroe County Courthouse at 39 West Main Street had two predecessors. It opened in 1896 and was another example of civic grandeur both inside and out.

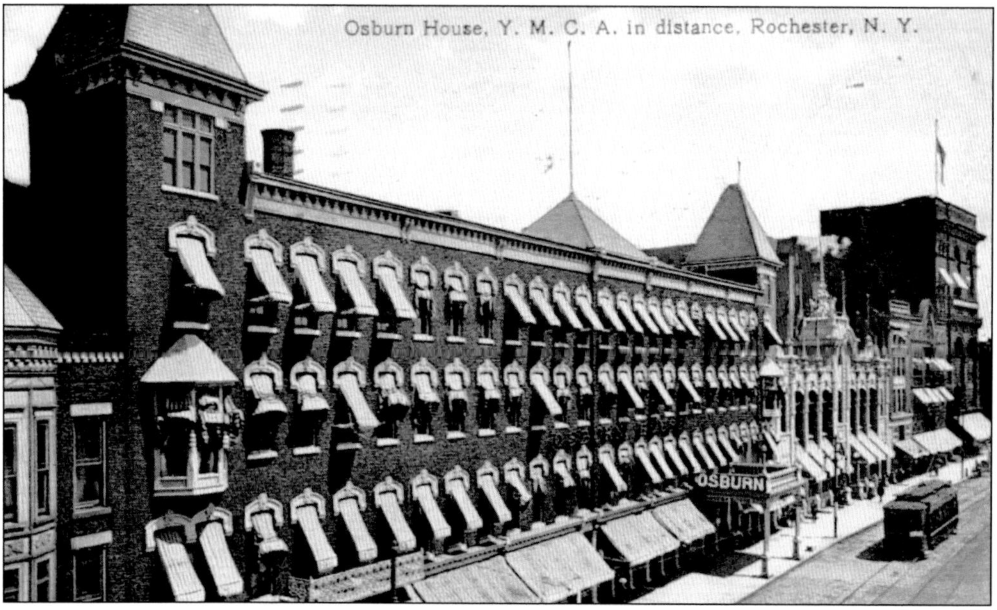

The Osburn House, Genesee Amusement Company, and YMCA are all pictured in this postcard dated 1910. In the 1898 *Souvenir of Rochester,* the Osburn House advertised that its then new location on South St. Paul Street offered free omnibus travel to and from depots, elevators as well as all modern improvements, including electric lighting and steam heat in every room. It offered electric cars to all depots and theaters and a large burglar and fireproof vault. Rates for a room were $2.00 to $2.50 per day.

The romanticized classicism of the Gay Nineties is evident in this interior view of the Monroe County Courthouse. Arcades sculpted from expensive marbles, hand wrought iron, brass railings, mosaics, and fine woods all applied by expert craftsmen gave the city a stunning interior that endures to this day.

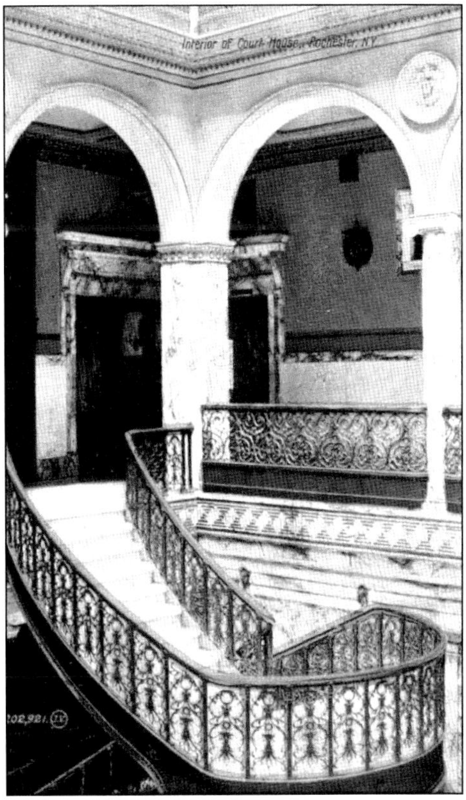

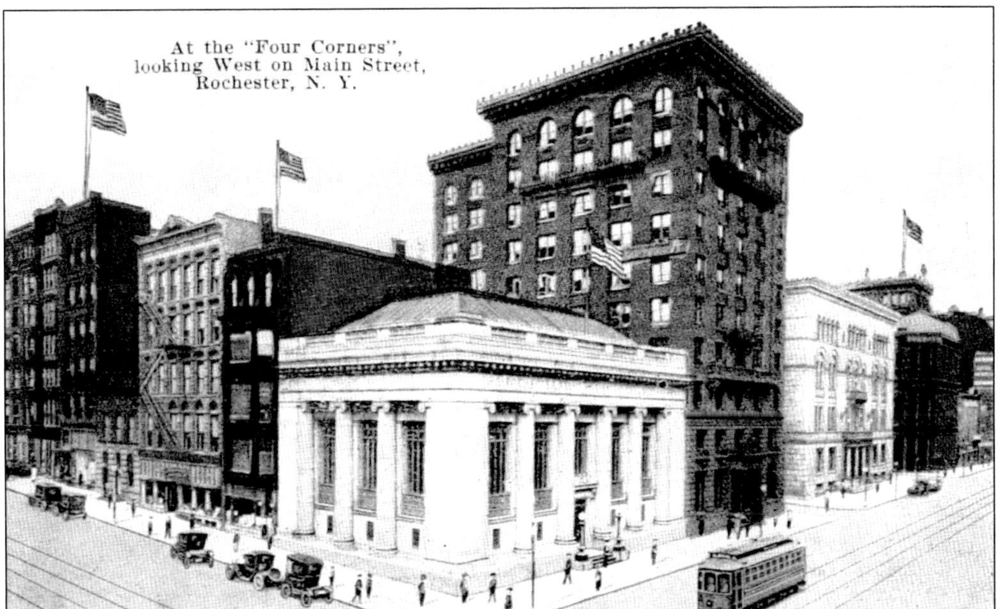

Nestled beside a towering neighbor, the Rochester Trust and Safe Deposit Company, located on the southwest corner of West Main and Exchange Streets, had a rock solid appearance that was intended to reassure depositors.

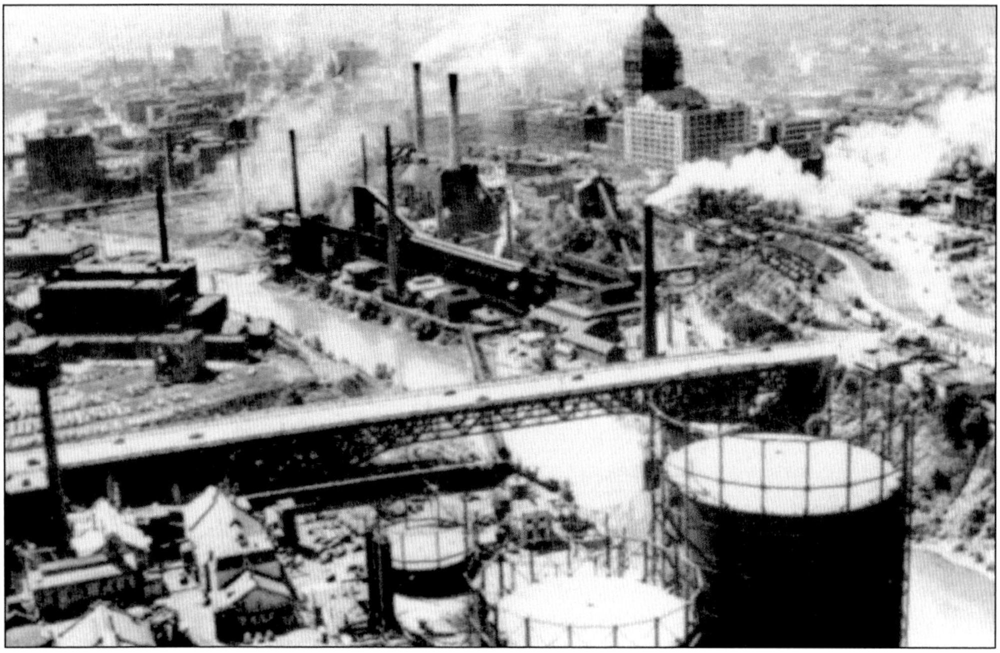

The proof of the devastating effects of industrialization on the environment is made quite convincingly. However, the free-enterprise system that created this was not long in finding ways to clean it up. This scene, from a souvenir flier, is much different today.

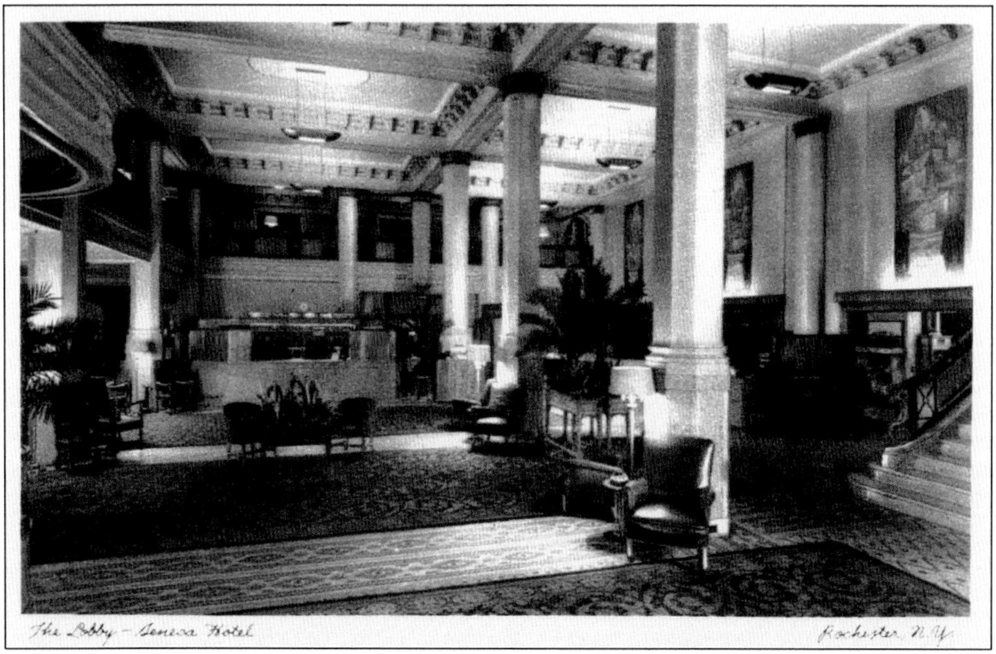

Another look at the Seneca lobby finds it again restful and inviting. The card explains that the hotel is spacious, cheerful, and comfortable. It is also "Popular for Conventions and Social Gatherings. Murals Depicting Historical, Industrial, Educational and Commercial Rochester, Painted by an outstanding Artist, Adorn the Walls."

The Richford Hotel at Elm and Chestnut Streets was not as elegant as the Rochester or Seneca, but it provided accessibility, comfort, and cleanliness all popularly priced. It later became the Cadillac Hotel.

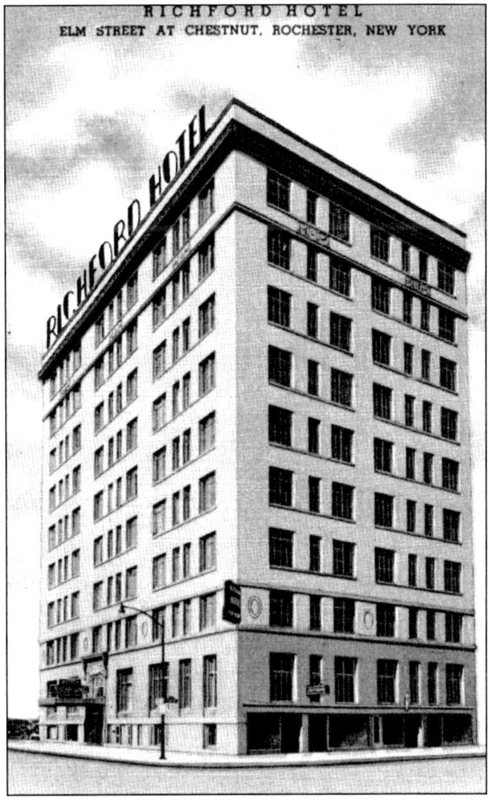

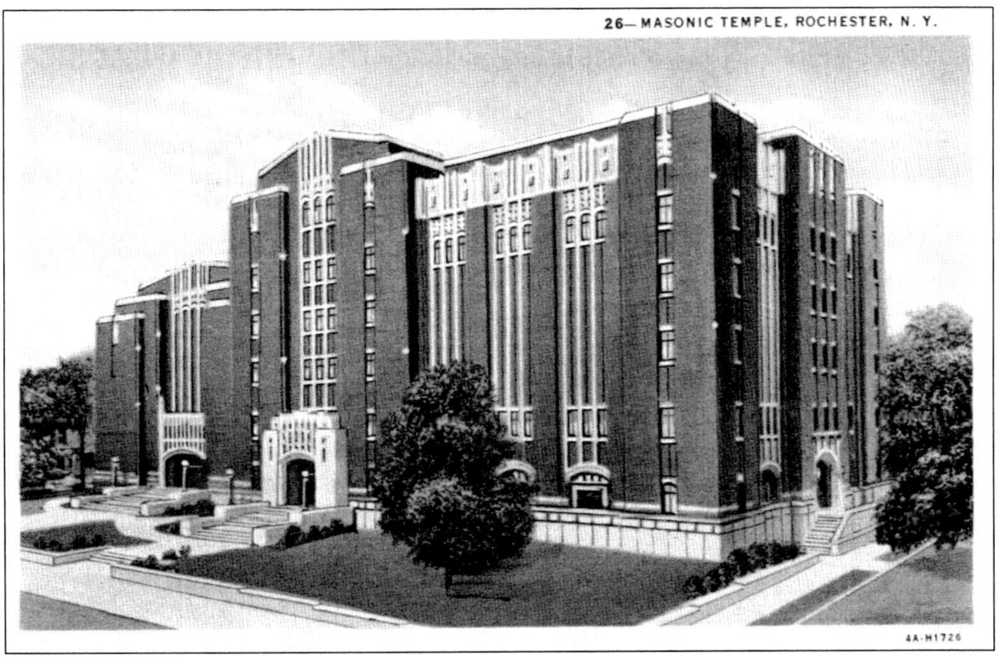

The Masonic Temple and Auditorium Theater on East Main Street are still in use today. The theater hosts some of Broadway's greatest triumphs, such as *The Phantom of the Opera.*

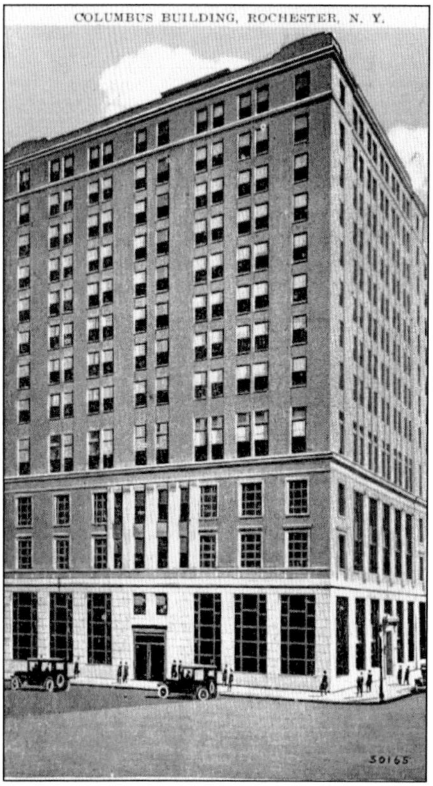

The Columbus Building bears the simple straightforward functional look of the Richford Hotel, its neighbor across Chestnut Street.

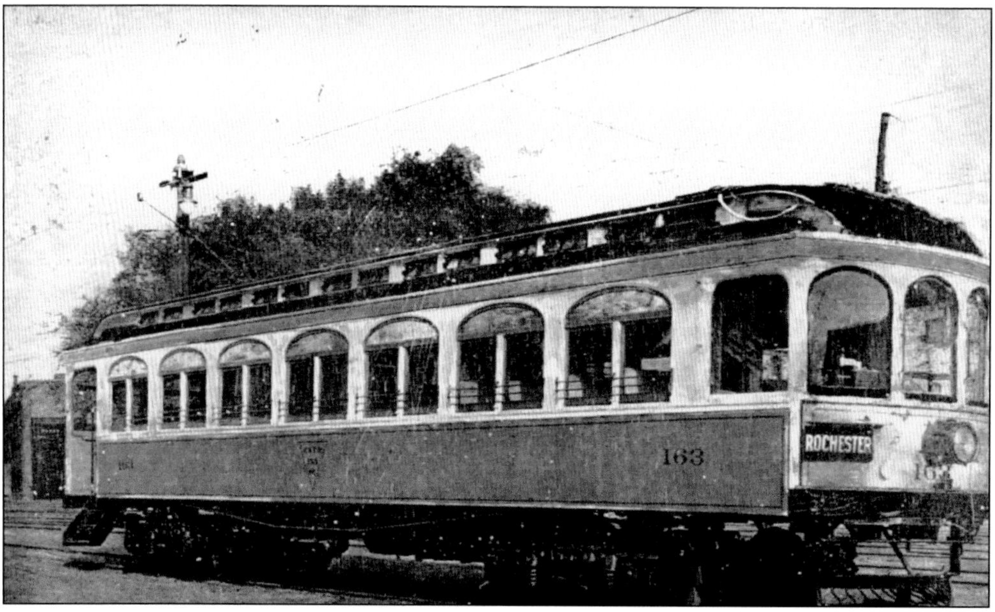

This handsome interurban is the Rochester, car No. 31 on the Rochester and Eastern Railway en route to Geneva in 1903. The car was painted yellow and cream. This William Gordon postcard even tells us the car weighed 71,000 pounds.

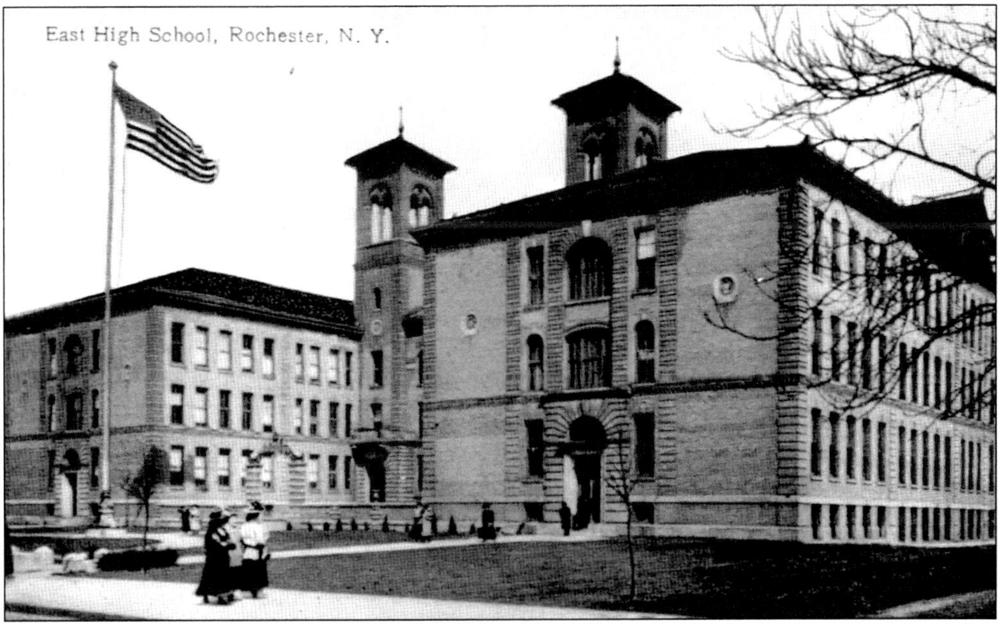

Education was taken very seriously throughout Greater Rochester—as it was in all American cities—and it became evident in the highly stylized and sometimes lavish schools that were built. People grumbled, but not for long, at the added expense of including a gymnasium in the new East High School. The school opened in 1903. For many years the Rochester school system was a model for cities across the country. Representatives came here to see how things were done.

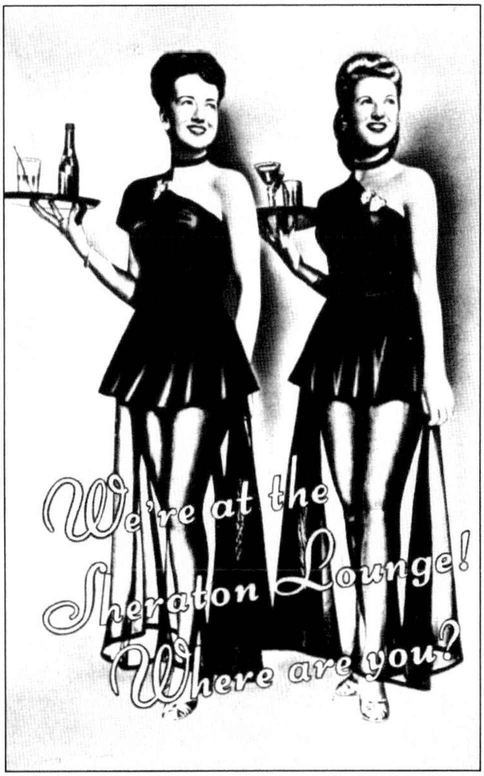

The Sheraton Hotel conveys on this card that it is "The Hallmark of Hospitality." They were not shy in their attempts to draw patrons to their Sheraton Lounge where they offered, "your favorite drink, mixed with a touch of genius . . .served with a touch of Venus."

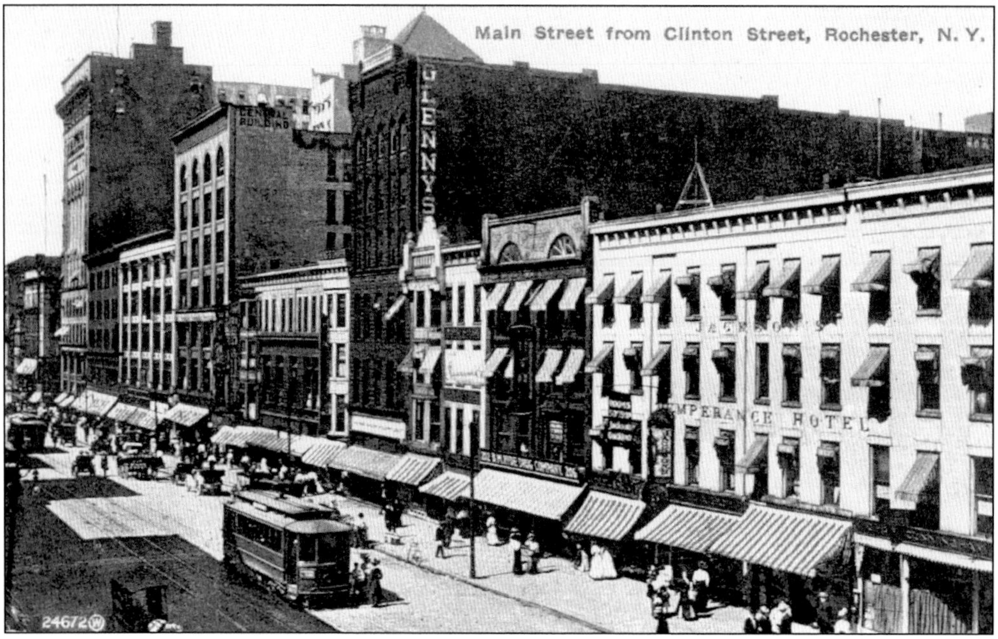

This view down Main Street from Clinton shows shoppers making use of the many awnings stores provided. By offering cool shade, the customer might linger in front of a shop window filled with dry goods and be inclined to make a purchase. The Temperance Hotel offered lodging to those unwilling to stay in establishments that offered guests spirits.

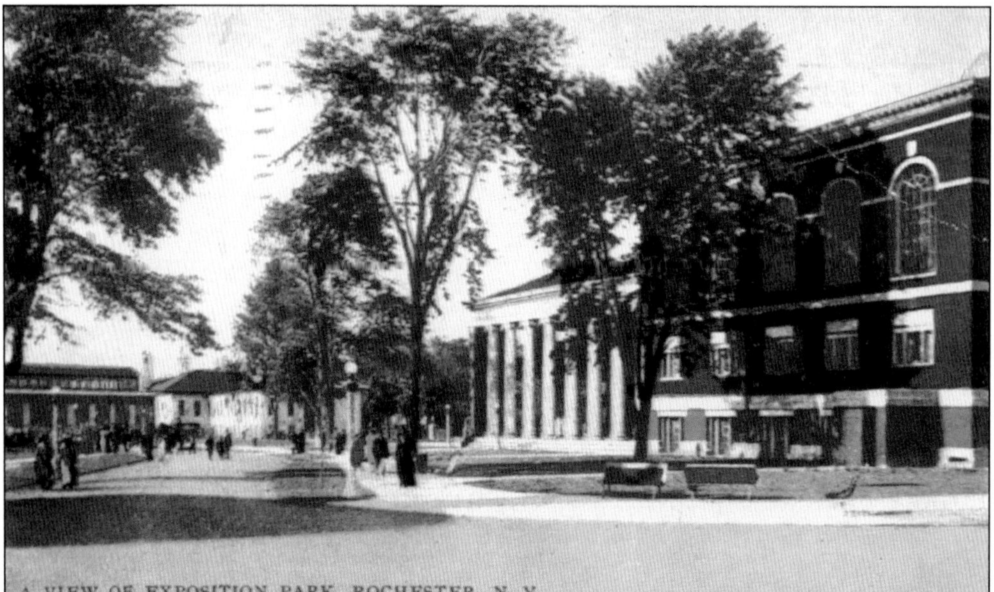

Exposition Park opened in 1911 on the grounds formerly occupied by the State Industrial School. It filled the area between Backus, Bloss, Dewey, and Emerson with exhibition halls where technological, agricultural, and industrial improvements were put on display.

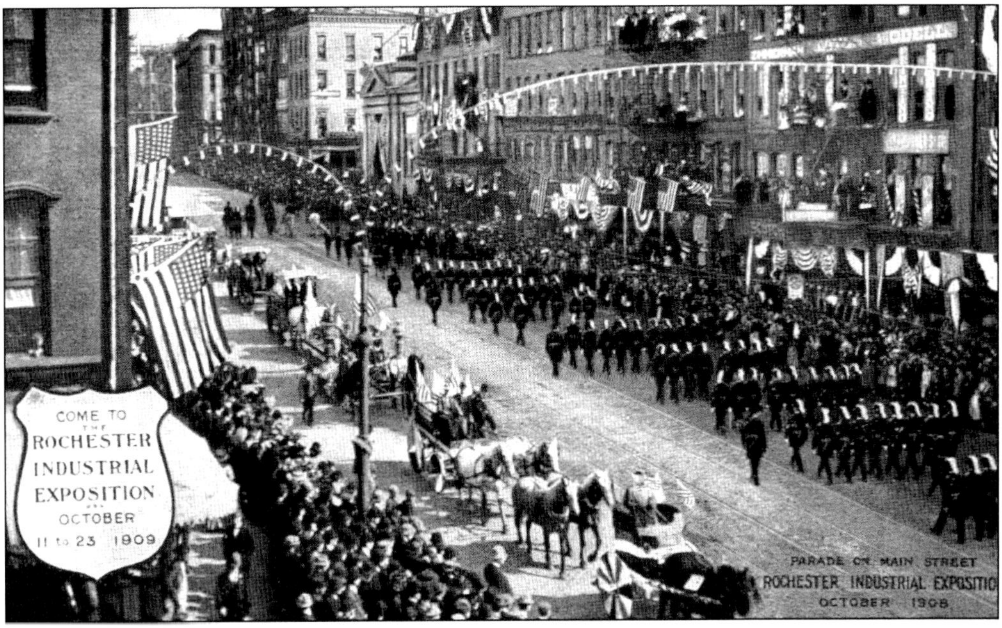

A special card was issued for the 1909 Rochester Industrial Exposition. Downtown is highly decorated and regaled in flags. The sender encourages her friend in Geneva to come to the city for the event: "You will miss half of your life if you don't!"

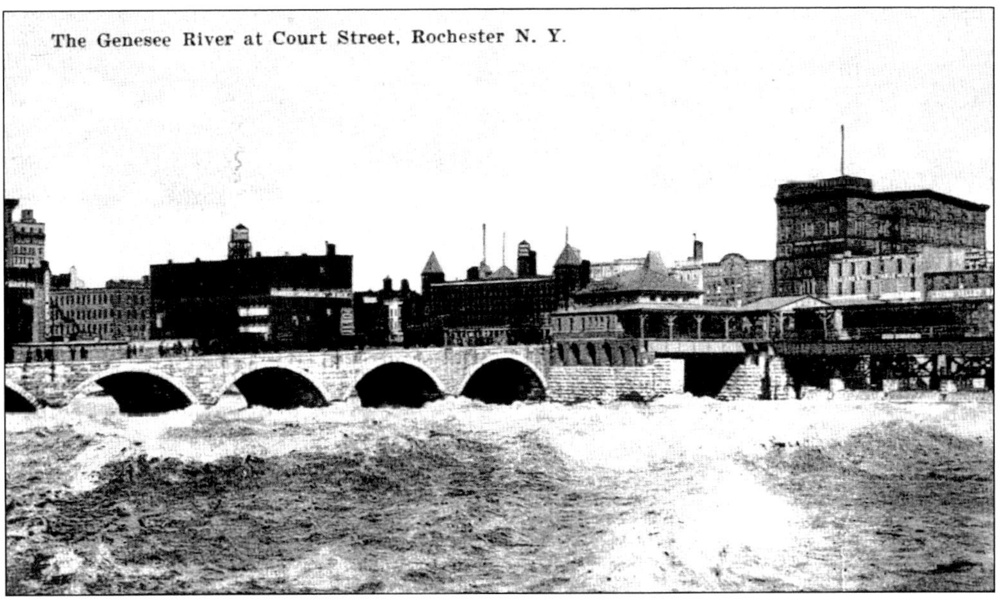

The river is turbulent as it passes under the Court Street Bridge. The platform and approaches to the Lehigh Valley Station on the right are suspended over the river. The twin towers of the Osburn House can be seen just in front of the station. The canal was an unwelcome feature of the city, and its days were numbered in this 1921 view. Plans were under way to install a subway in its bed.

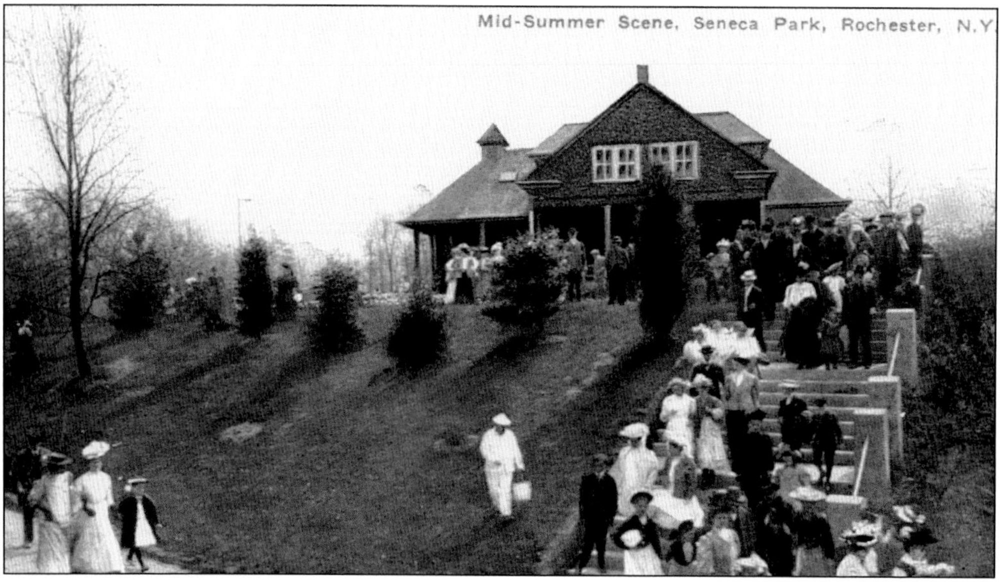

In the 1890s, the newly formed Parks Commission wisely sought the expertise of Frederick Law Olmstead, the nation's leading park designer. Seneca Park, along the river, was one park Olmstead contributed to heavily. A creek was dammed to form Trout Pond, and roads were laid out along old Indian trails. Outings were important in those days of hard labor. Visitors would wear their Sunday best, as evidenced by these leisurely strollers at Seneca Park in 1910.

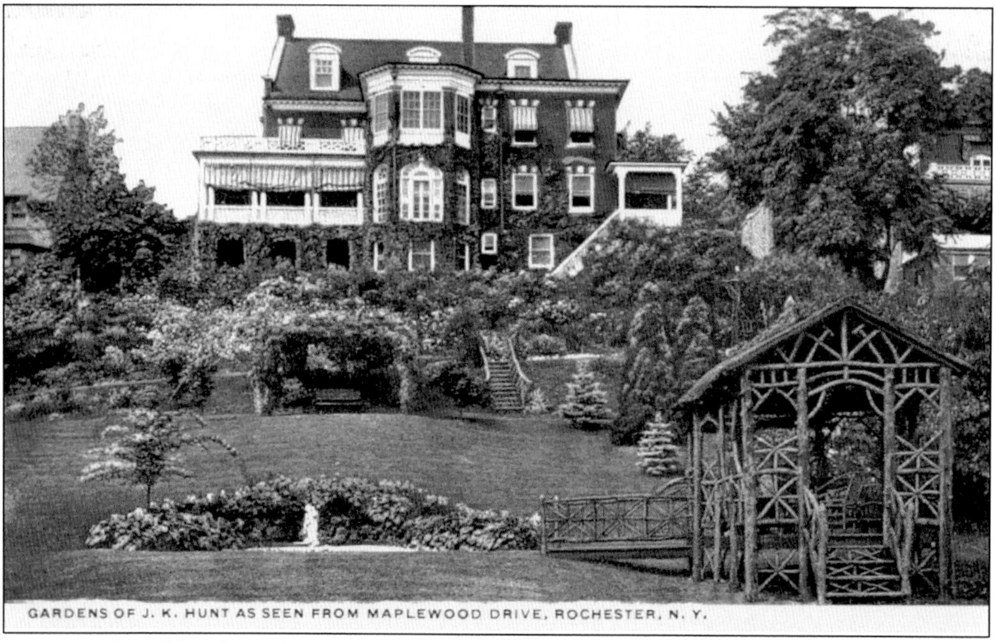

Renowned worldwide as the "Flour City" because of the tons of flour ground at the milling complexes around its falls, Rochester would have that torch seized by Midwestern states. The city then became nationally famous as the Flower City because of its fabulous nurseries and parks. Neighborhood parks resplendent with flowers and fountains appeared, and homeowners at every level continued the tradition of exceptional gardens in their own yards. These are the J.K. Hunt gardens in 1919 as they appeared behind his ultra-fashionable home on Maplewood Avenue.

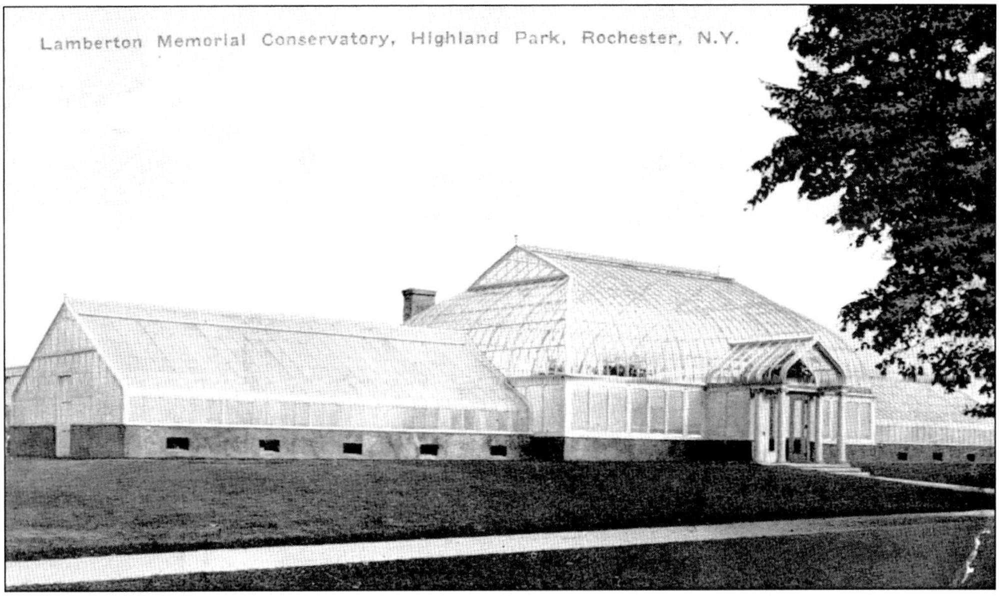

The Lamberton Conservatory opened in 1911 in Highland Park. It was named after Alexander B. Lamberton, a former president of the parks board. The glass enclosed structure remains in use today, providing a Victorian-era facility for floral exhibits year-round. Highland Park continues as a nationally famous horticultural preserve and is considered one of Olmstead's greatest local works.

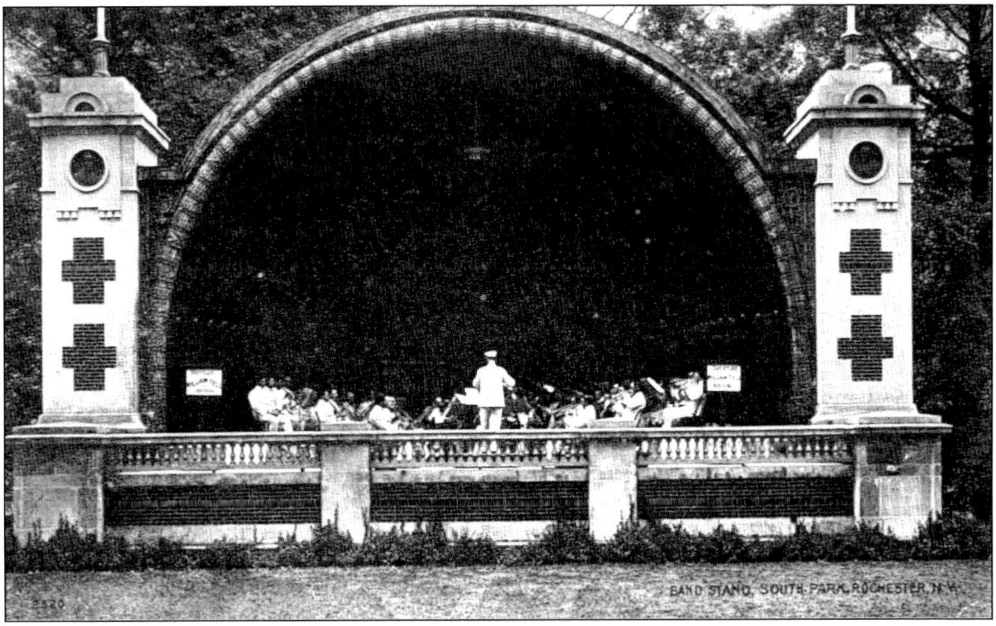

South Park (Genesee Valley Park) was laid out by Olmstead to make use of the pastoral fields and shadowed solitudes along the gentle banks of the Genesee south of the city. This was in stark contrast to Seneca Park that was sculpted along the river's precipitous gorge. Band concerts were well attended in the days before radio and television. Rail lines were run to the parks to make attendance easier. The band, pictured here in the South Park band shell, is playing the *William Tell Overture*.

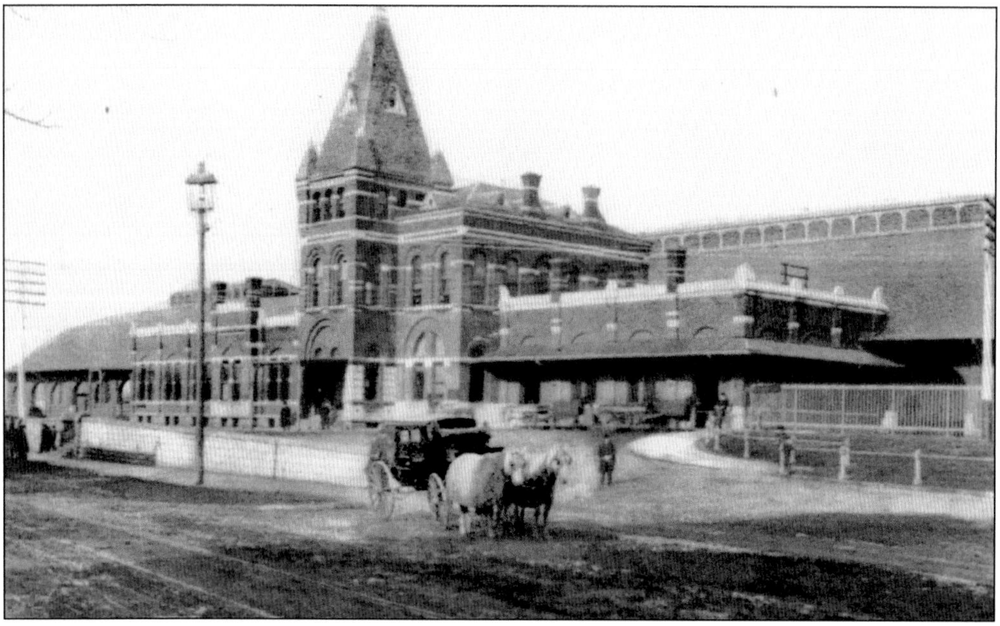

This New York Central and Hudson River Railroad depot at Central Avenue and St. Paul provided service from the 1880s through the first decade of the 20th century. The station's massive train shed, which provided shelter for passengers in harsh weather, can be seen behind the station. This William Gordon postcard uses a *c.* 1882 image.

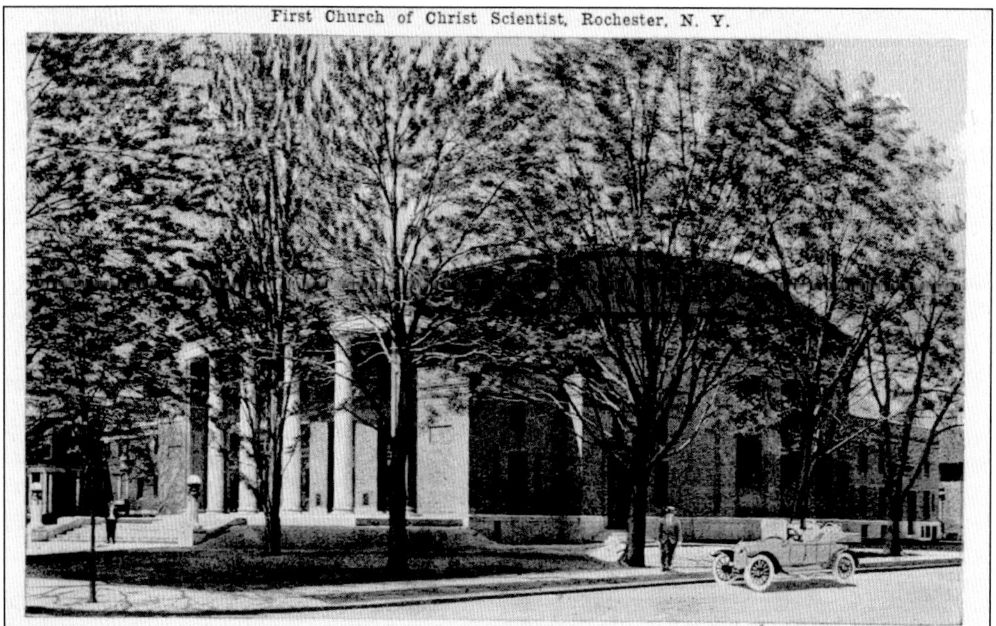

The impressive First Church of Christ Scientist is located on East Avenue beside the Hiram Sibley Mansion.

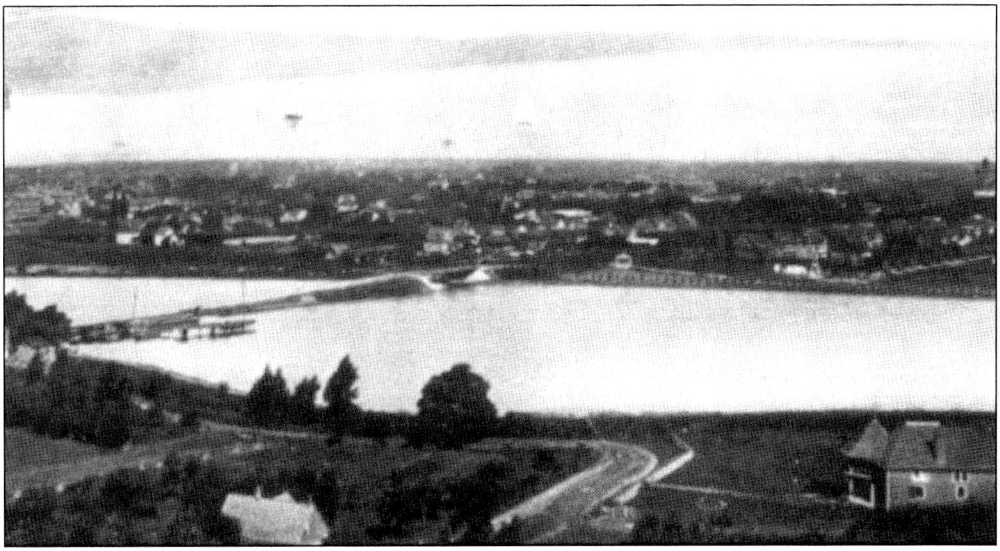

A wonderful example of artistic license is found in this postcard view of the western Wide Waters, an enlarged basin on the Erie Canal. The German artist was told Rochester was near Lake Ontario so he painted in a lake, complete with shoreline and sailboats where there were none. He did not do a bad job, actually.

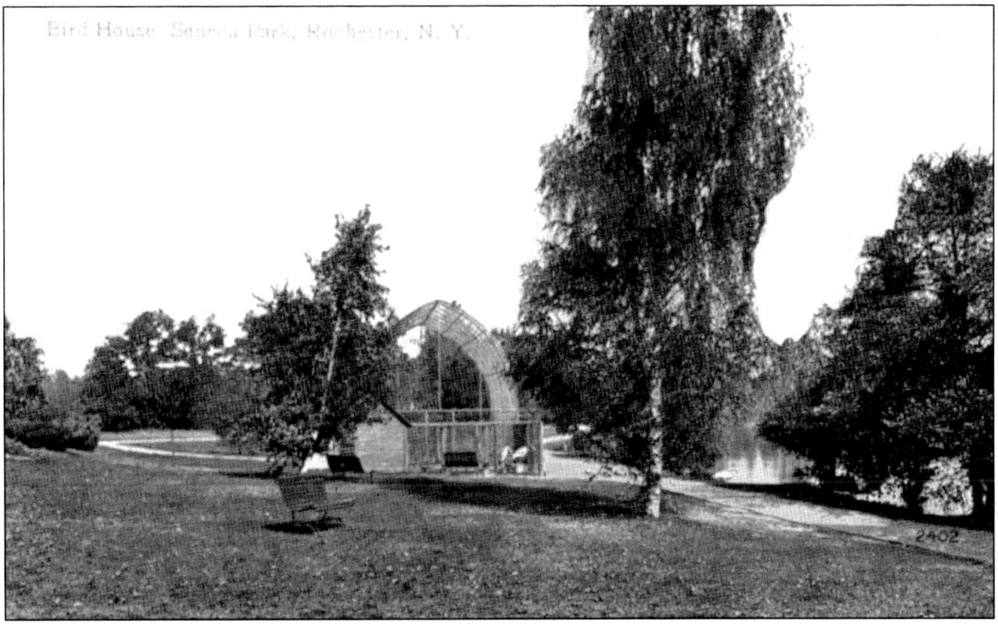

The birdhouse, or aviary, at Seneca Park housed many species of birds. The park had a small collection of animals. At South Park, a herd of sheep was used to keep the grass low.

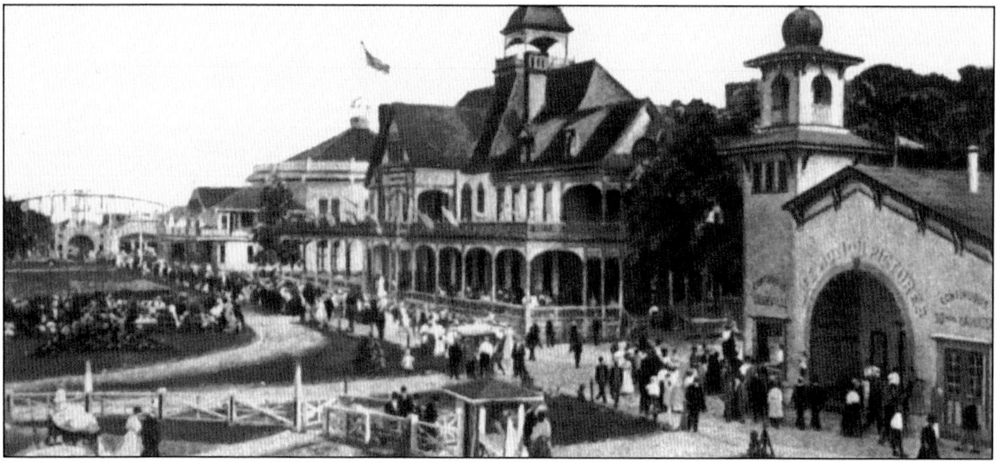

Ontario Beach Park on Lake Ontario opened in 1906 and quickly grew into a major amusement park, attracting visitors from Canada, Pennsylvania, Ohio, and other parts of the Northeast. Its offerings of fine dining and accommodations, lake and land activities, boardwalks, midways, and amusement rides brought trolley and trainloads of fun seekers every weekend. Quickly, more lakeside resorts opened along the lake. Some of the areas most fascinating postcards are of that era.

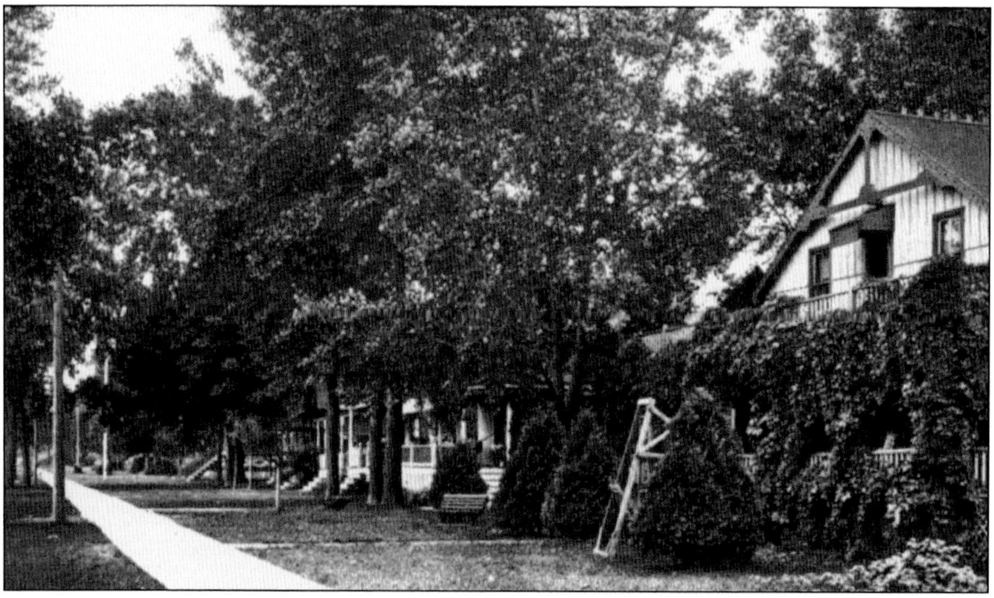

In the turn-of-the-century *Souvenir of Rochester,* Ontario Beach Park is already being called "The Coney Island of the West." Other resorts within easy reach were Windsor Beach, Sea Breeze, Summerville, Forest Lawn, Sodus Bay, Long Pond, Manitou Beach, and others around Irondequoit Bay. Pictured here is the Promenade at Summerville. Along its five streets, leading to the lake, were cottages set into small lush parcels.

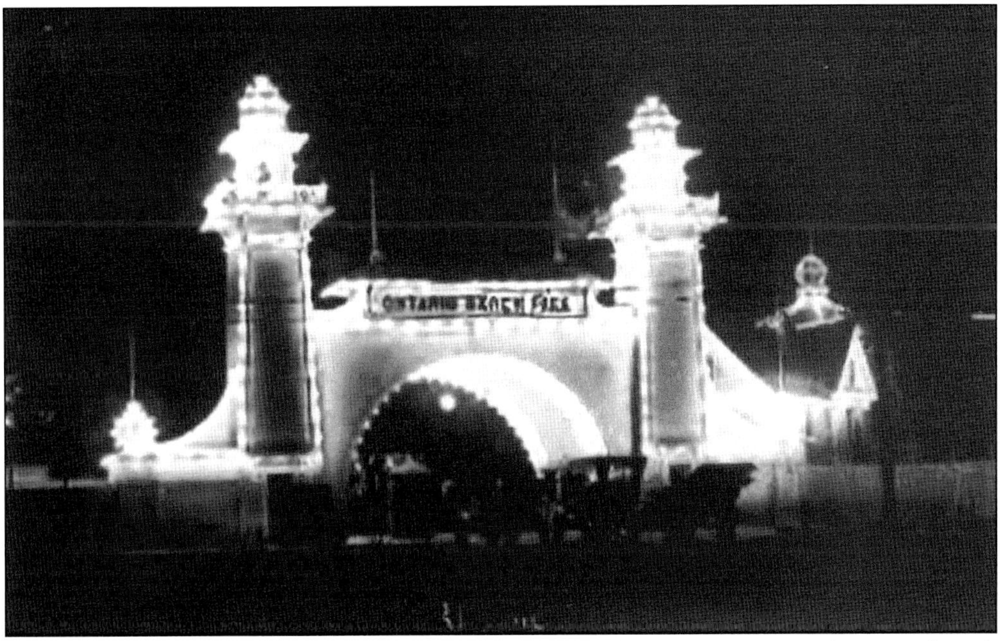

This dramatic night image of Ontario Beach Park is classified as a real photograph postcard. Each one was an actual photograph print from a negative. The back of the card was then imprinted with a place for a message and address.

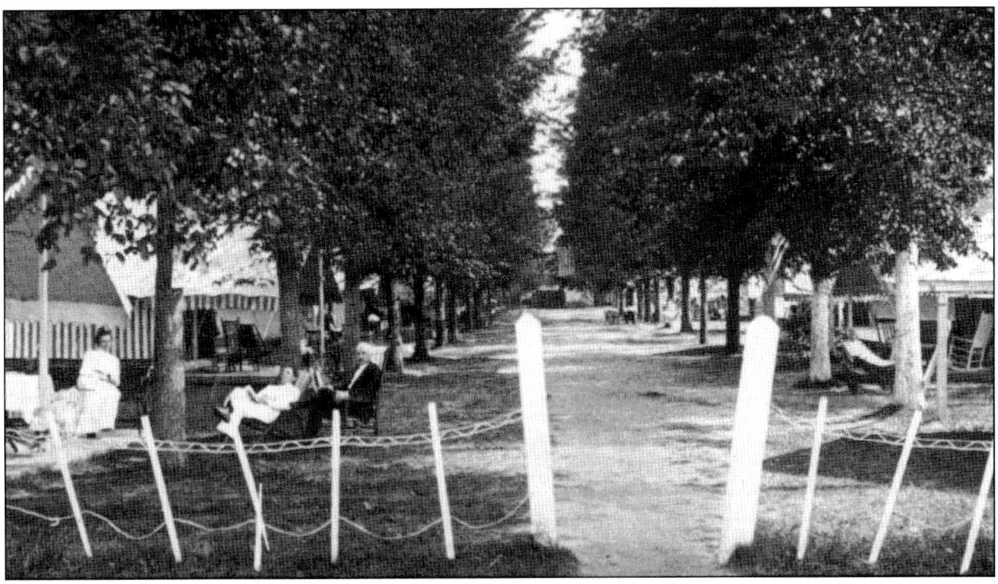

White City was a small summer colony near Windsor Beach. The name comes from the sophisticated white canvas tents families set up along the city's eight streets. Most were put on platforms or skids, and the interiors were often separated into a few rooms by canvas walls. Gardens and picnic areas added to the resort's homey atmosphere.

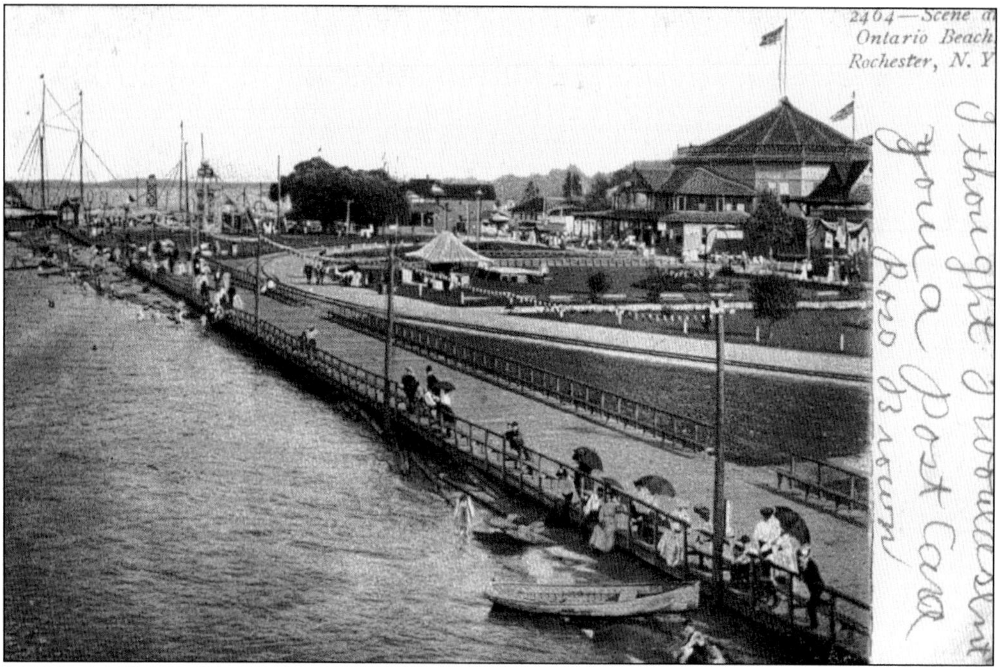

Perhaps the simple message written here is enough: "I thought I would send you a post card," signed Ross Brown. The card conveys visually the excitement of Ontario Beach Park. The lake and boardwalk are shown. Along the upper left, the Genesee River can be seen. A small schooner may be dropping off cargo at the Port of Rochester. The river enters the lake here. Large ferries that took passengers to and from Canada would tie up at piers.

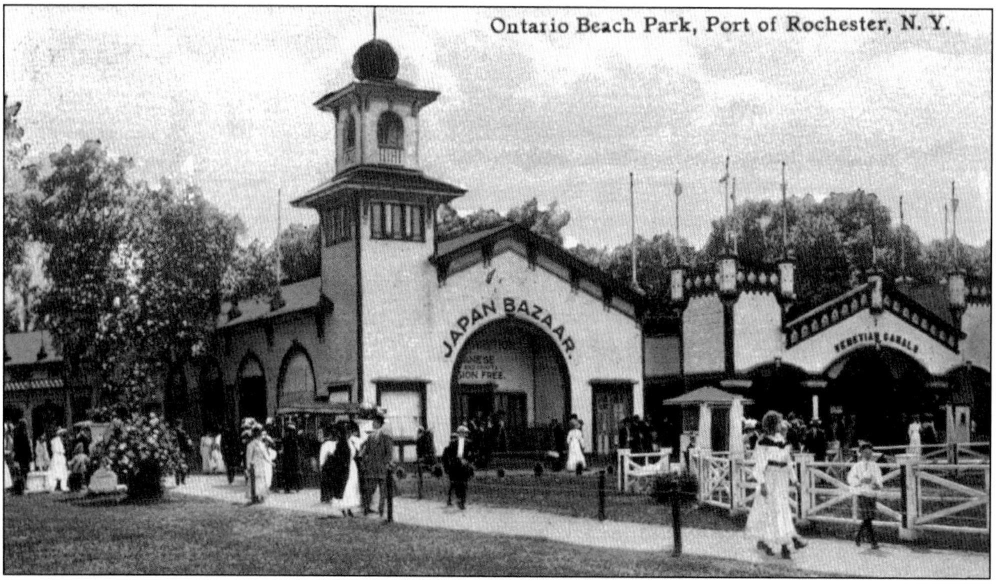

The message on the back of this Flower City series card is from R.J. to Mrs. Woodward at General Railway and Signal Works, a major industry less than 10 miles away. He tells her: "Going to stay three weeks instead of two! Having a wonderful time." The Japan Bazaar opened into a wonderfully tacky and vividly colored Japanese village where visitors could stroll among images, sounds, and fragrances associated with the Orient.

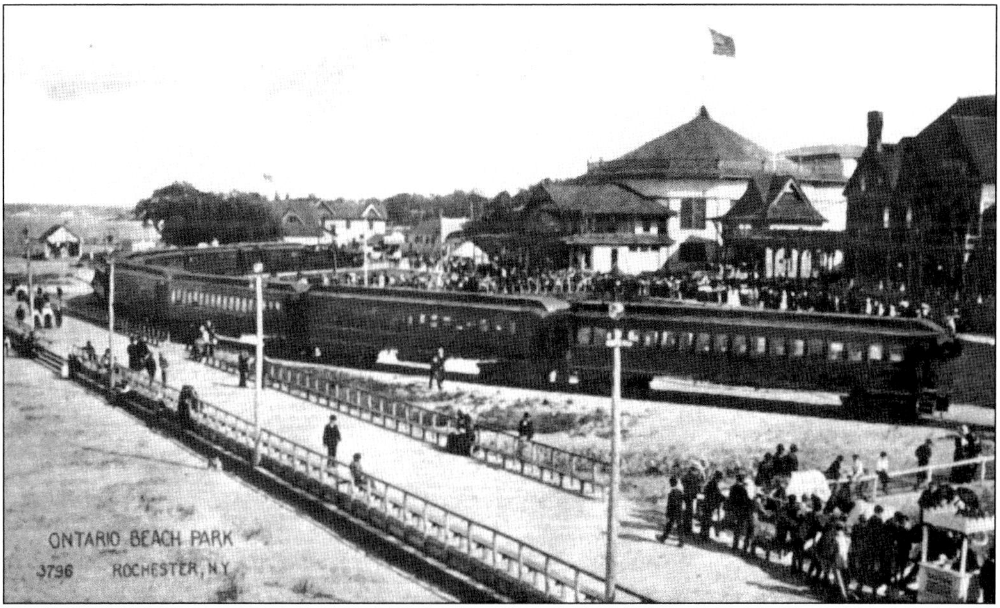

The arrival of trains with packed coaches and trolleys from numerous city and rural lines was endless on weekends. Eventually, this track was relocated outside the park for safety reasons and to lessen tie ups.

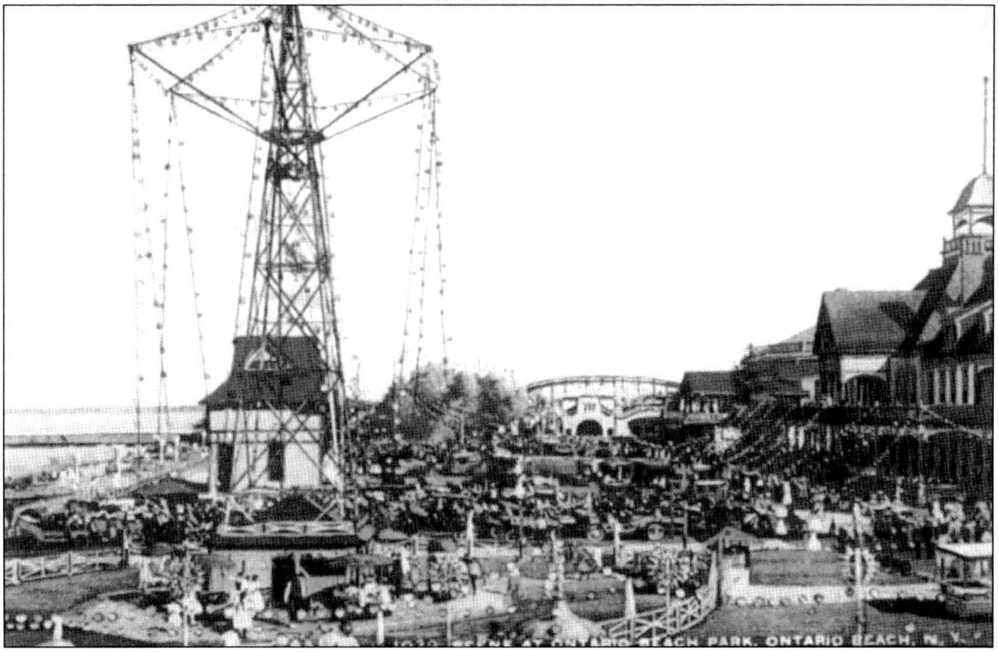

The park clearly made use of every inch of real estate. Of course the congestion of the Victorian grounds was preferable to that of the teaming city. Although fine food was available, carnival fare was most likely preferred, especially by the young who could not wait to have their insides suitably churned on one of these spindly amusement rides.

Amusement parks really come to life at night when gloriously illuminated in colored lights. This *c.* 1909 real photograph postcard of Ontario Beach Park gives us an idea of what passengers on the big steamers would have seen when making port at Rochester.

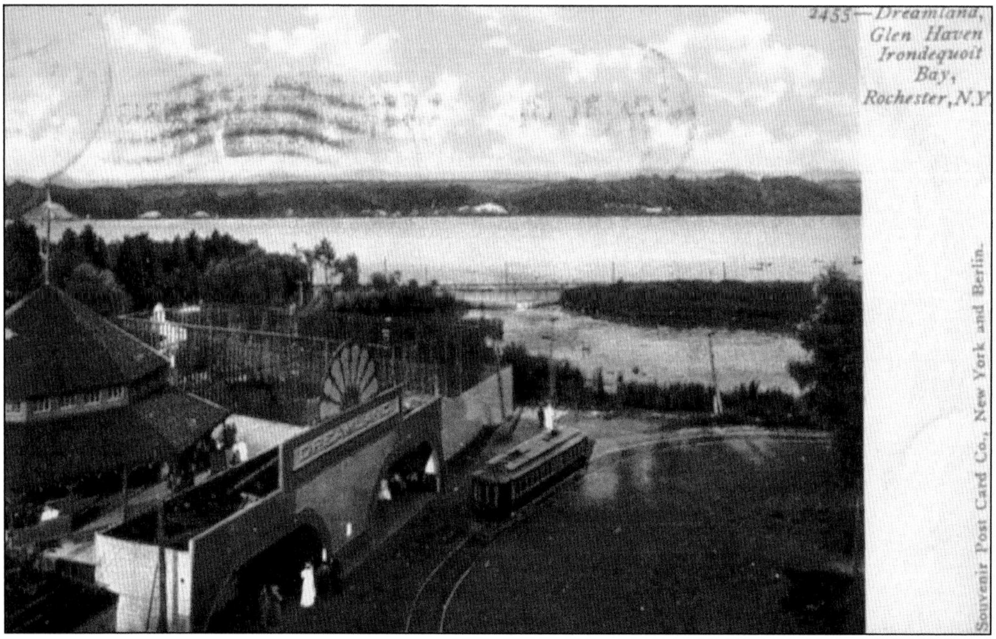

A trolley enters the loop at Glen Haven's Dreamland Park on Irondequoit Bay after its half hour ride from the city. On the back of this card the writer laments, "Having a good time here. I don't want to come home." This view is dated 1908.

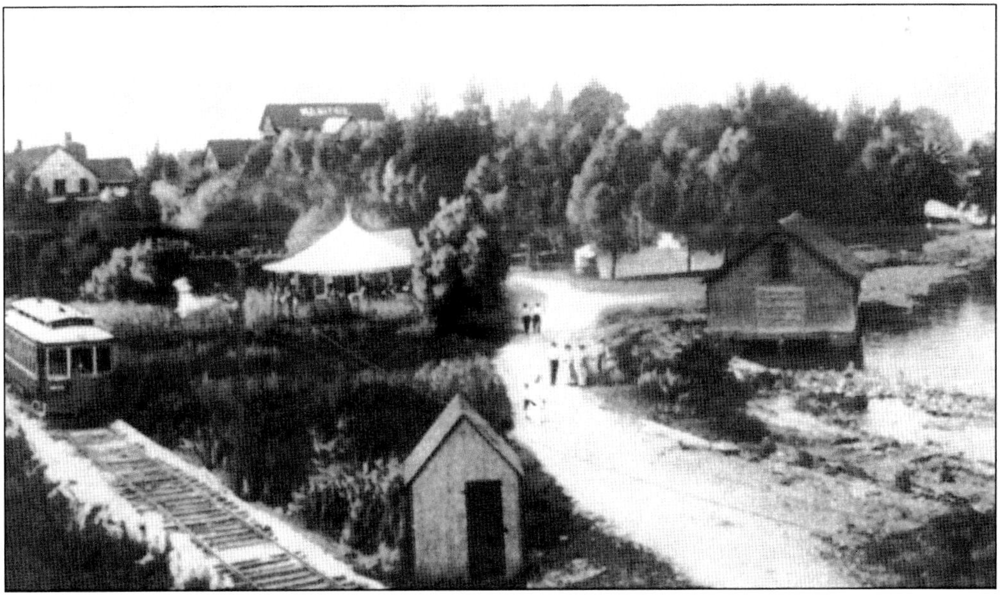

The Rochester, Charlotte and Manitou Railroad promised the "most beautiful ride in the Empire State" along its eight miles of shoreline track. The ticket agent was housed in the Powers Arcade where church, society, and outing club excursions could be arranged. The cars stopped at resorts at Crescent Beach, Round Pond, Island Cottage, Grand View Beach, Braddock's Bay, Cranberry Pond, and here, at Manitou Beach.

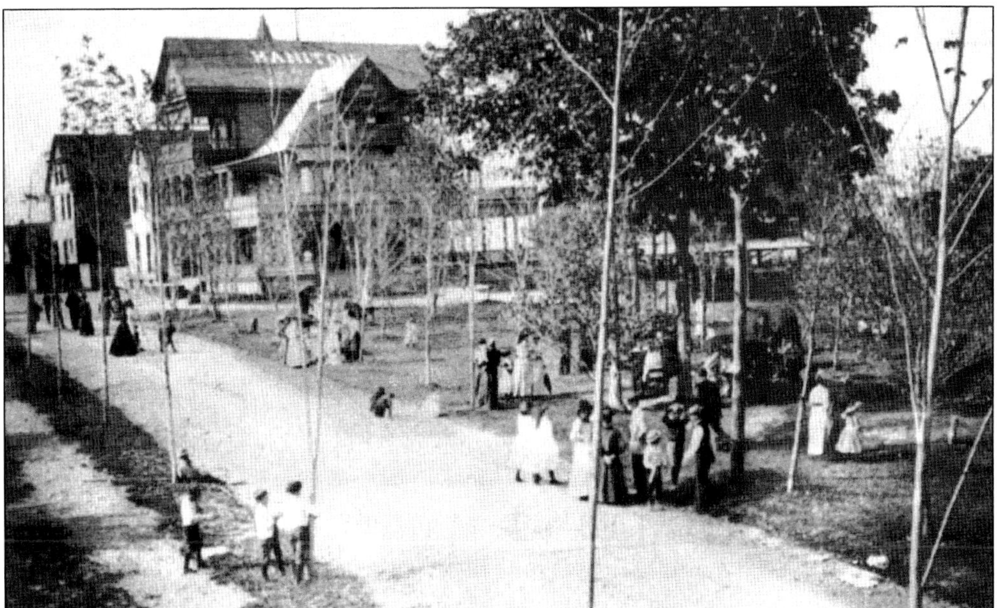

The promenade leading to the grand Manitou Hotel is enjoyed by guests. Again, most are wearing their best clothes. Cool lake breezes offered a refreshing respite from the belching smokestacks of the city. The messages on the backs of these cards show that leaving these resorts was done only with the deepest regrets, especially for children.

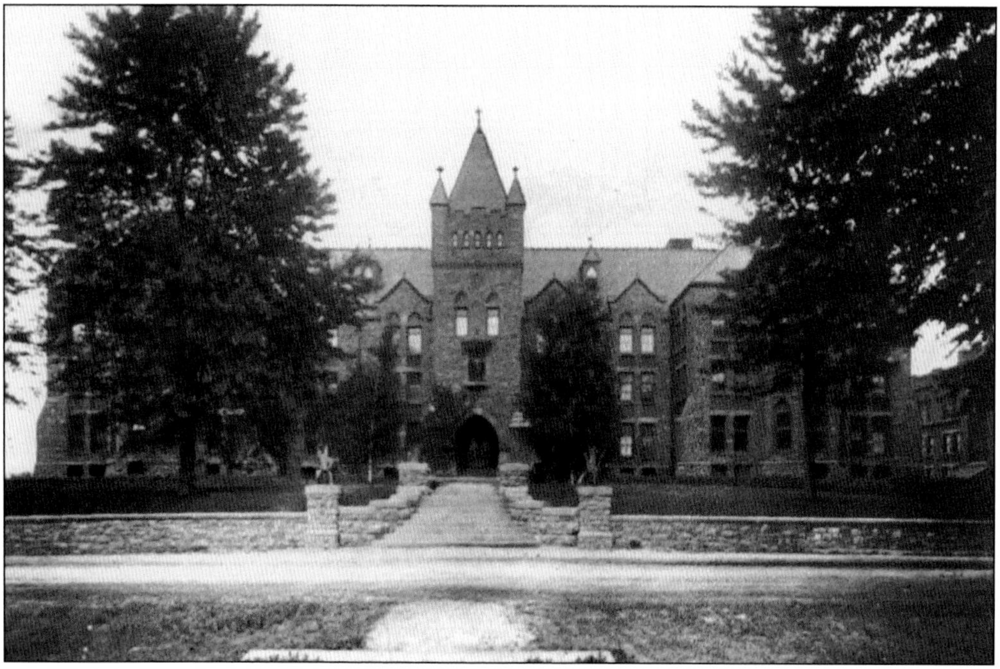

Travelers to resorts that used Lake Avenue trolleys would pass St. Bernard's Theological Seminary. Built between 1891 and 1893, during the leadership of Bishop McQuaid, this building was a great accomplishment for another local architect, Andrew J. Warner.

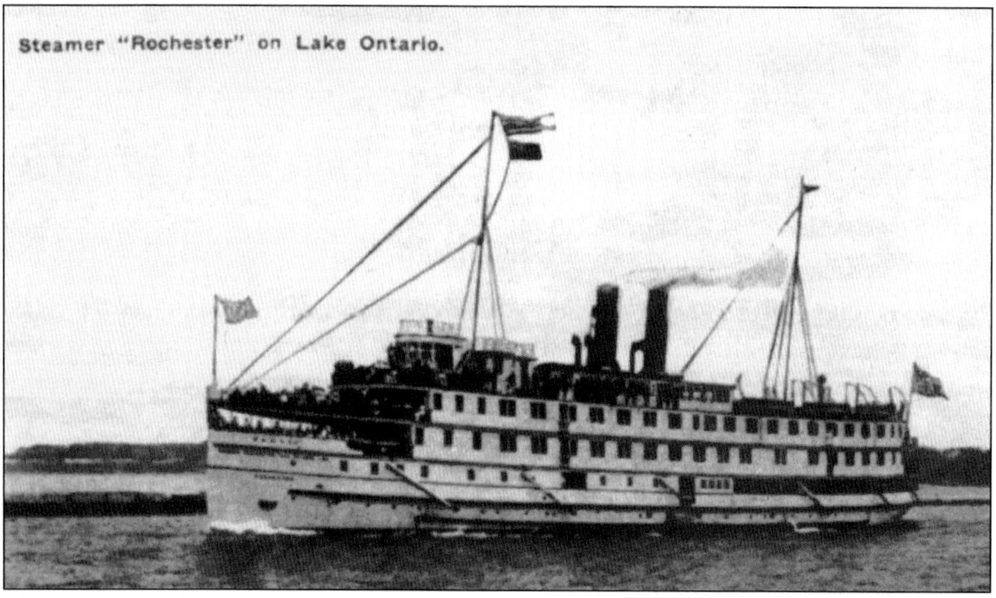

The steamer *Rochester* makes for the open waters of Lake Ontario after casting off its moorings up river at the Government Pier. A stone lighthouse set back downriver guided early schooners and steamers to safe harbor before the pier was extended out into the lake. The port at the river in Charlotte handled ships of all sizes, from Great Lake schooners to ocean going vessels, during the heyday of Great Lakes shipping and touring.

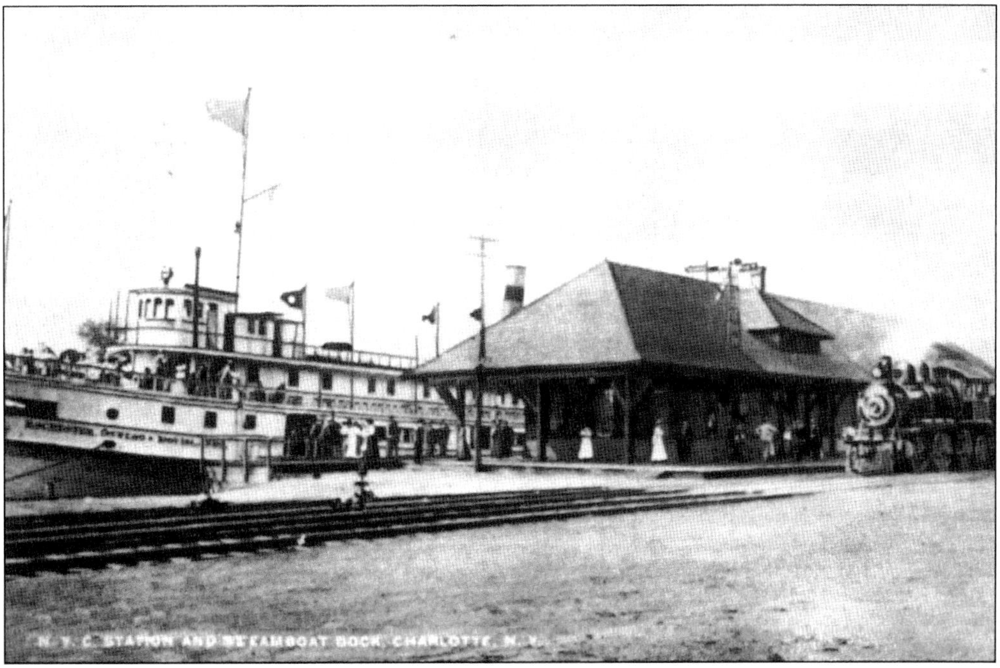

The New York Central Station on the Hojack line servicing Charlotte was a busy place in this *c.* 1914 postcard view. Passengers are boarding a steamship that makes stops at Rochester, Oswego, and the 1,000 Islands.

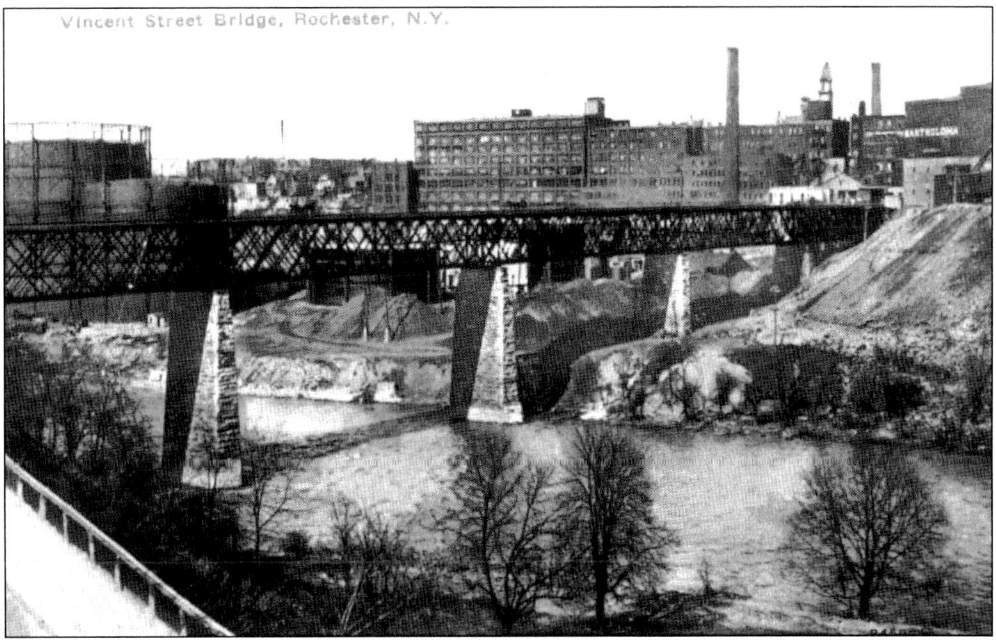

Here, the Vincent Street Bridge crosses the Genesee at the Rochester Railway & Light Company power-generating plant in 1916. The behemoth tanks on the upper left held gas. Towering smokestacks usually blanketed this part of the city beneath a smoldering haze from coal burned for power generation.

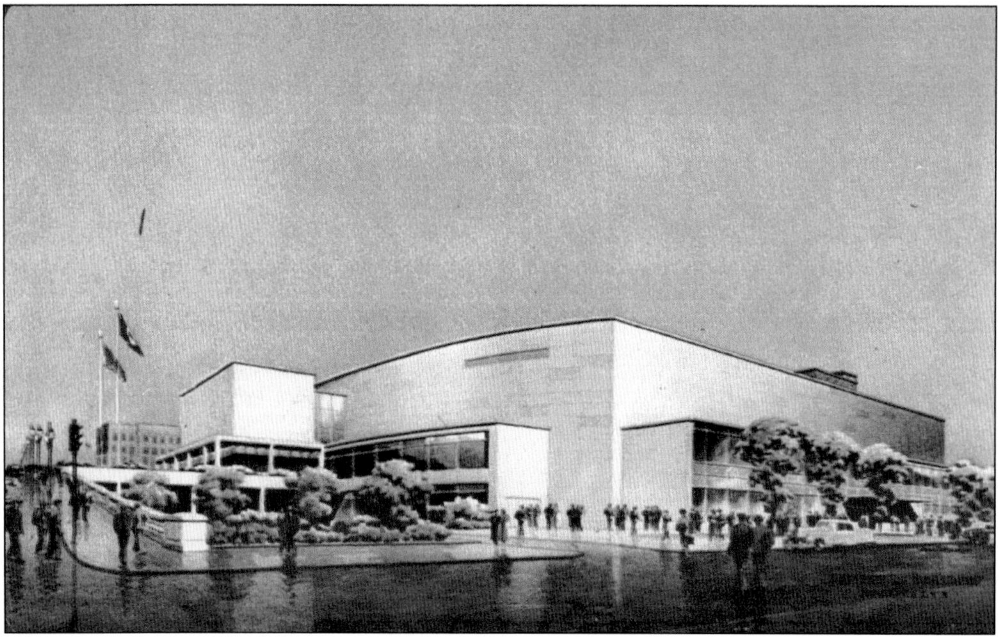

The Rochester War Memorial Auditorium and Exhibit Hall was built in the 1950s beside the river downtown on the site once occupied by the Kimball Tobacco factory. During excavation of the auditorium, the ruins of arched foundations for Benjamin Campbell's mill, which occupied an island in the 1830s, were unearthed. The tobacco company filled the area before building their factory, contributing to the gradual elevating of the city.

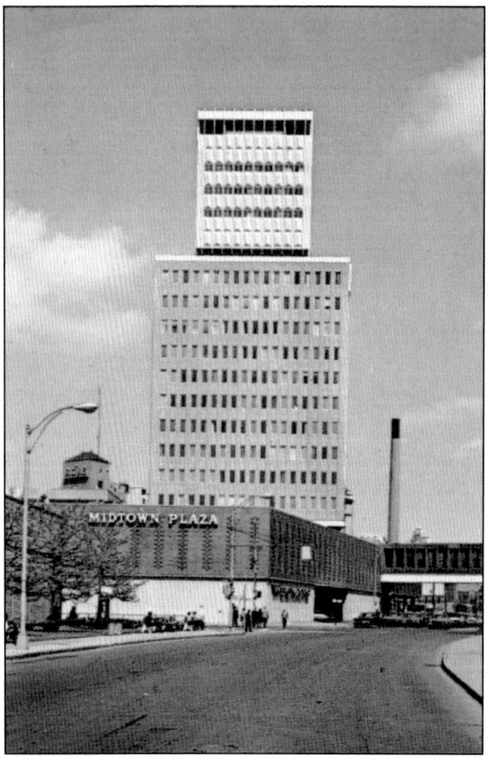

Midtown Plaza was built in the early 1960s and represented one of the first enclosed malls built in an American city. During a visit, Walt Disney praised the ambitious venture, admiring its vast openness. The plaza encompassed seven and a half acres of mostly retail space, all of which was built over an underground garage.

"Meet me at the clock," usually meant joining a friend at the plaza's Clock of the Nations. The card explains, "It marks the time with a colorful pageant, as twelve nations are depicted with dancing puppets and folk tunes of the country fill the air. The romance and enjoyment of the traditional European village square have been recaptured at Midtown Plaza."

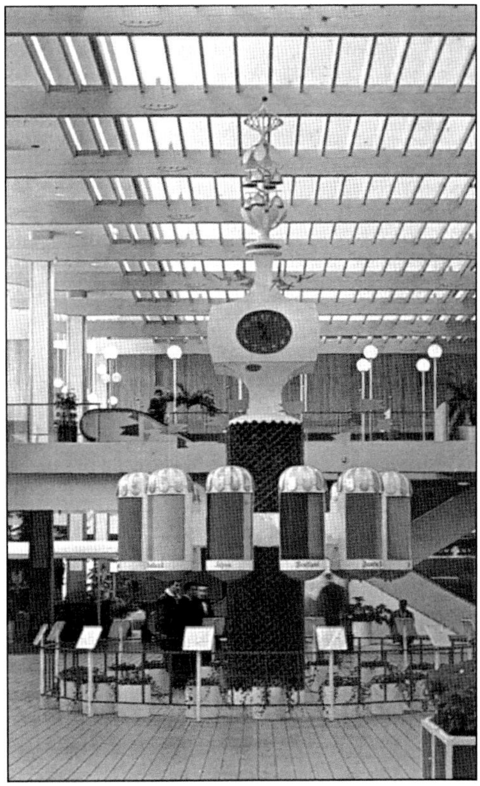

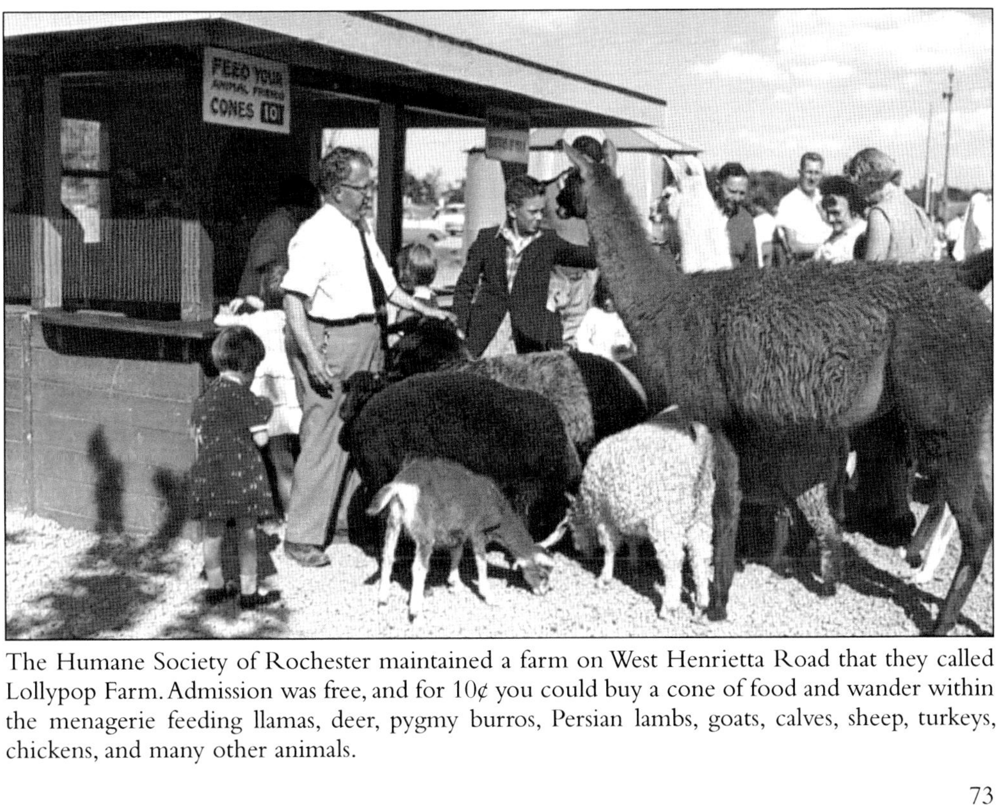

The Humane Society of Rochester maintained a farm on West Henrietta Road that they called Lollypop Farm. Admission was free, and for 10¢ you could buy a cone of food and wander within the menagerie feeding llamas, deer, pygmy burros, Persian lambs, goats, calves, sheep, turkeys, chickens, and many other animals.

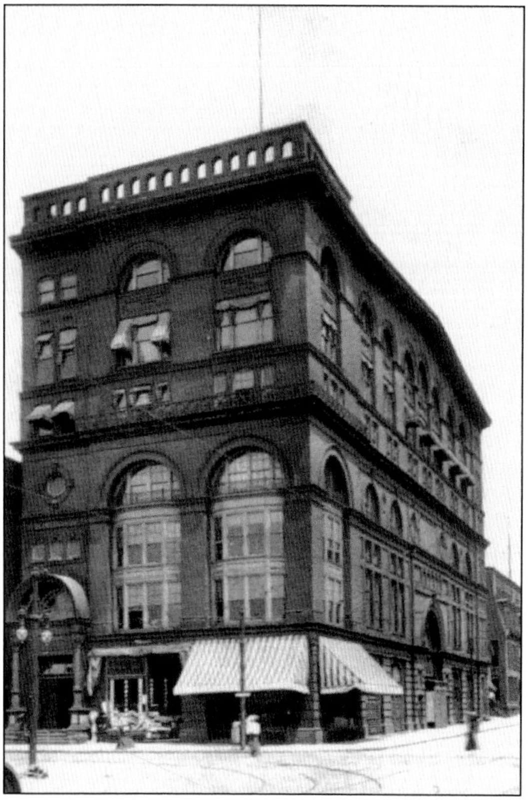

The YMCA located at South Avenue and Court Street as pictured in a turn of the century *Souvenir of Rochester* booklet shows a blending of two styles vying for importance at the end of the 19th century: Romanesque and Renaissance.

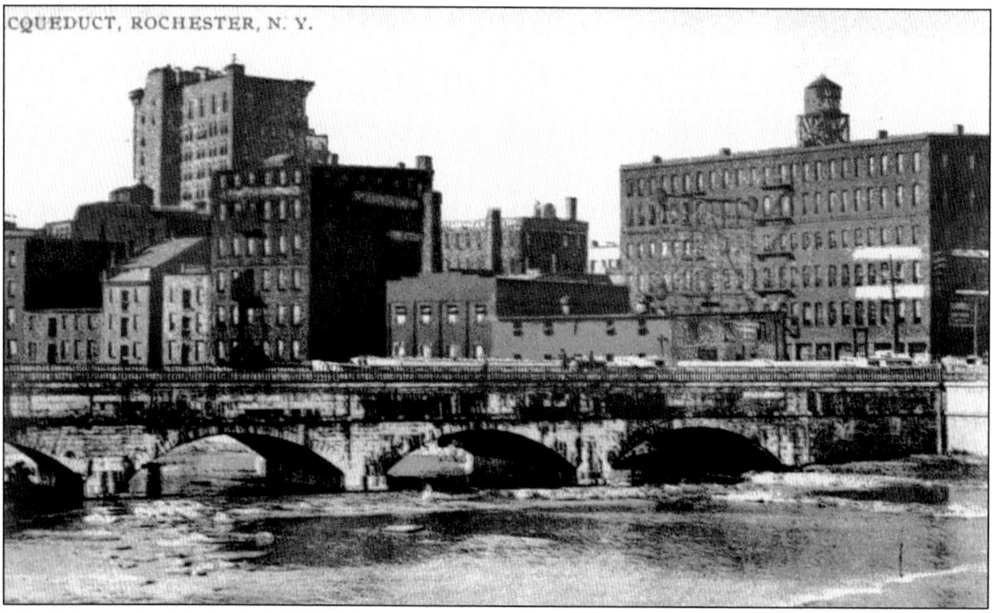

The Roman aqueduct looks a bit ruddy in this northeast view.

Two

THE POWERS BLOCK

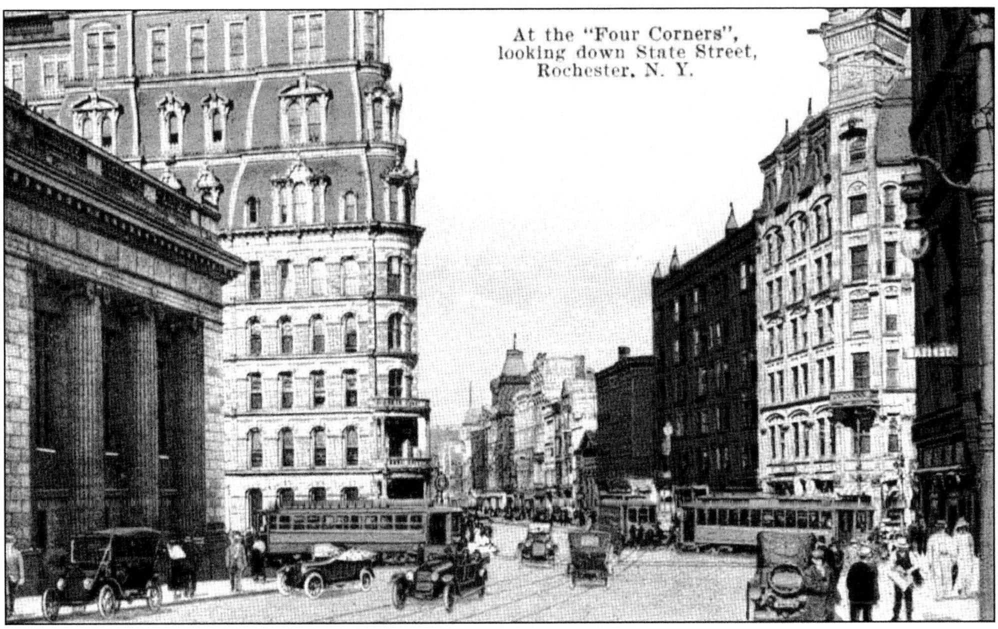

The history of Rochester is retained in the Powers Block in many ways, including bearing a marker where Hamlet Scrantom, one of the first settlers, built his cabin. Monroe County is fortunate to have this block relatively intact when similar blocks have perished from most cities. Daniel Powers, a wealthy merchant, developed his Powers Banking House into a distinguished block after the Civil War with a fascinating Second Empire building that glorifies commerce. This view looks north towards State Street.

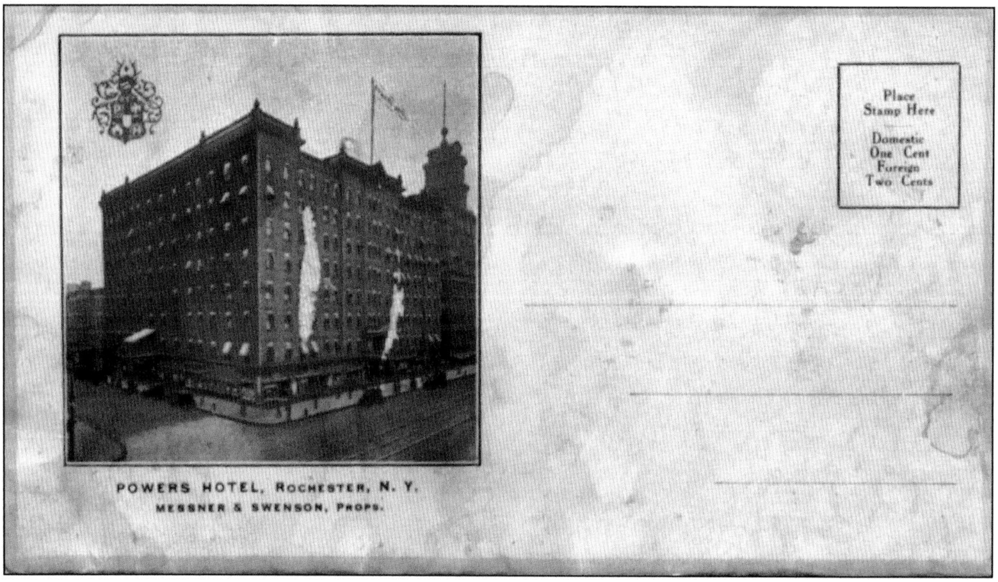

The Powers Hotel offered its guests souvenir books such as this one. It contains not only pictures but also a wealth of knowledge about the golden days of hotels. Additionally, it provides fascinating tidbits of information about the city.

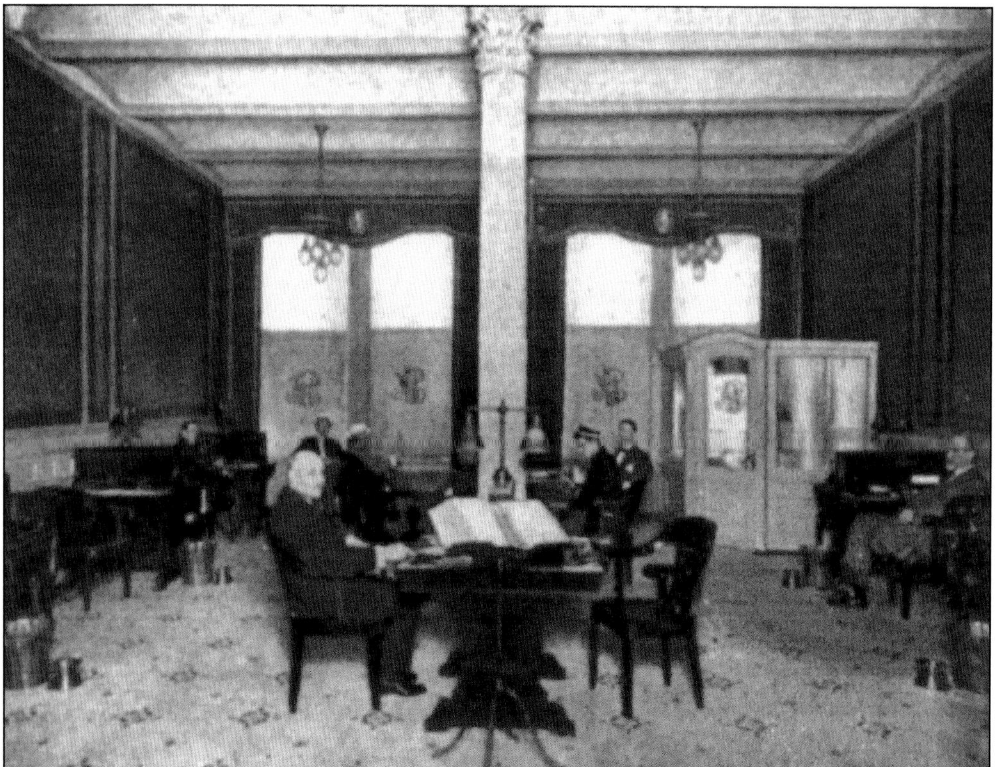

The Writing Room provided 10 double desks, excellent light, professional journals, and a compartment for a stenographer and typewriter. There was an entrance from this room to nearby bond and stockbroker's offices.

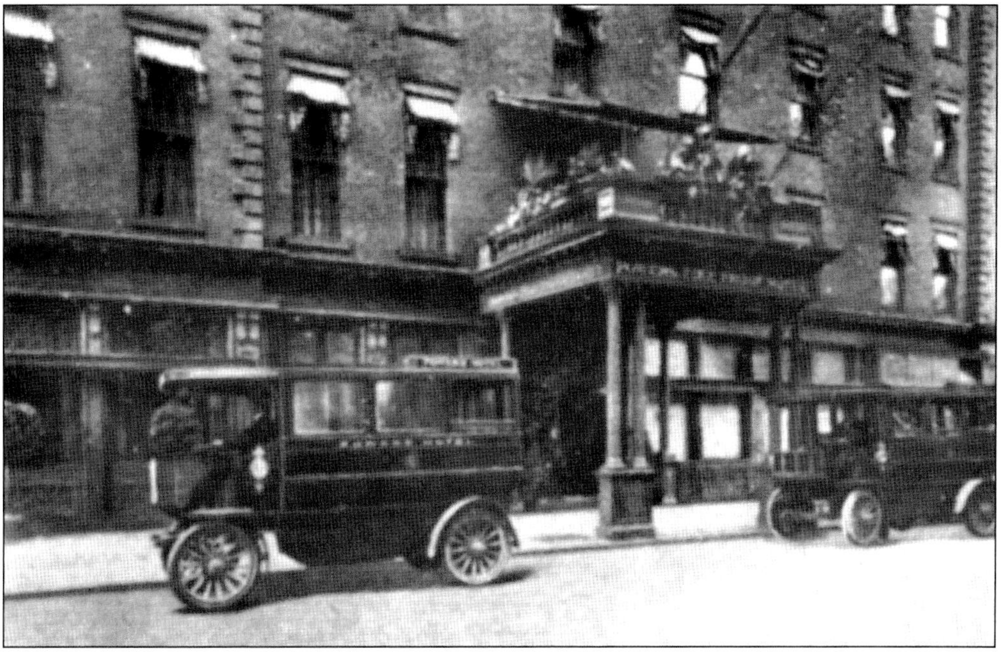

Omnibuses waiting outside the ladies' entrance provided transportation to any downtown location. The souvenir folder mentions that Rochester is first in the production of photographic supplies, seed and nursery stock, and optical instruments; it has 15 mills producing about 1,000,000 barrels of flour annually. Eight steam railroads and seven trolley railroads entered the city.

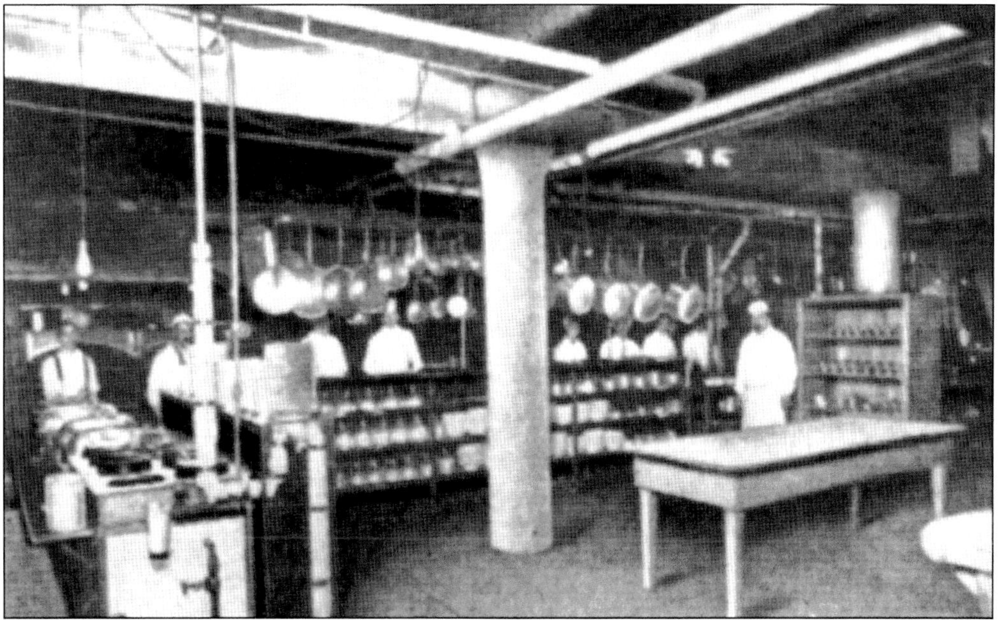

A rare view of a kitchen in one of these giant hotels lets us see how big an operation it was. Note the large kettles and line of gas-fueled stoves. Through the doors were an adjacent butcher shop, storeroom, and refrigerators. The refrigerating plant had a capacity of 30 tons of ice (made from distilled water) per day.

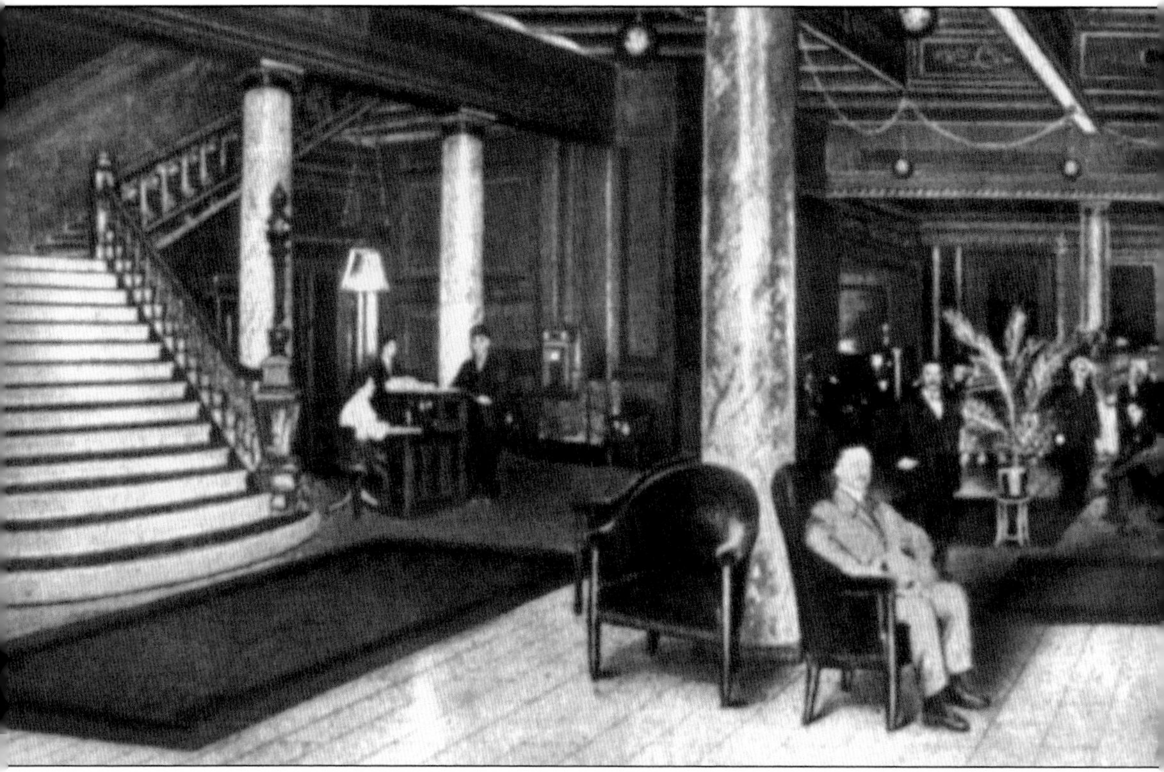

The first impression of the hotel was the lobby. It is one of refined and subdued elegance. The electric fixtures in the lobby of this "fire proof" hotel were verde antique bronze. In the

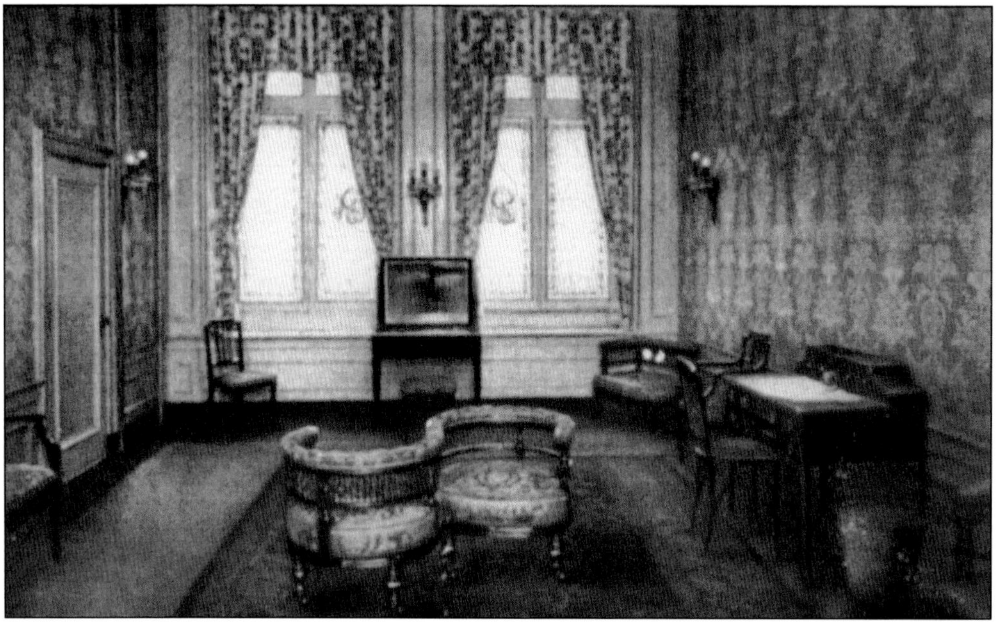

Here is a look at the ladies' reception room on the lobby floor. Not much is said about it, but we do learn that guests can visit six libraries in the city and six theaters: the Lyceum, Temple, Cook's Opera House, Baker, National, and Corinthian.

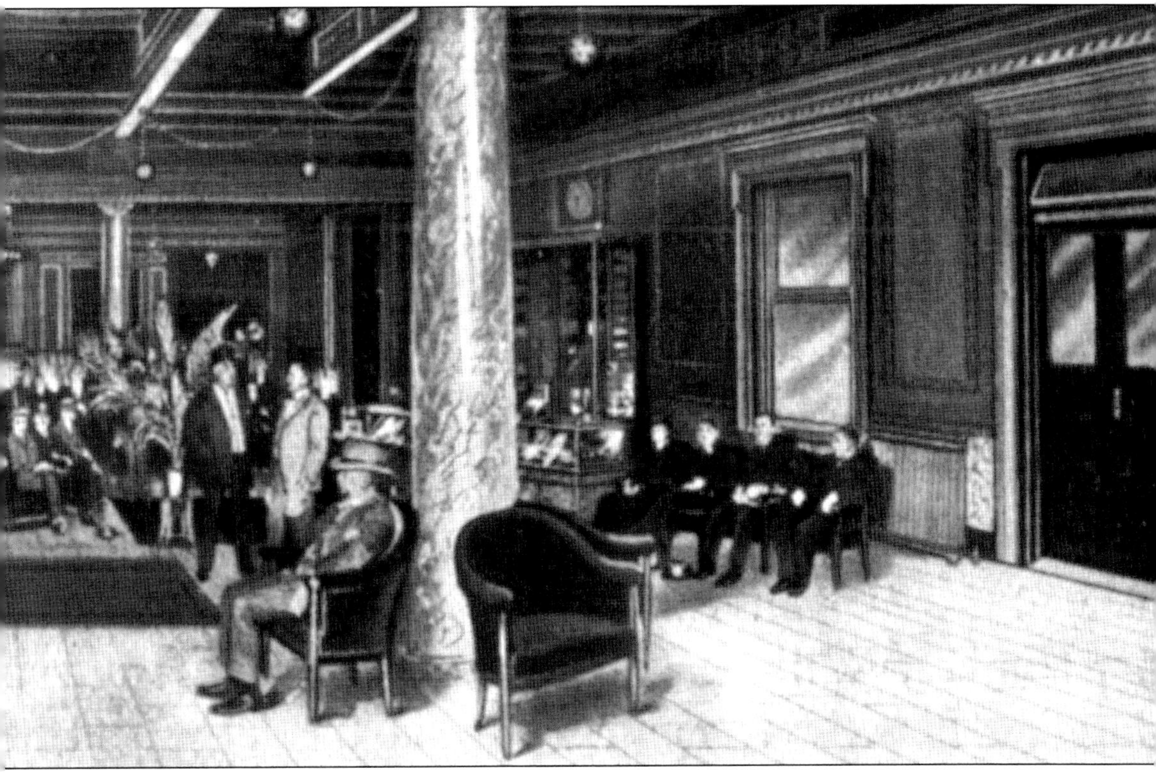

center of the room was a magnificent candelabrum. Marble statues were set at each side of the main vestibule.

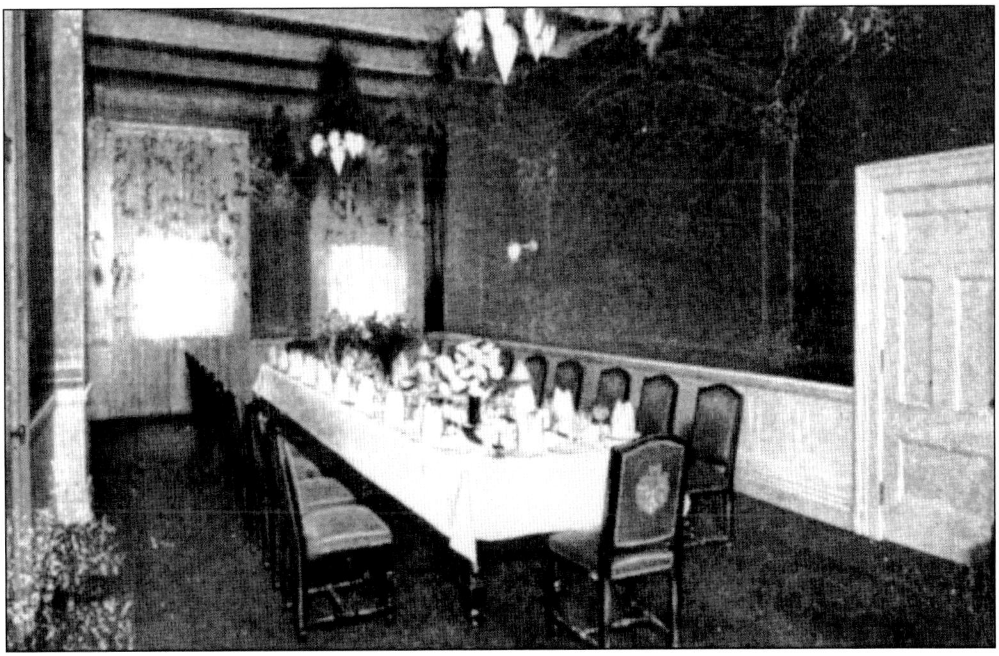

Private banquet rooms were available for luncheons and dinners. The management prided itself on offering "cosmopolitan cuisine with delicacies from home and abroad."

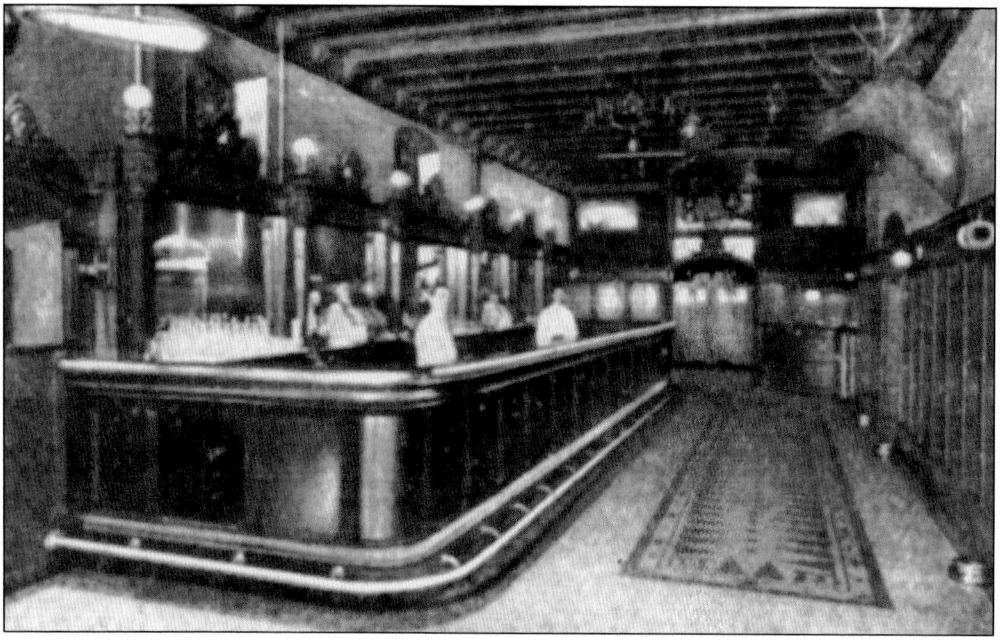

In the buffet was found "the choicest brands and vintages, dispensed by skillful and courteous attendants." Gentlemen at the bar might discuss, over a few stouts, other information made available in this souvenir folder, including that Rochester had 54 boot and shoe manufactories.

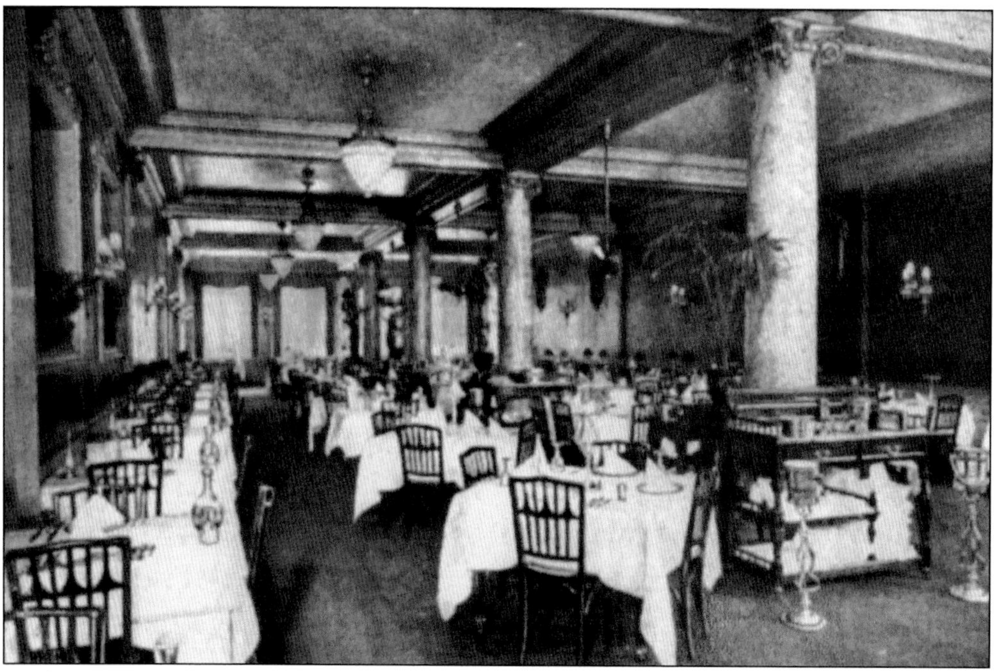

In the main dining room, "a splendid orchestra with auxetophone [an early amplifier] gives concerts during dining hours."

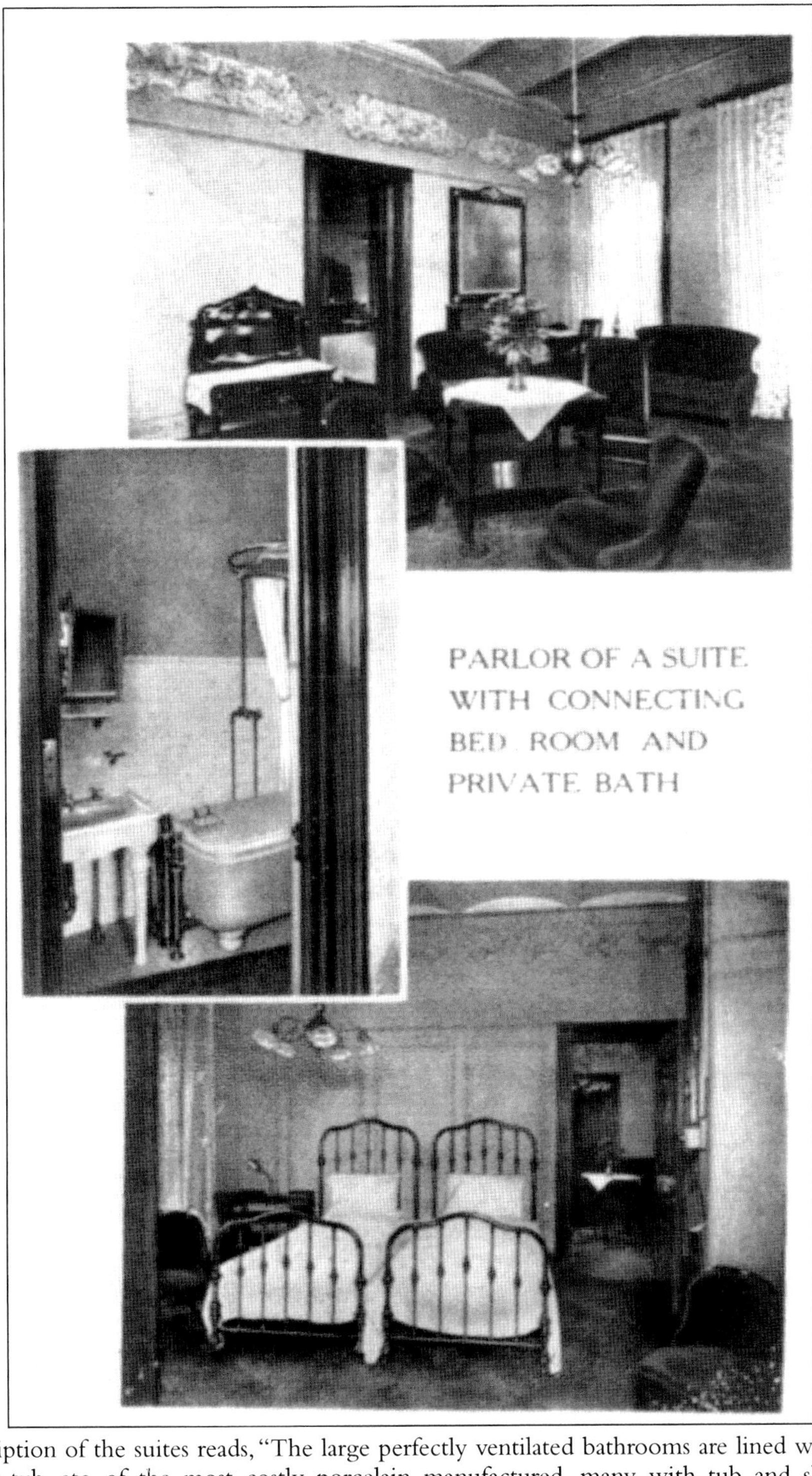

A description of the suites reads, "The large perfectly ventilated bathrooms are lined with white tile, the tub, etc. of the most costly porcelain manufactured, many with tub and shower in combination; all fixtures are of nickel. There are no noisy radiators; the walls, carpets and furniture are cleaned by the vacuum system, thus making the rooms perfectly sanitary."

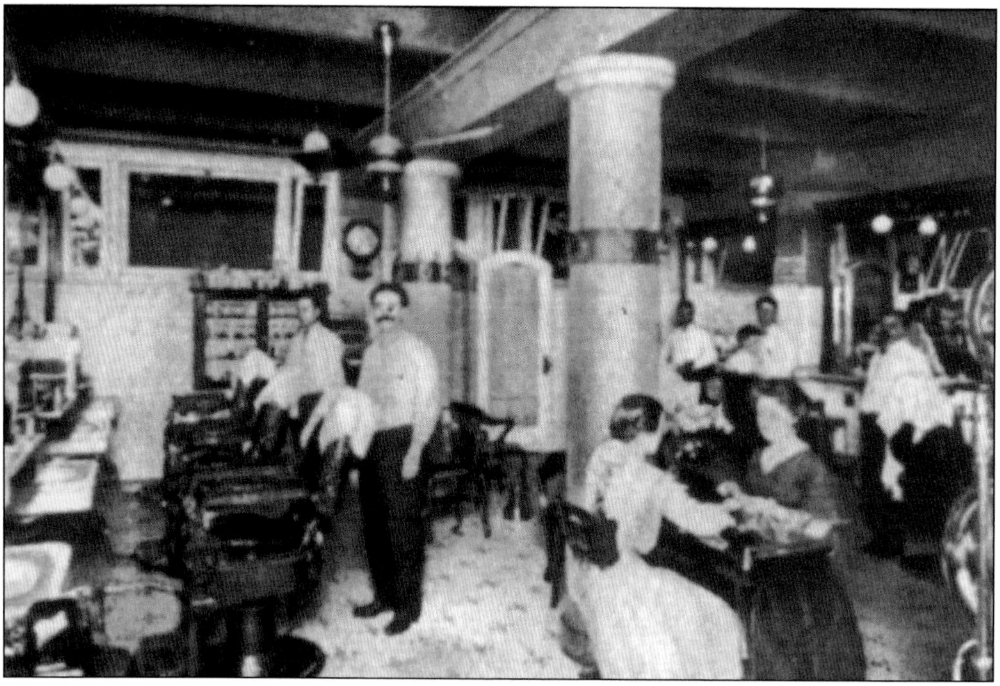

This is a view of the barbershop and manicure room.

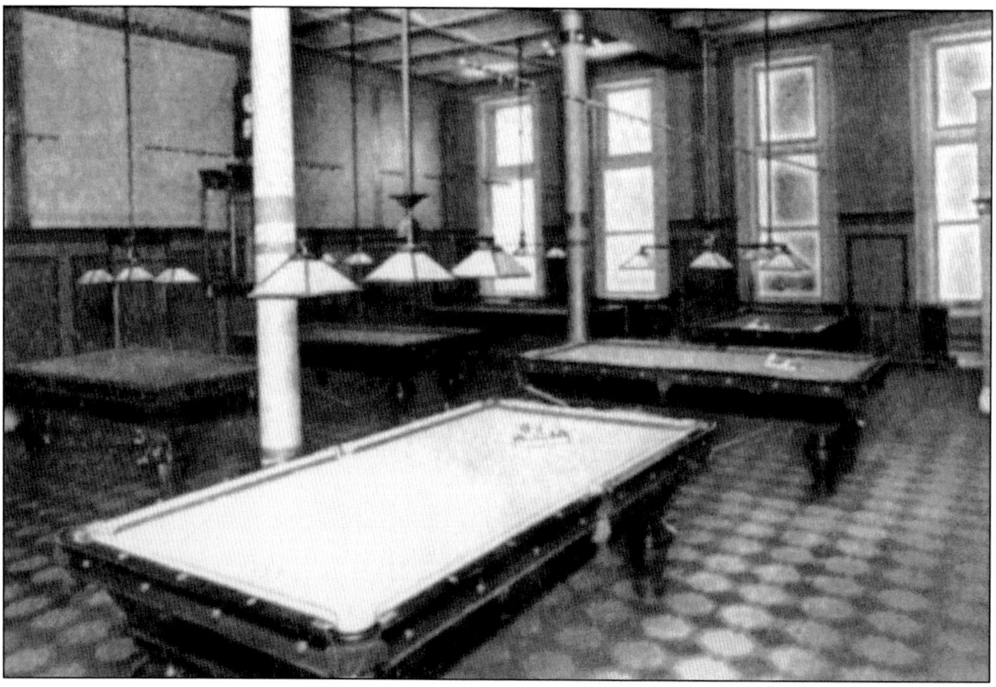

The hotel may have done better showing their billiard room with a few guests enjoying themselves.

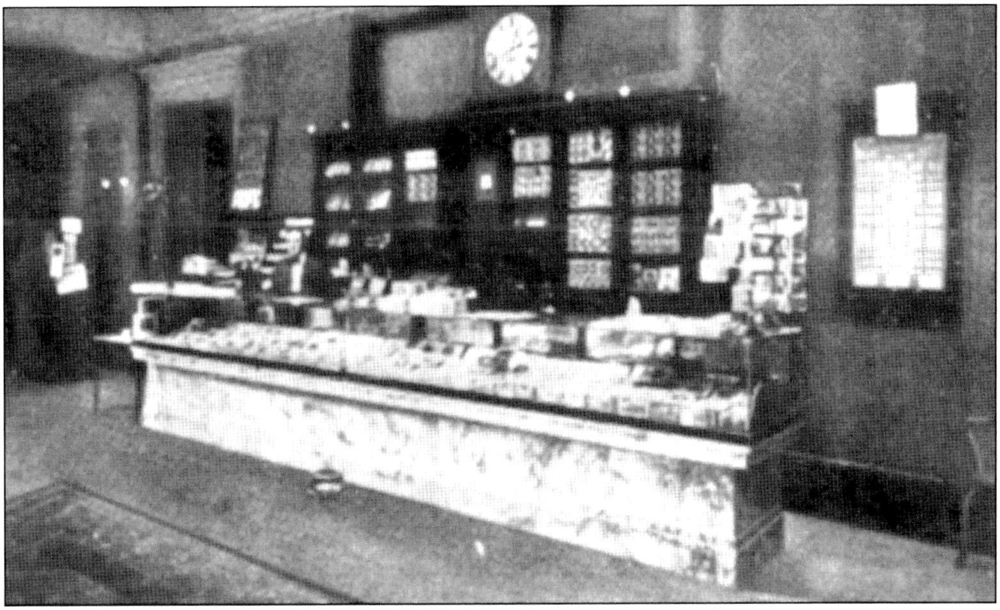

The cigar stand was made of the same Sienna marble used in the lobby's columns and pilasters. The wainscoting was of beautifully grained Tennessee marble. The mural decorations were Roman Renaissance carried out in Tuscan gold. There appears to be a wire rack of postcards on the right end of the counter. On the floor, about midway along the counter, is a spittoon, or slop pot.

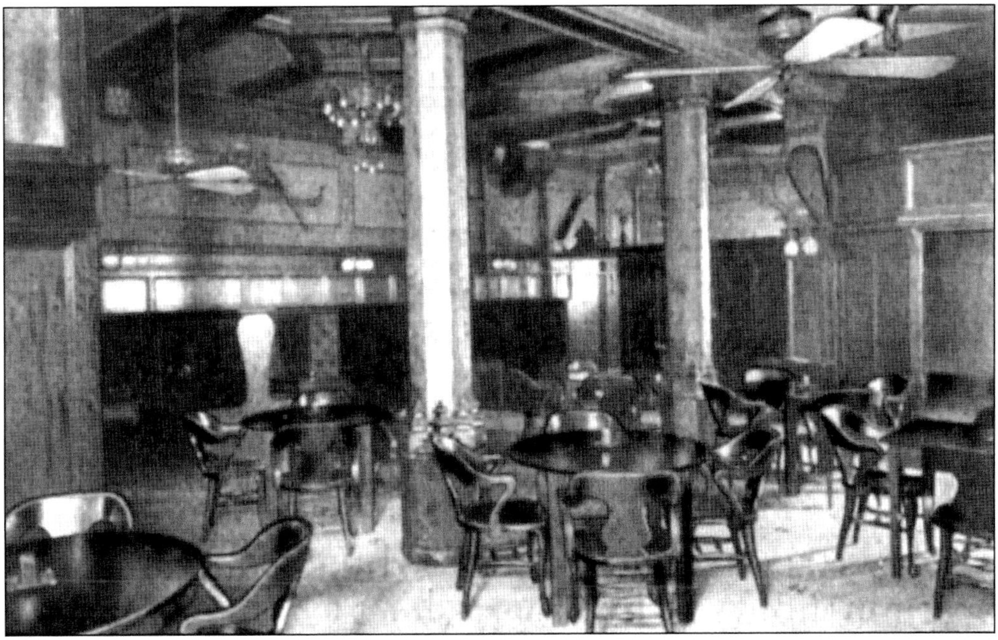

The Hunt Room was "one of the most beautiful gentlemen's cafes in the country. It is a reproduction of a Trophy Hall in a famous Feudal Castle in Hungary embellished with escutcheons of the Knights of Old." The hotel's most famous restaurant was the Rathskeller, also known as the Town Hall Cellar. In the ancient town halls of Germany, town fathers made plans over "bumpers of old amber-colored Rhine Wine."

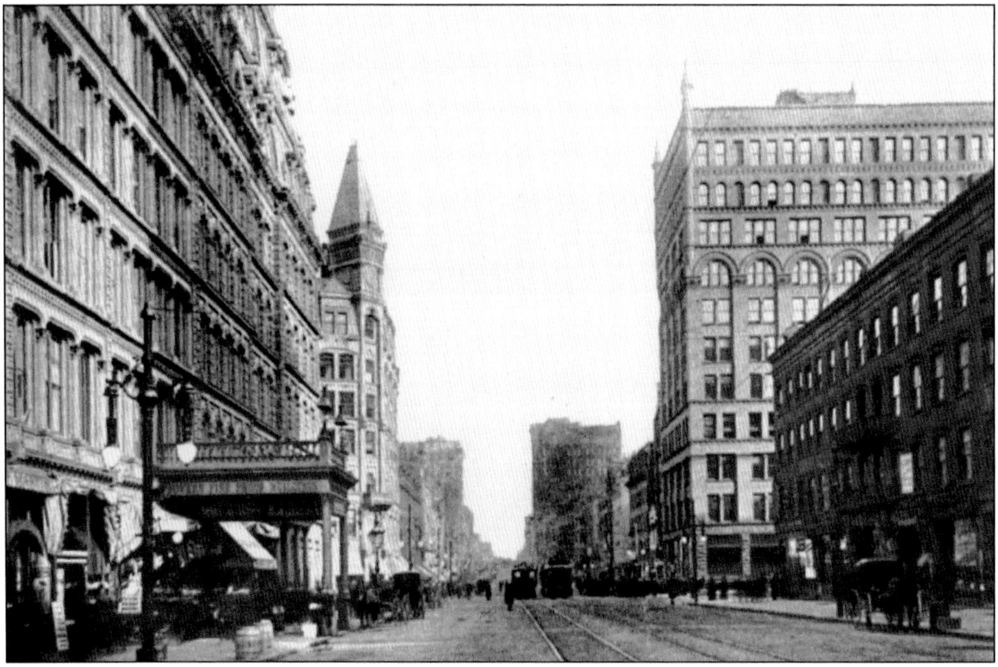

The entrance on the left reads Powers Fire Proof Building in this *c.* 1898 view looking east on Main Street.

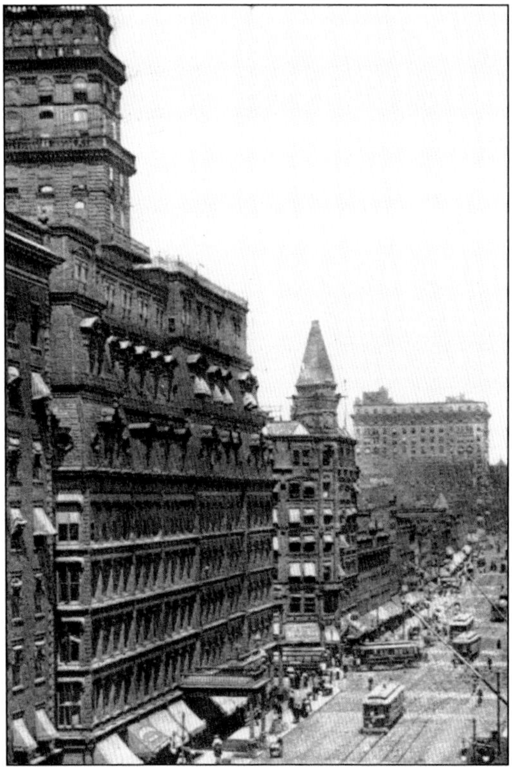

This 1890s view of Main Street showing the Powers Building was used for many postcards. In some, the buff-colored façade has been colored red to look like brick.

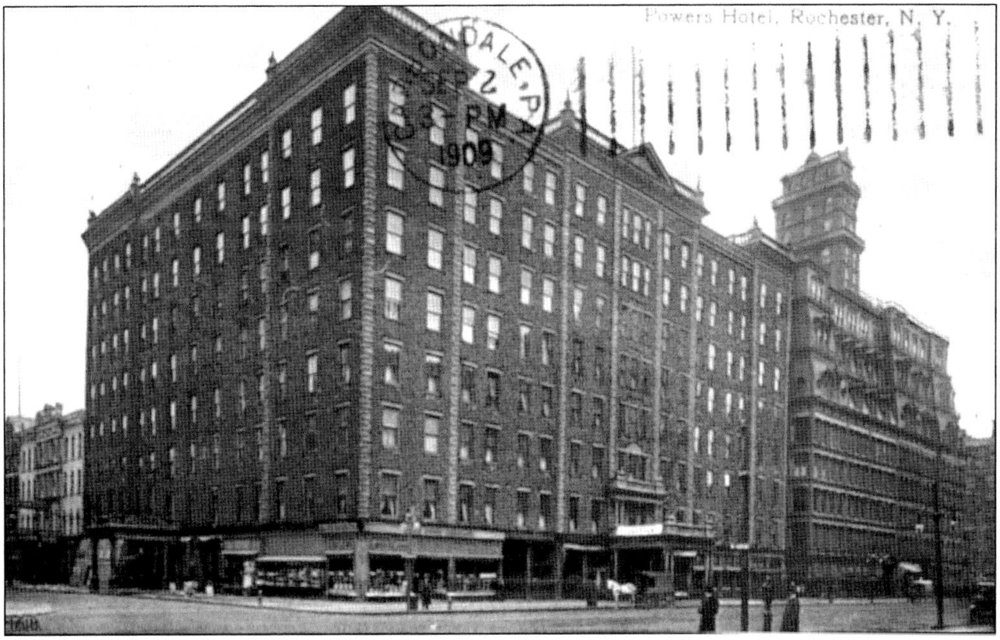

The perspective in the view on this postcard, which was mailed in 1909, was slightly compressed to give the hotel height and drama. By squeezing a photograph, the corners of buildings could be distorted to alter their appearance. This effect could make a structure look taller and bolder than it may have been.

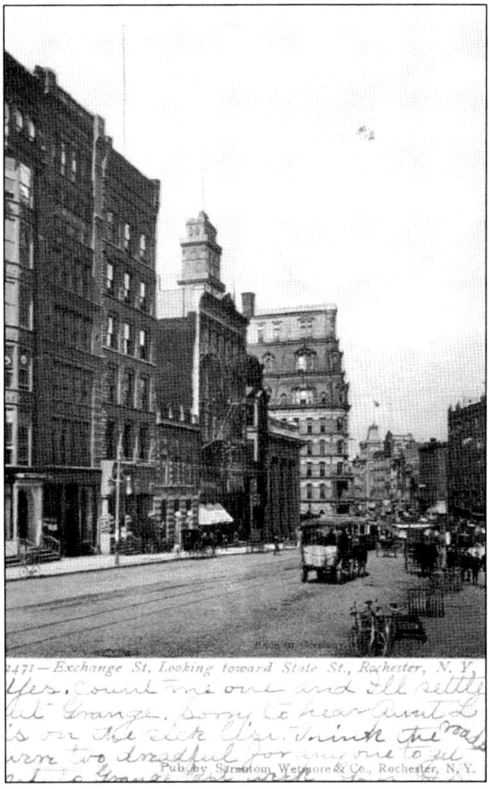

In this 1907 postcard published by Scrantom, Whetmore and Company of Rochester, the Exchange Street section of the Four Corners is shown. Exchange Street became State Street on the north side of Main Street.

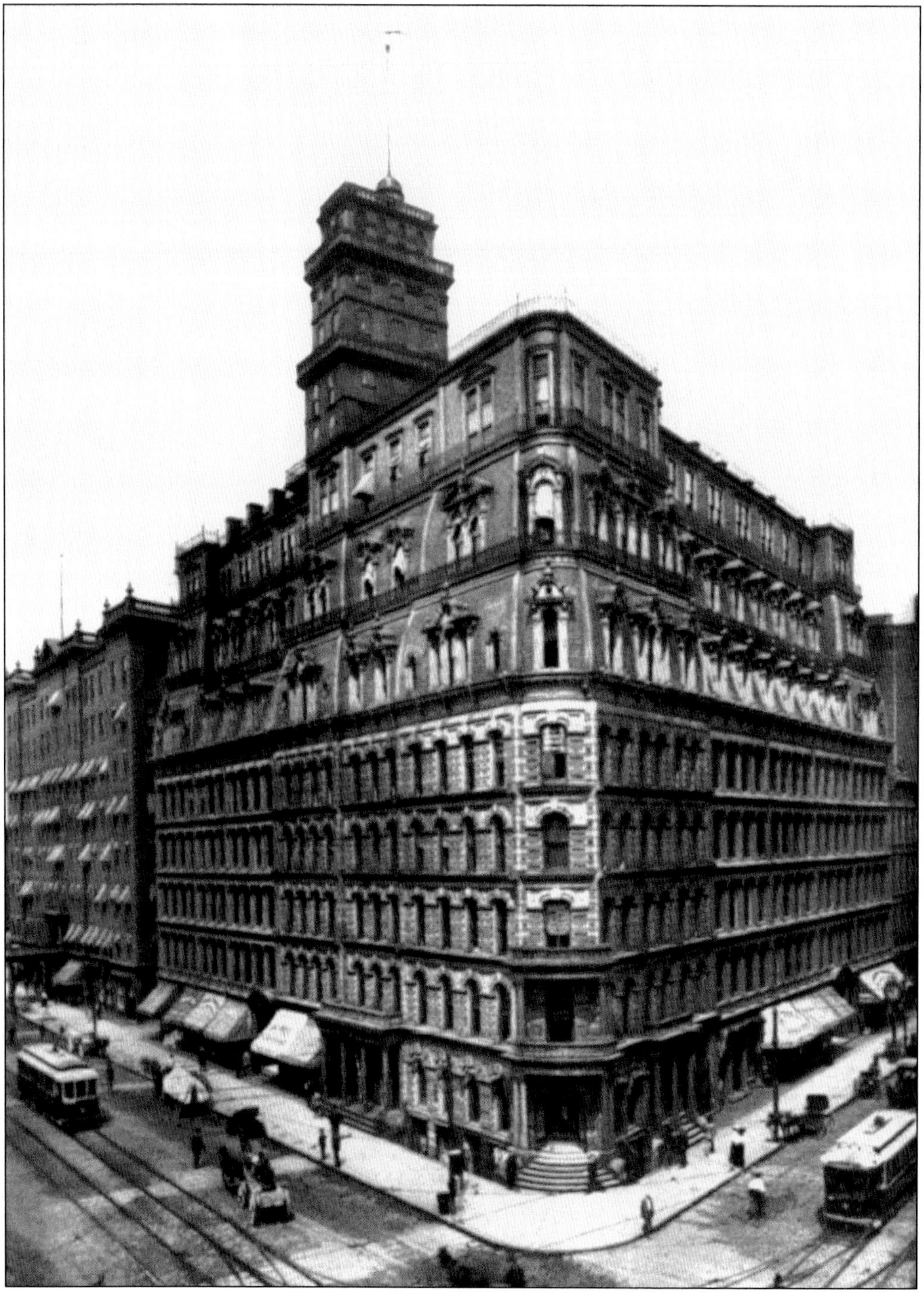

The first part of the Powers Building opened shortly after the Civil War and was steadily expanded. Built with Second Empire elements, it is very French. The addition of more floors, mansard roofs, and an ever growing tower that kept it the king of the skyline for years, it was considered magnificent by many, and vulgar and eccentric by others. This original 1898 souvenir view was altered for numerous postcards.

The lasting quality of the original is proven in this highly altered rendering sent in 1911, 12 years after the original appeared in the *Souvenir of Rochester.* An artist has skillfully transformed it into a night scene, carefully illuminating nearly every window. Were it not for the overstatement of the beams of light from the trolley headlamps, this image could have been mistaken for an actual nighttime exposure.

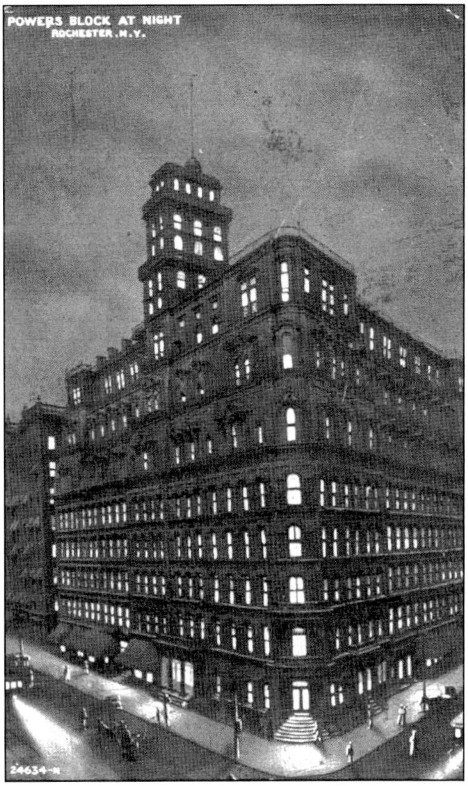

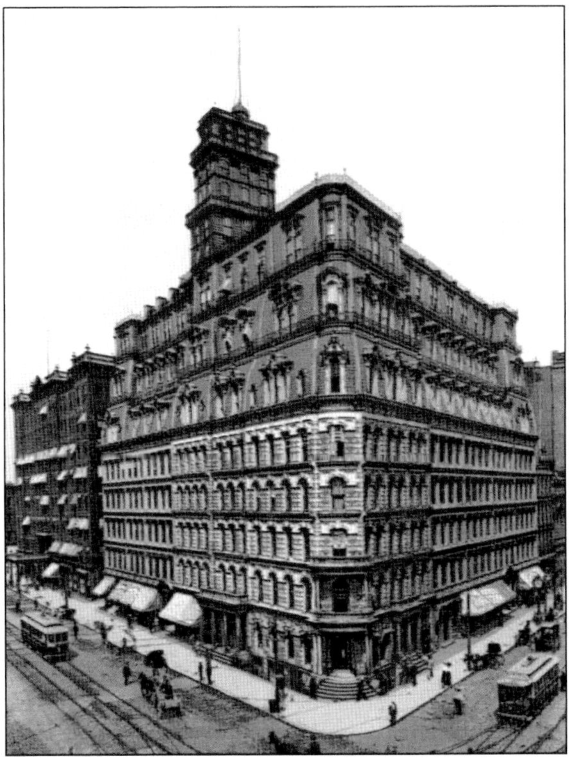

This pristine card from a German printer shows the original image having been lightly colored. None of the exquisite detail has been ruined. The trolleys retain their fine details. In many ways, this beautiful rendering is more appealing than the original.

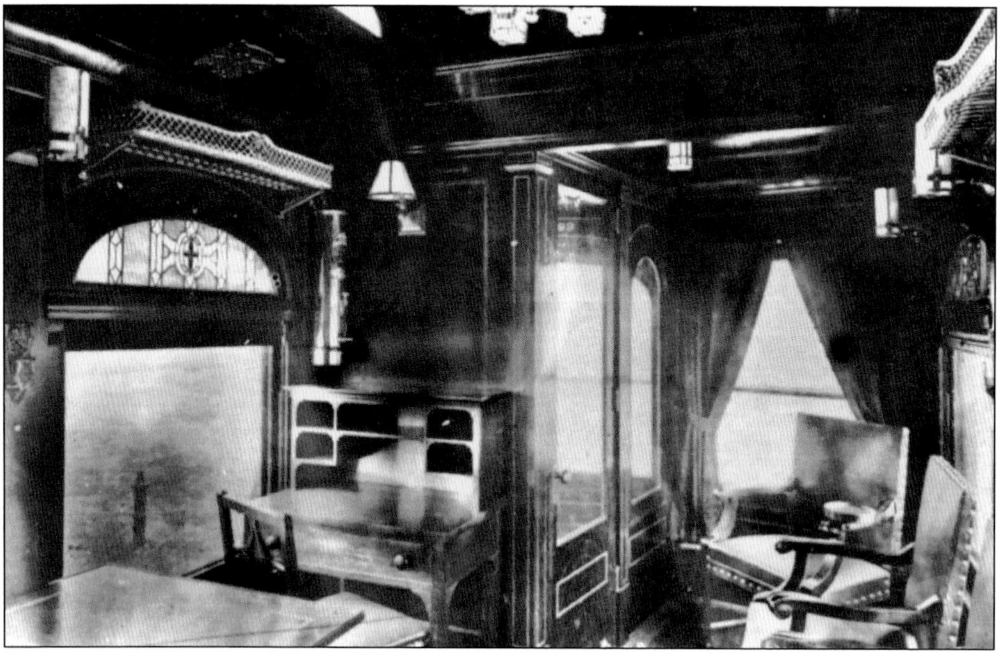

The posh interior of private car No. 999 of the Rochester, Syracuse and Eastern sparkles in this William Gordon postcard. There are stained-glass windows, hardwood paneling, velvet chairs, and lots of polished brass.

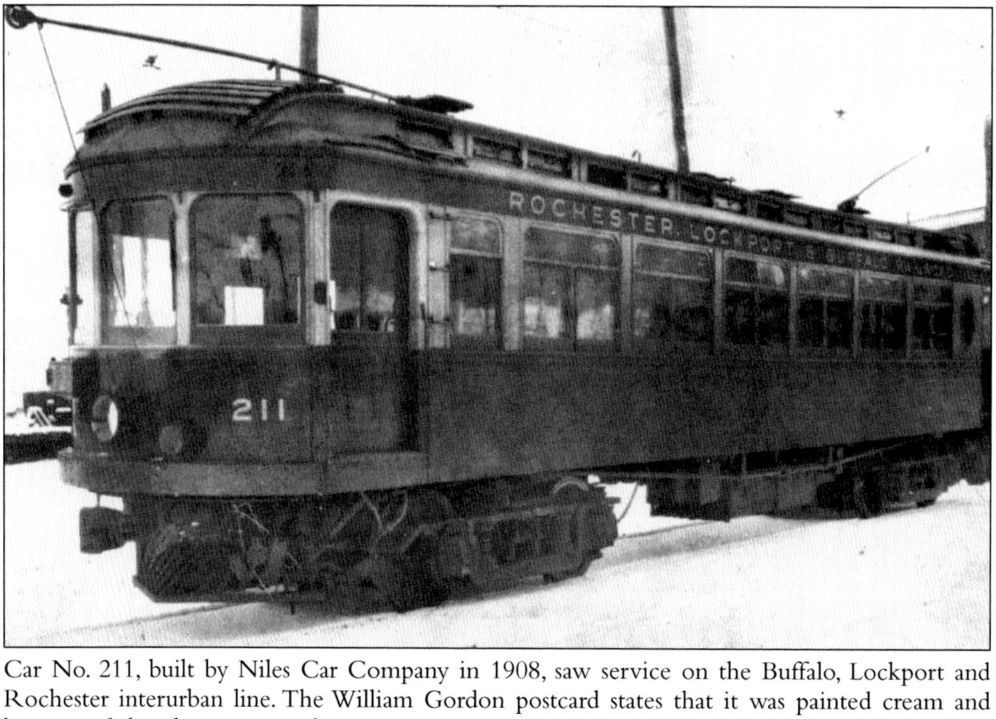

Car No. 211, built by Niles Car Company in 1908, saw service on the Buffalo, Lockport and Rochester interurban line. The William Gordon postcard states that it was painted cream and brown and that the car entered service in Rochester in 1918.

Three

Views of the Genesee-Finger Lakes Country

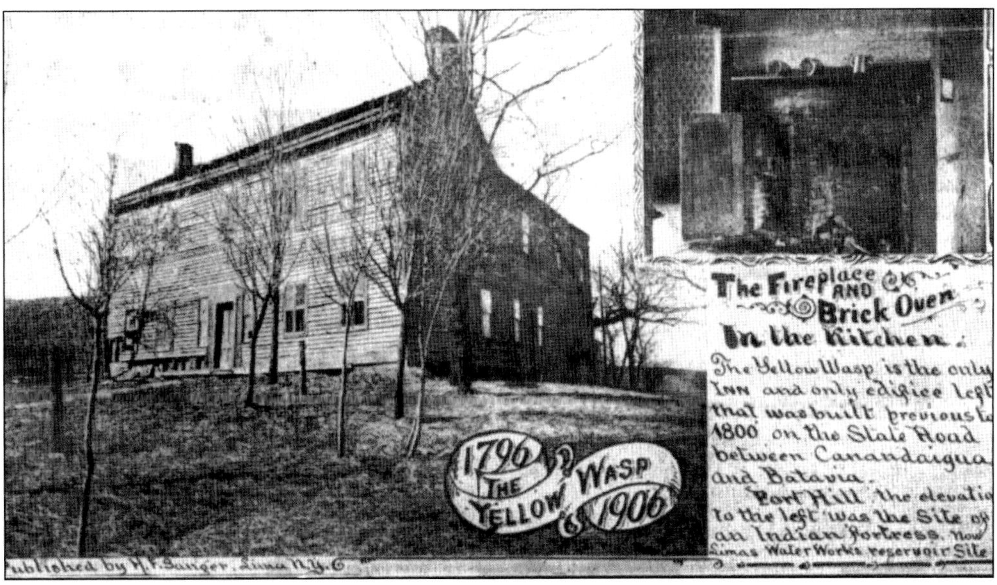

Travelers on the old State Road that ran from the Hudson west to the Niagara River would have passed numerous inns such as this one in Lima. It was built as the Nash House in 1796 and became the Yellow Wasp in 1816. It survived until 1906. In this H.F. Sanger postcard, the fireplace and brick oven have been included.

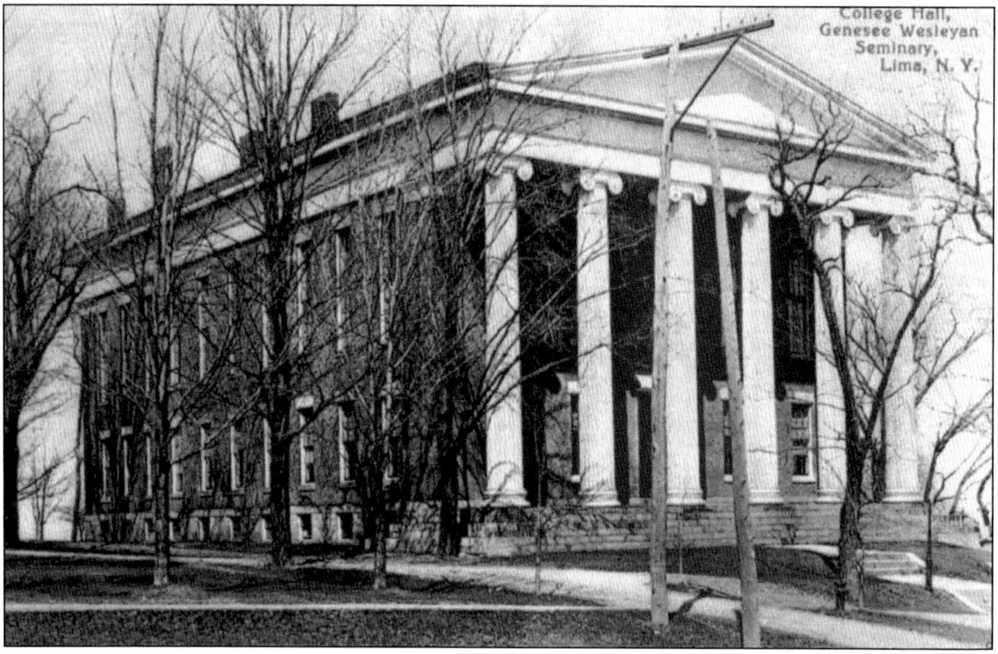

Hundreds of Lima postcard views were taken. Many of them were of Genesee Wesleyan Seminary. This is College Hall, built *c.* 1850. Elim Bible Institute took over the campus a century later in 1950 and continues it as a place of learning.

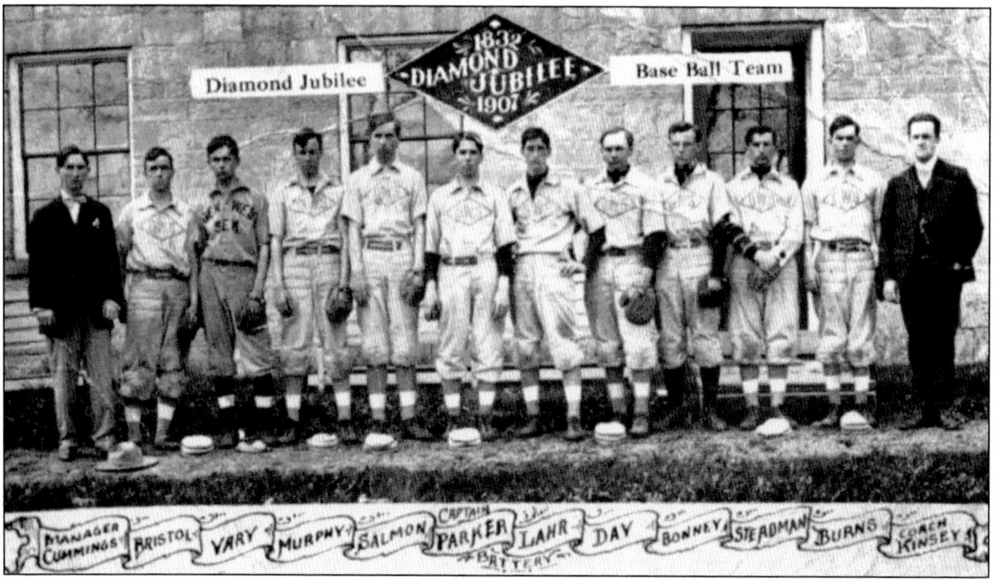

The seminary's baseball team poses for its Diamond Jubilee celebration in 1907.

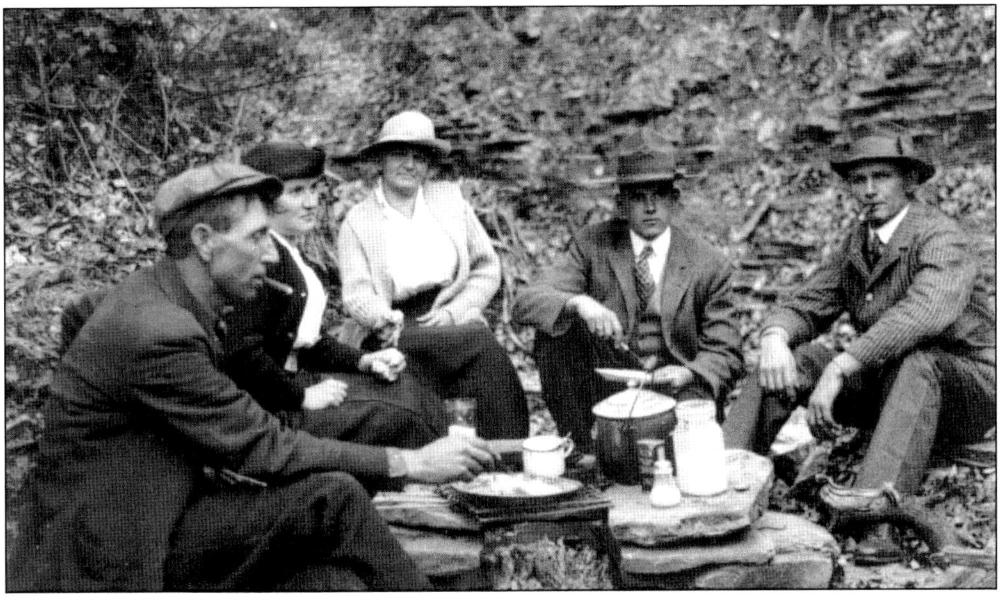

This photograph was taken *c.* 1915 by Bruce Corby and imprinted as a limited edition postcard by his brother George, the young man in the center-right. It was taken in the Letchworth State Park area. The Corby family has stopped for a roadside picnic.

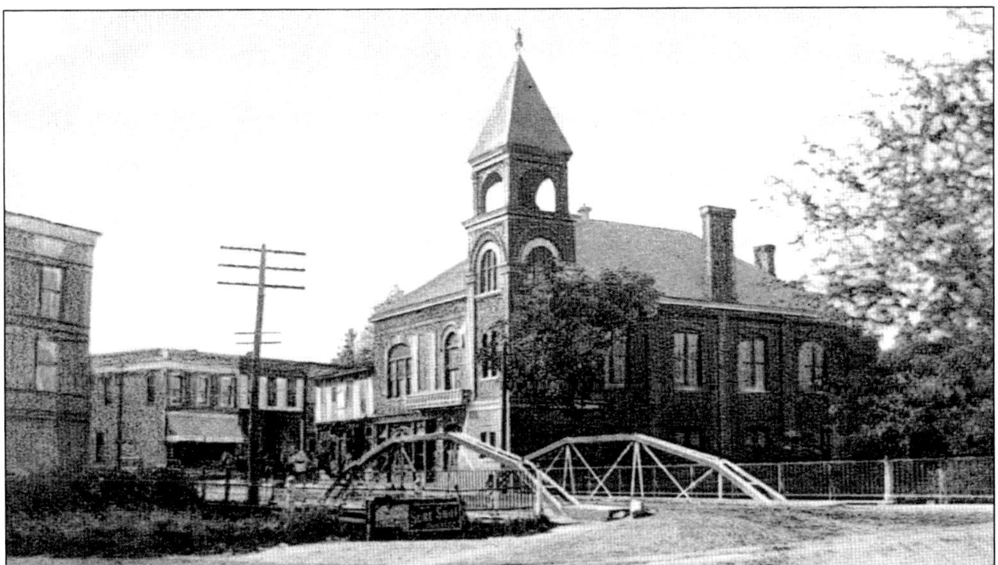

Picturesque Honeoye Falls prospered from Honeoye Creek, whose swift running waters were harnessed to power large mills. At one time, a covered wooden railroad bridge spanned the creek in the village. The village hall, pictured here, was home to the fire department for several decades.

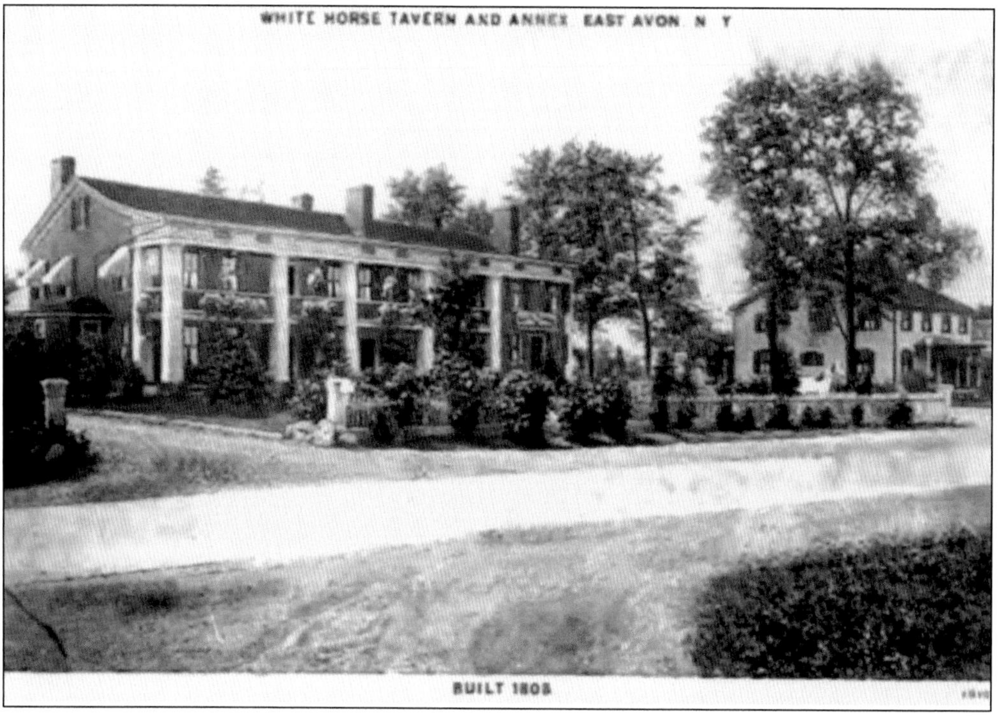

The White Horse Tavern was built in 1808 in East Avon by John Pierson. It hosted many Genesee Valley foxhunts in its time. Avon was built around mineral springs. Thousands traveled here from around America and other nations for water treatments at a time when it was believed that sulphur water had healing powers.

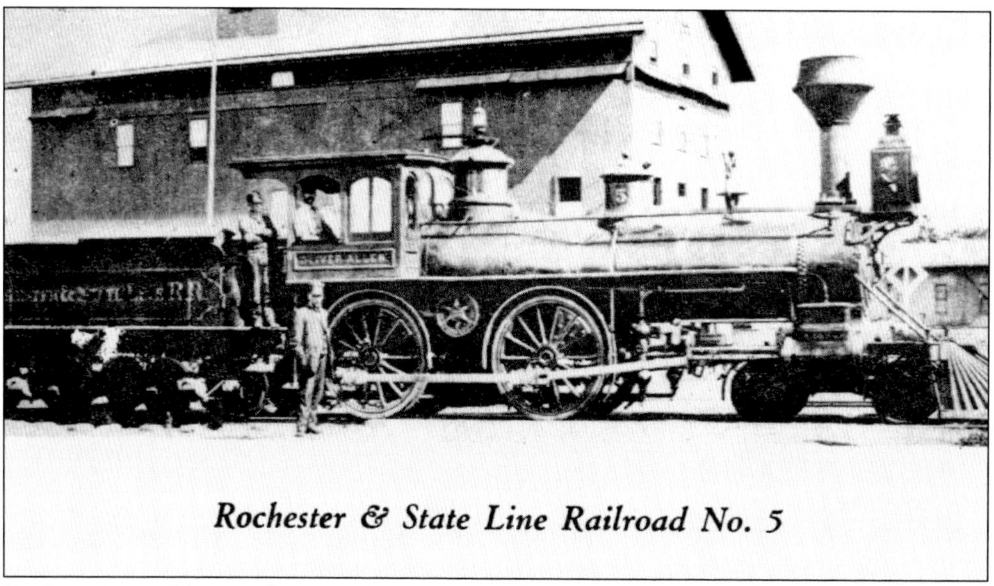

Engine No. 9 of the Rochester and State Line Railroad is seen in Mumford, according to this William Gordon postcard. The photograph was taken in 1877.

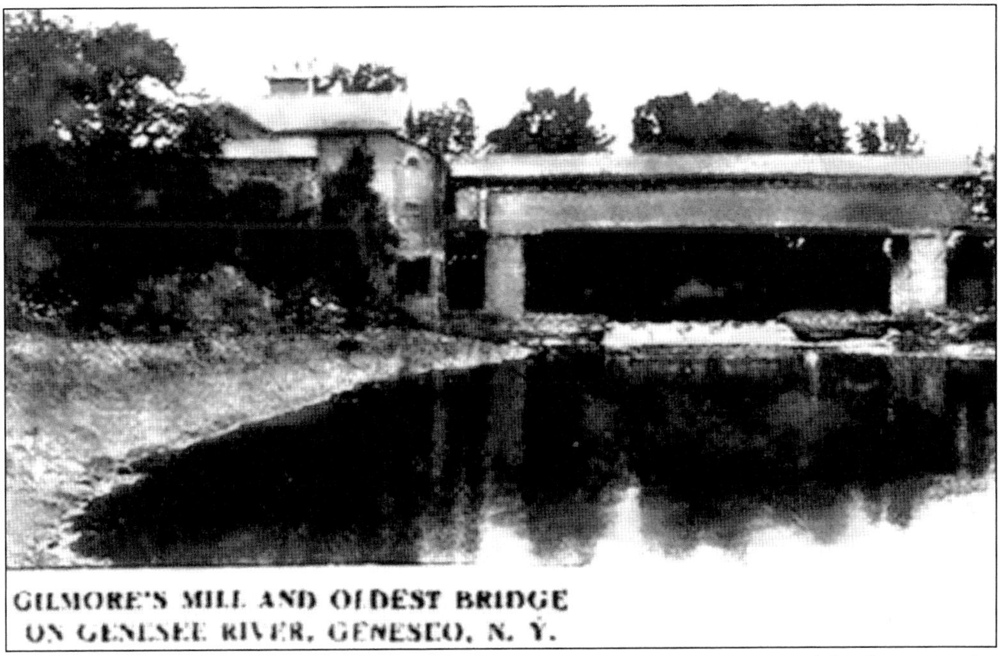

A romantic setting in Geneseo, encompassing Gilmore's Mill and a covered bridge over the Genesee River, gives us an idea of what things looked like in the pioneer days.

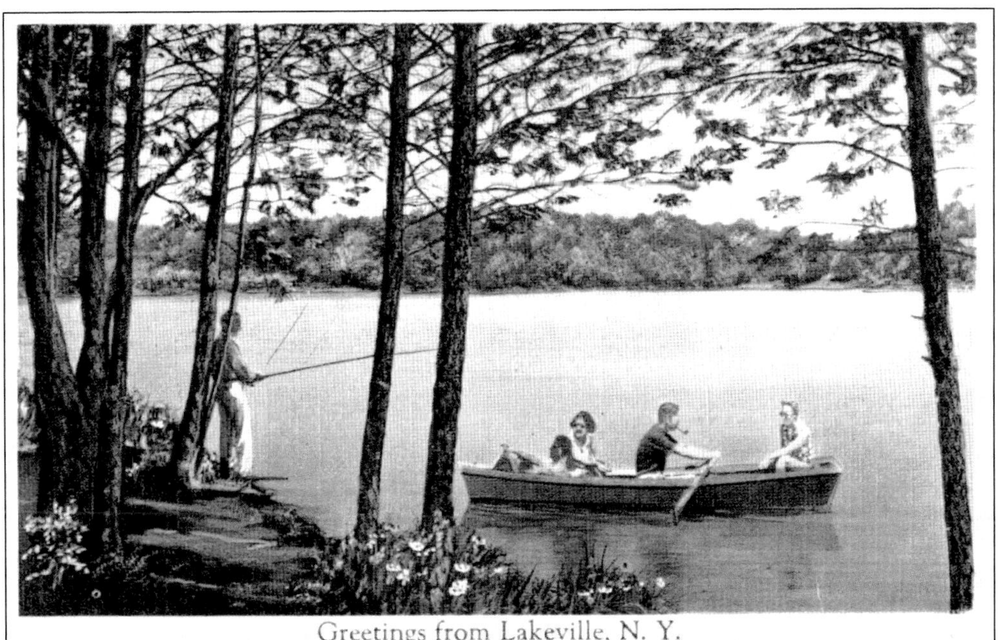

Conesus Lake has been a favorite vacation spot since the 1880s. One of the ways tourists could reach it was on the Livonia, Lakeville and Avon Railroad.

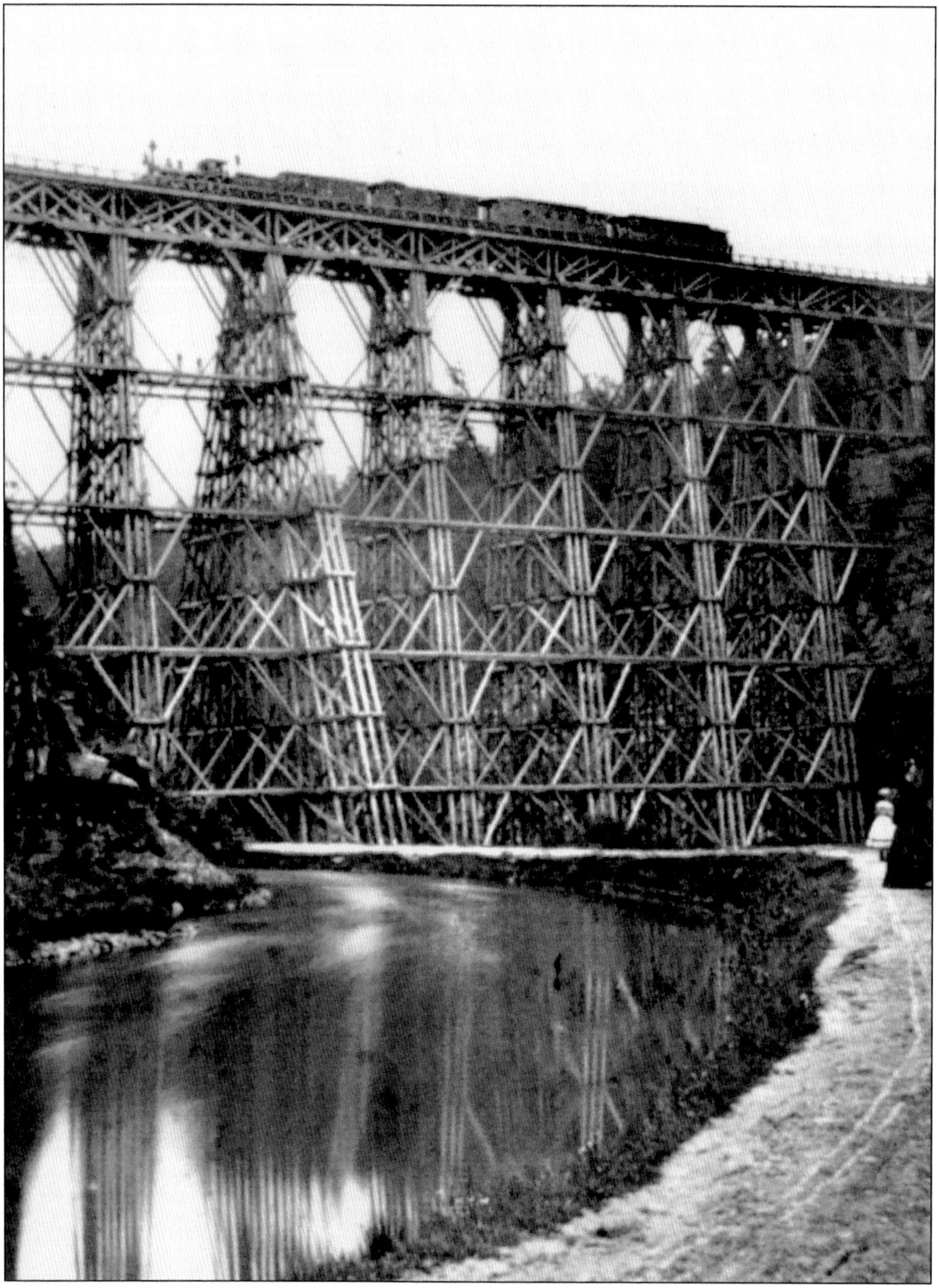

The original for this often-used souvenir image is a stereo view. The determination to overcome seemingly impossible obstacles is conveyed by these two ambitious engineering feats. The Erie Railroad Bridge built at Portage opened in 1852. It soared 235 feet above the riverbed and stretched 820 feet across the gorge. Construction on the Genesee Valley Canal, pictured here, started in Rochester in 1837 and finished in 1847. Essentially a branch canal for the Erie Canal, it ran south from Rochester to Mill Grove near Olean—a distance of about 124 miles.

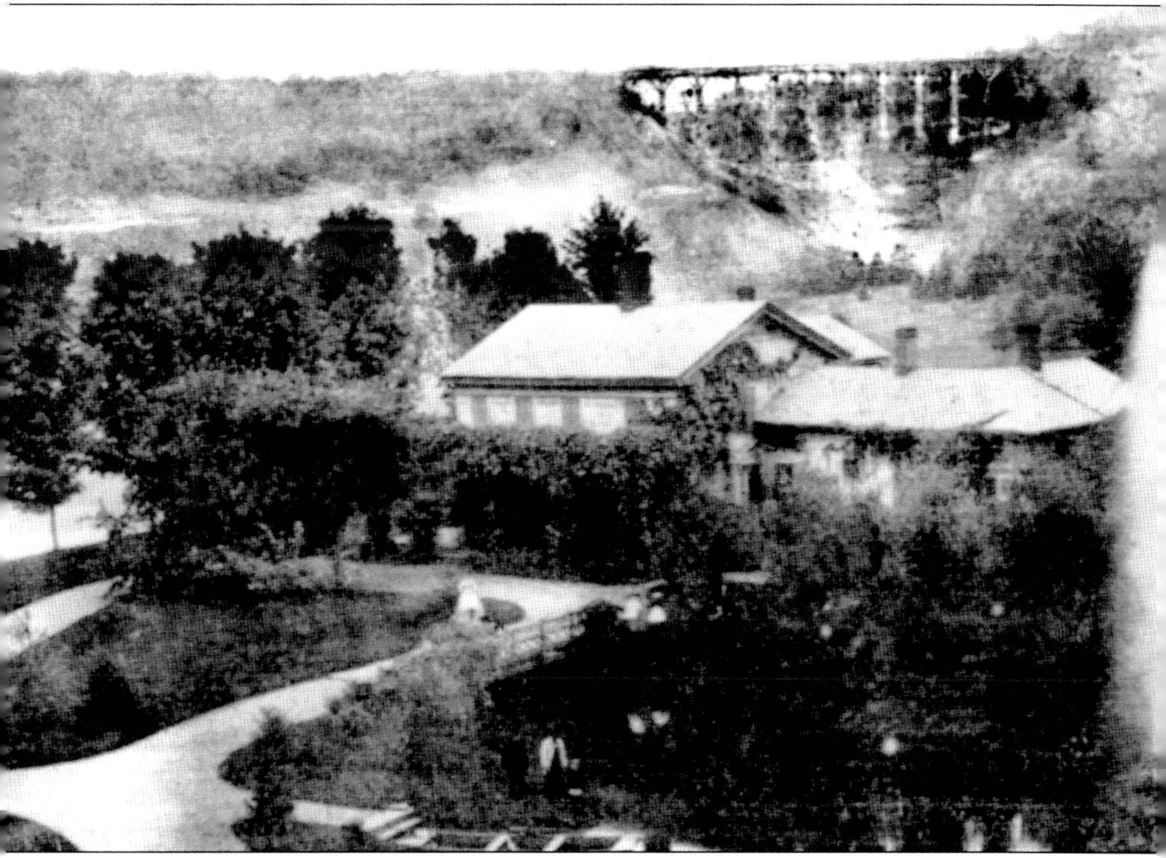

The waterfalls at the southern end of the Genesee River fared differently than those at Rochester. William Pryor Letchworth purchased approximately 1,000 acres that was threatened by loggers and other industries and made it his estate. He called his house Glen Iris, pictured here with its fountain in operation. The distant Erie Railroad Bridge burned in 1875 and was quickly replaced with an iron bridge still in use today. The thin line visible over the trees in the center is the Genesee Valley Canal.

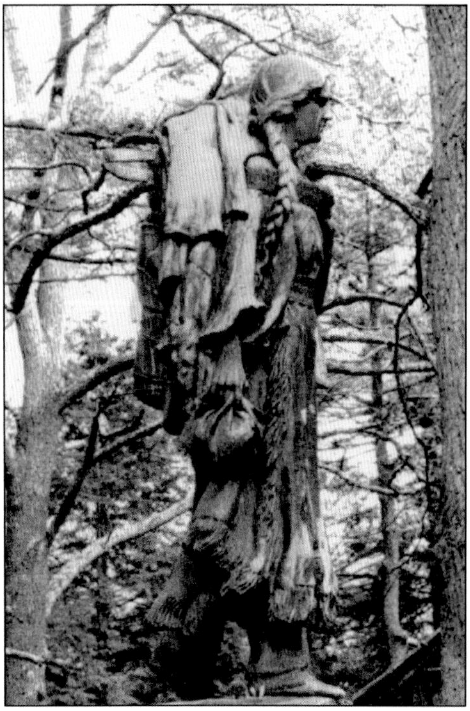

The most enduring figure of the Genesee Valley is Mary Jemison. She survived the massacre of her family and came to live with the local Iroquois. She raised a family at the northern end of the gorge and although she had opportunities to return to her people, she chose to live with the Iroquois people. Letchworth was so absorbed with her story that he had her remains removed from a Native American cemetery near Buffalo to a secluded knoll near his house. He then commissioned this statue, insisting that her face reflect both beauty and character. To complete the site, he had a deteriorating Seneca council house moved to the knoll and a cabin built by Mary Jemison situated nearby.

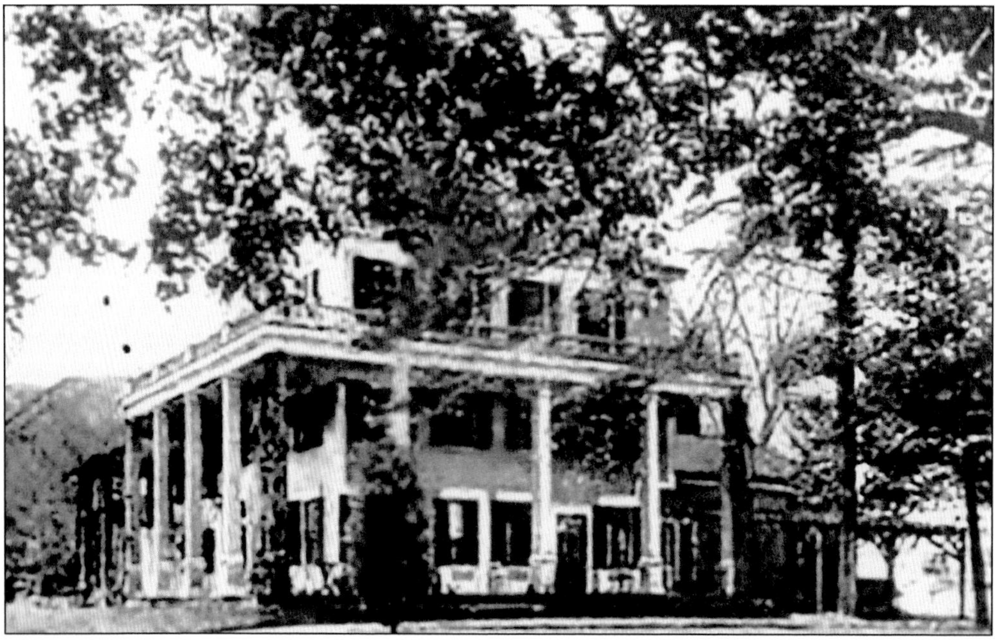

Glen Iris was built to allow views of the gorge, falls, and railroad trestle.

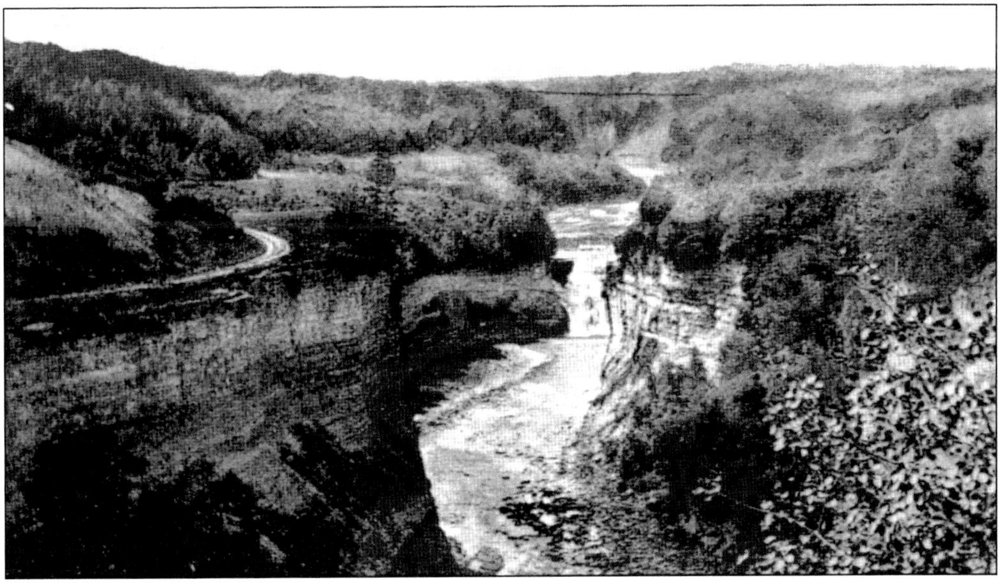

Sent in 1907, this German printed card shows the Portage Bridge in the distance and the Pennsylvania Railroad following the original path of the Genesee Valley Canal on the left. The canal never came close to the spectacular success of the Erie. It was a leaky, burdensome, high-cost nightmare with over 130 locks to maintain along its 124-mile route. In fairness, it created many industries along its towpath. It closed in 1878 and was sold in 1880 to the Genesee Valley Canal Railway Company.

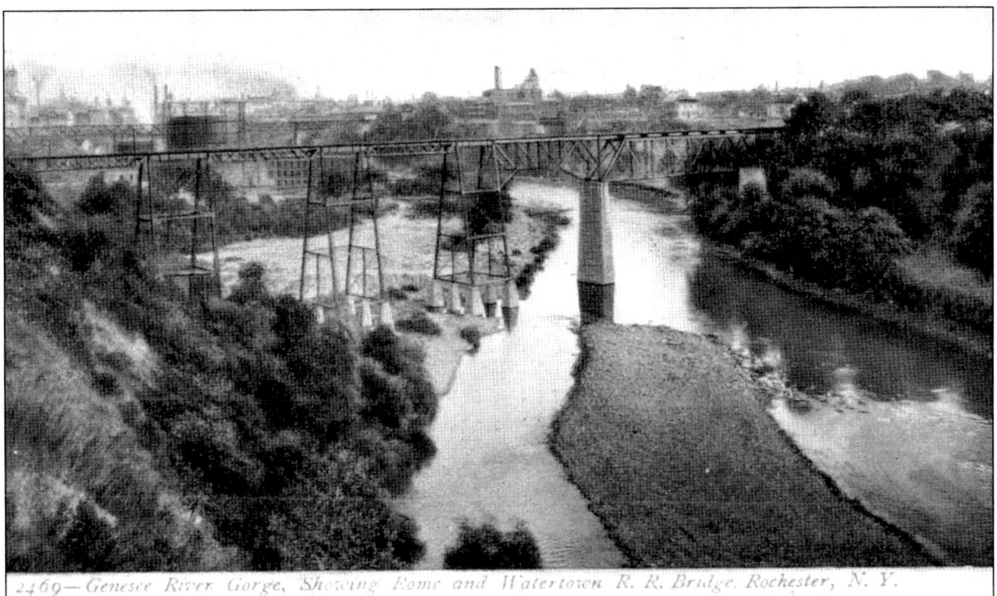

It is interesting to see how the Genesee River gorge was developed at Rochester in comparison to its journey through Portage. The bridge spanning the gorge is for the Rome, Watertown and Ogdensburg Railroad.

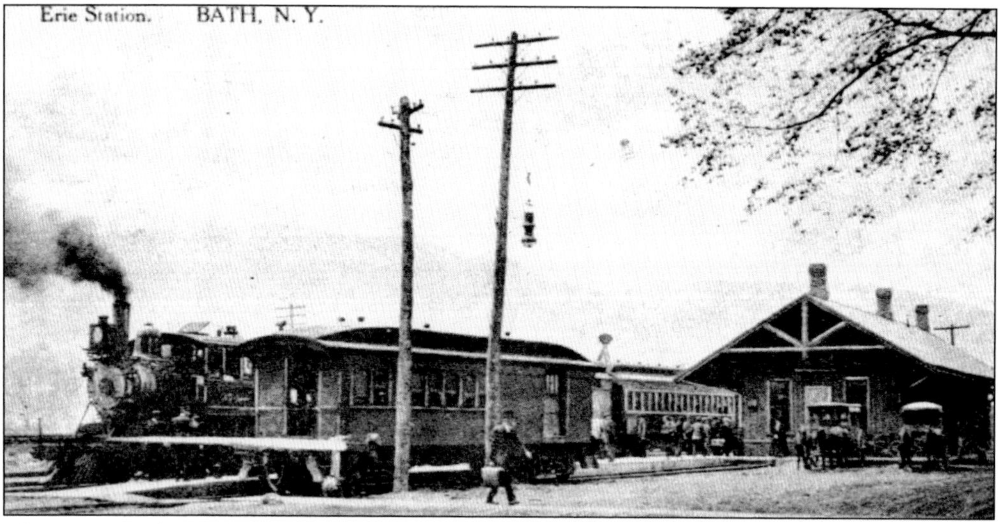

The Finger Lakes offered *c.* 1900 tourists steamboat rides, camping, hiking, boating, and tours of the vineyards. The small engine pictured in this William Gordon postcard has just arrived from Rochester on the Erie Railroad. It would then head for Corning and Elmira. The picture dates back to 1900, when the Bath and Hammondsport Railroad and the Erie Railroad serviced the station.

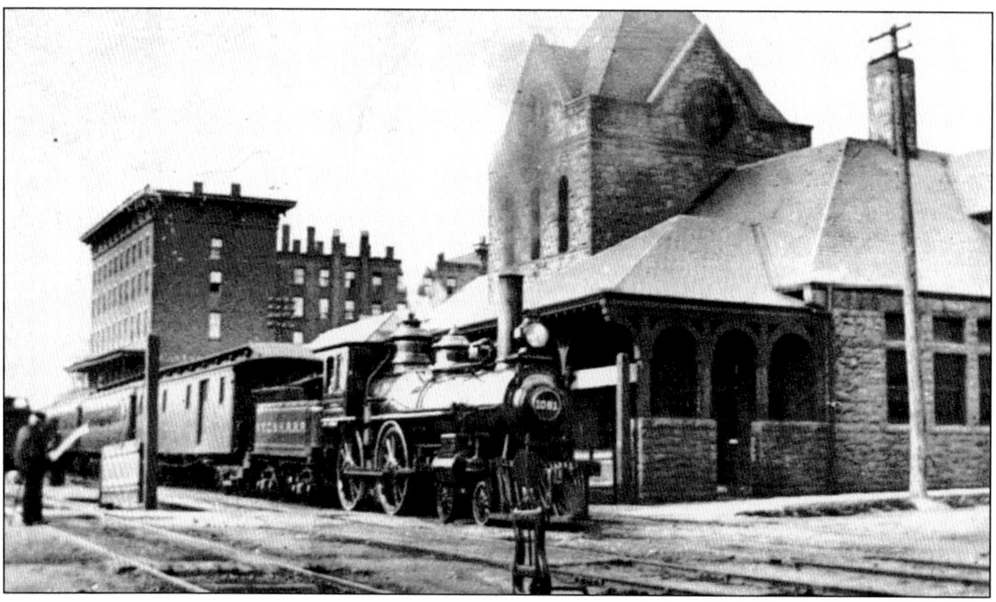

A New York Central and Hudson River Railroad passenger train waits at the Canandaigua Station. Most railroads, because of competition, made a point of keeping their passenger engines and cars clean and attractive. Freight engines were occasionally steam cleaned but were usually left spattered and streaked with grime, rust, mud, oil, and soot. This is a William Gordon postcard.

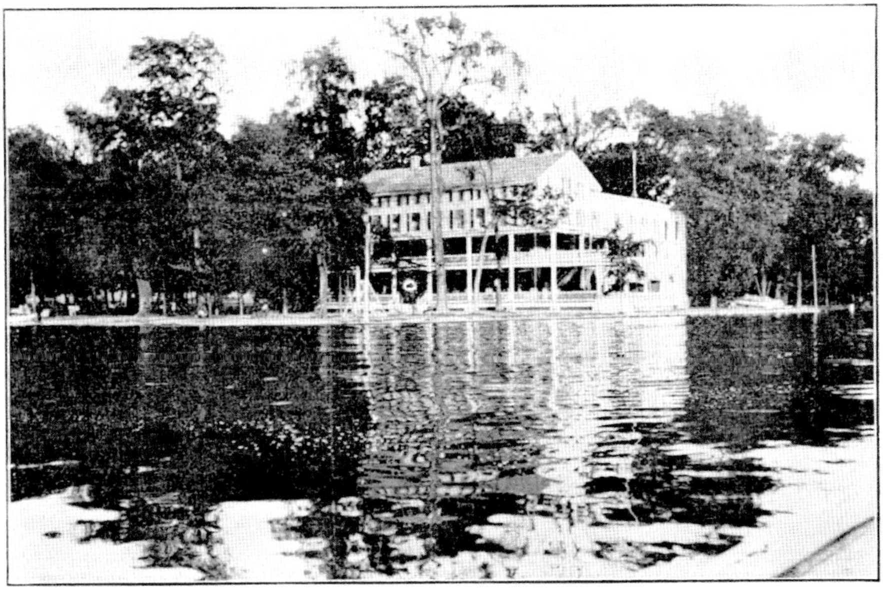

LIVINGSTON INN, CONESUS LAKE

The message on this card, "It is lovely up here. We are having a fine time," was sent to Mendon—not all that far from this spot. Postcards like this one, which features a 1909 view of the Livingston Inn on Conesus Lake, are hard to come by. Small steamboats and naphtha (gas) launches carried tourists around the lakes, often stopping at larger inns for a meal. A boat could be chartered by an organization like a church or school class for a day outing.

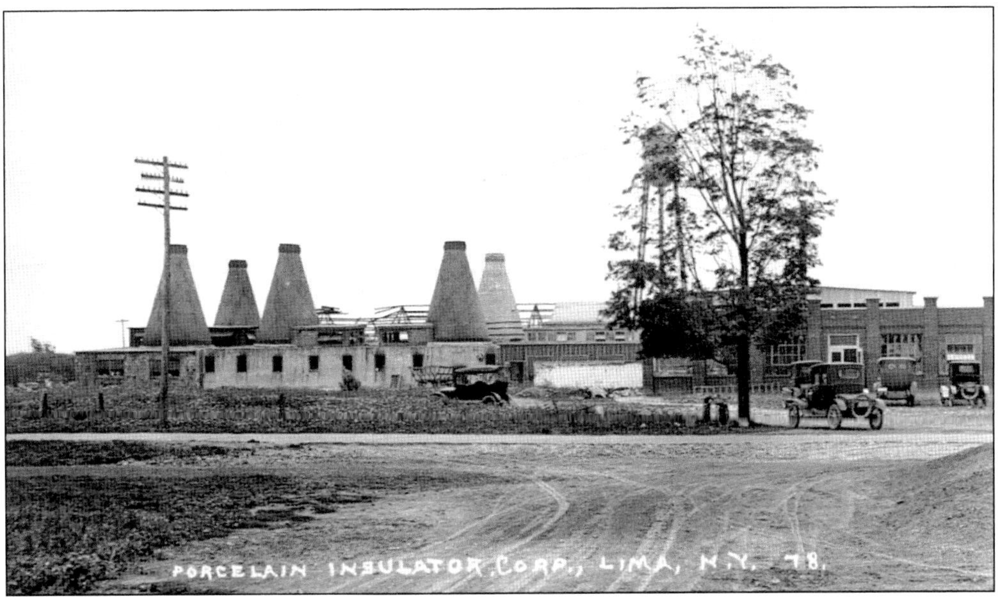

PORCELAIN INSULATOR CORP., LIMA, N.Y. 78.

Somewhere in the book of courtship there must be the statement "Never send your sweetheart a postcard of the blast kilns at Lima." A kind of postcard madness must have gripped the photographers here. Some small towns are lucky if they can scrape together a dozen postcard views. Lima had hundreds produced and, because of that, we have a vivid record of small-town life.

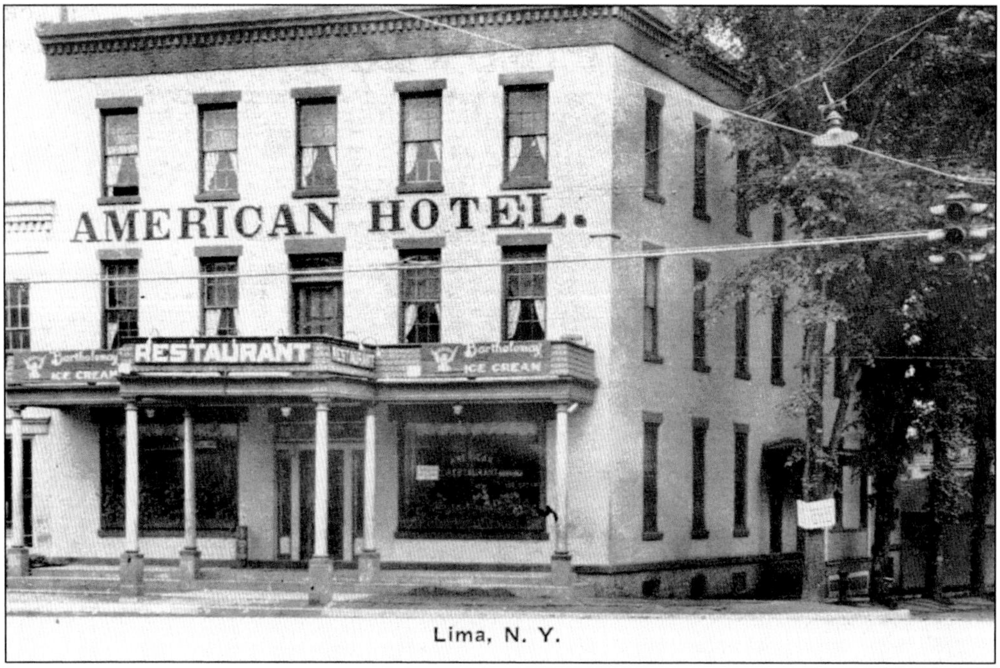

Seen here is the venerable American Hotel at the crossroads in Lima.

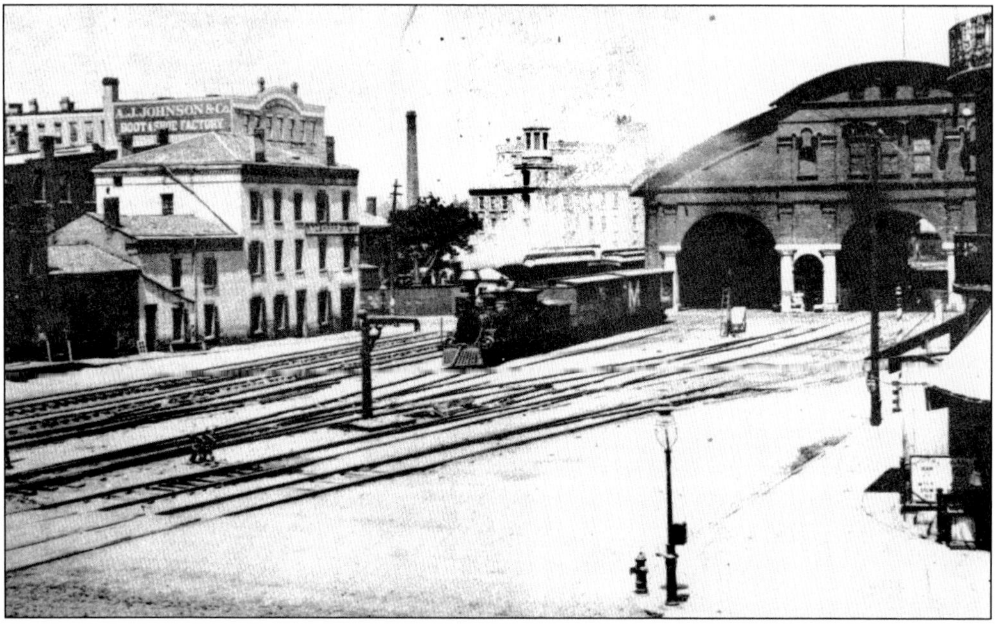

A small passenger train chuffs out of the cavernous train shed of the New York Central and Hudson River Railroad depot in Rochester. It was here that Lincoln came twice, first during his inaugural trip and then when his funeral train stopped briefly while en route to Springfield, Illinois. The tracks crossing State Street in this William Gordon postcard caused terrible hardships, as accidents occurred here, and traffic was often backed up throughout the city. They were eventually elevated.

Four

In Our Midst

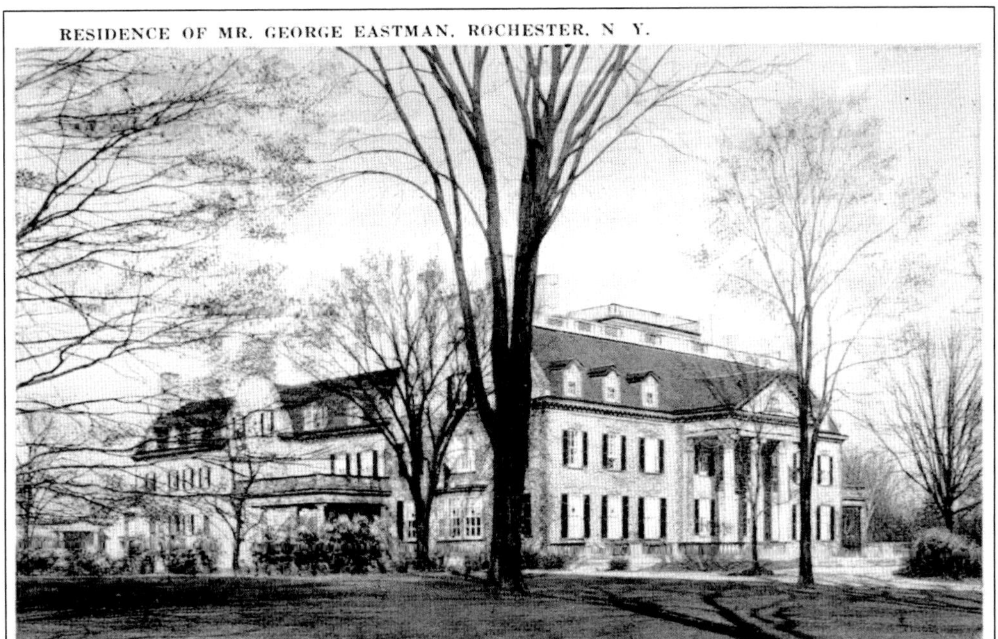

The little village by the river, founded by Rochester, Carrol, and Fitzhugh, became the nation's first true boomtown; its population tripled in five years, from 1820 to 1825. George Eastman was always positive about the city's potential. From small rented rooms on State Street, he built an empire that established Rochester as the "Image Center of the World." This is his East Avenue mansion. He chose East Avenue over Lake Avenue because it did not have noisy trolleys. That move established the grand corridor where Rochester's wealthy would build their estates.

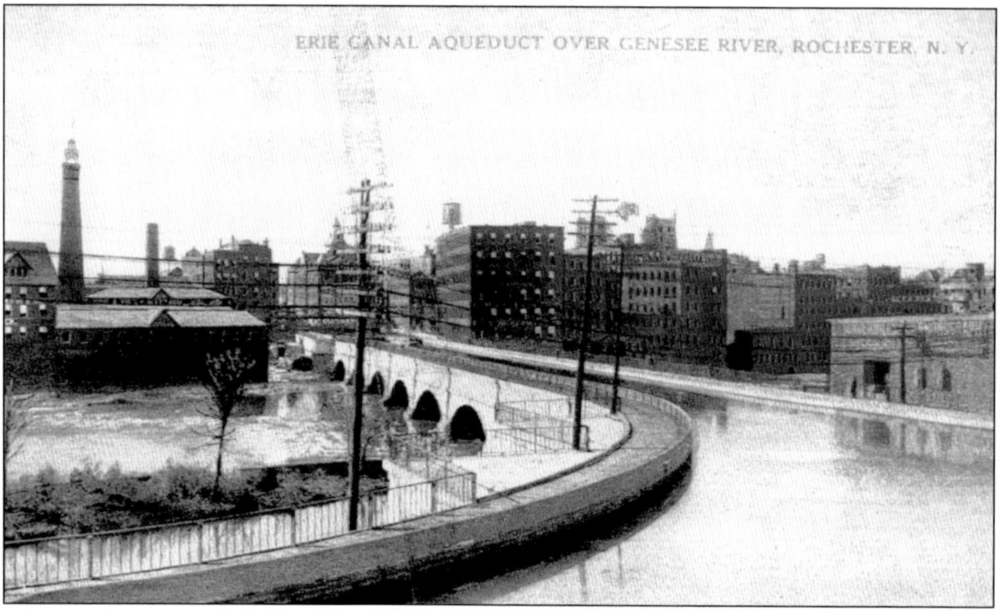

The combination of the Erie Canal with the milling complexes led to explosive growth. Immigrants set their differences aside and built fortunes together. Education and cultural institutions had to be of the highest quality as if to legitimize the burgeoning city.

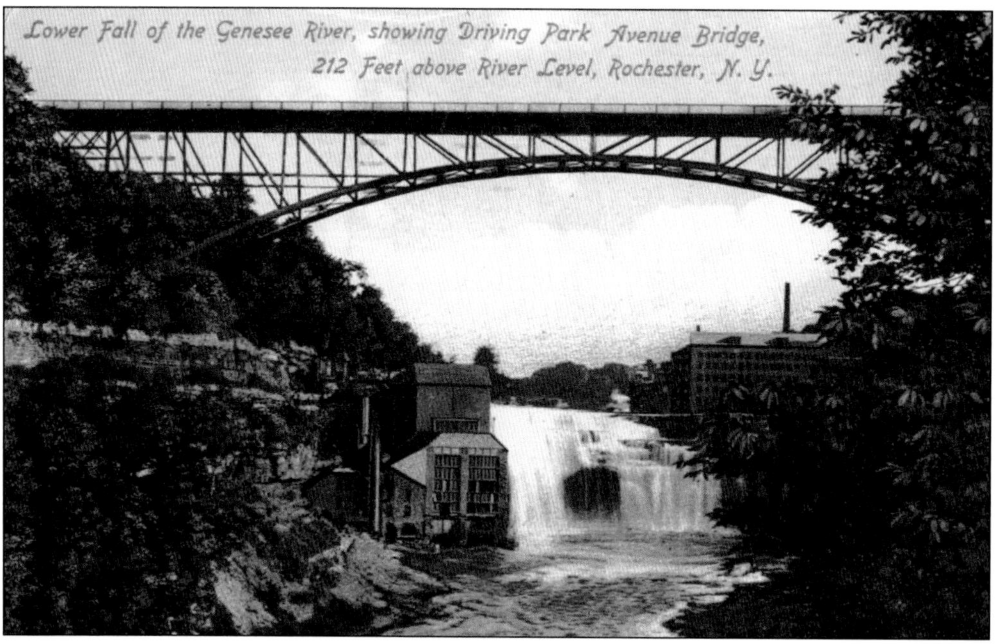

The Lower Falls and river beneath the Driving Park Bridge was a fascinating place to young Seth Green who lived here when it was Carthage. He fished the "giants" that came up river—the 15-pound bullhead and the 150-pound sturgeon that local inns served as Albany beef. He also developed a method of artificial fish propagation that won him worldwide notoriety as the father of fish culture.

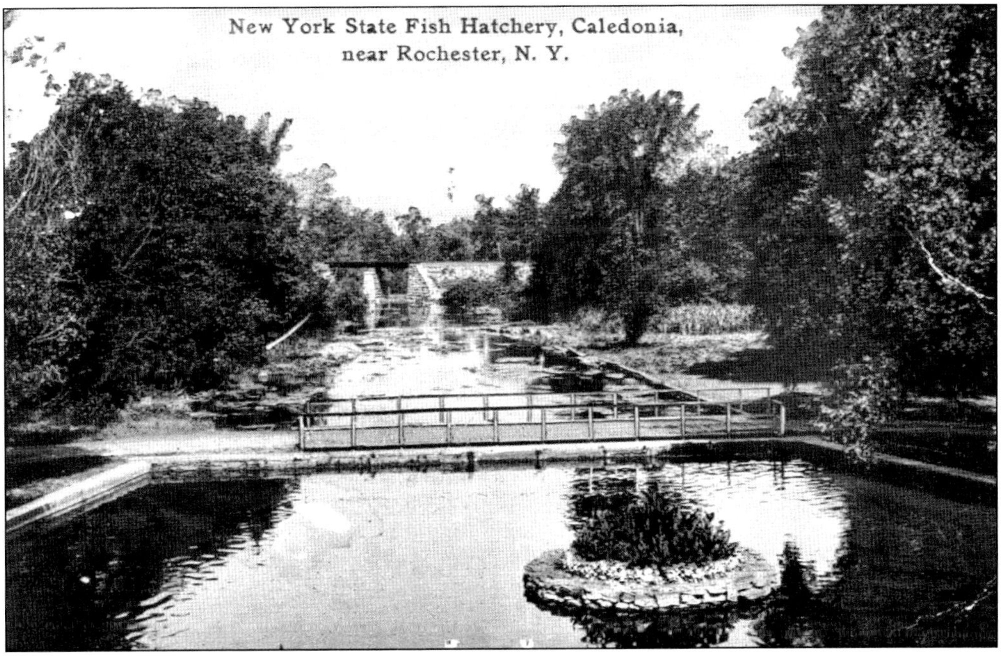

In 1864, Seth Green purchased land in Caledonia and used its cool creek waters to establish his fish propagation market. He eventually raised shad, trout, whitefish, and others. He would create a system of restocking water systems with healthy fish around America and the world. He once traveled to Sacramento on a train with four milk cans filled with 12,000 shad beside him. The fish hatchery in Caledonia still offers visitors a fascinating look at a system of providing fish to the world that was started by a sensible young man from Carthage.

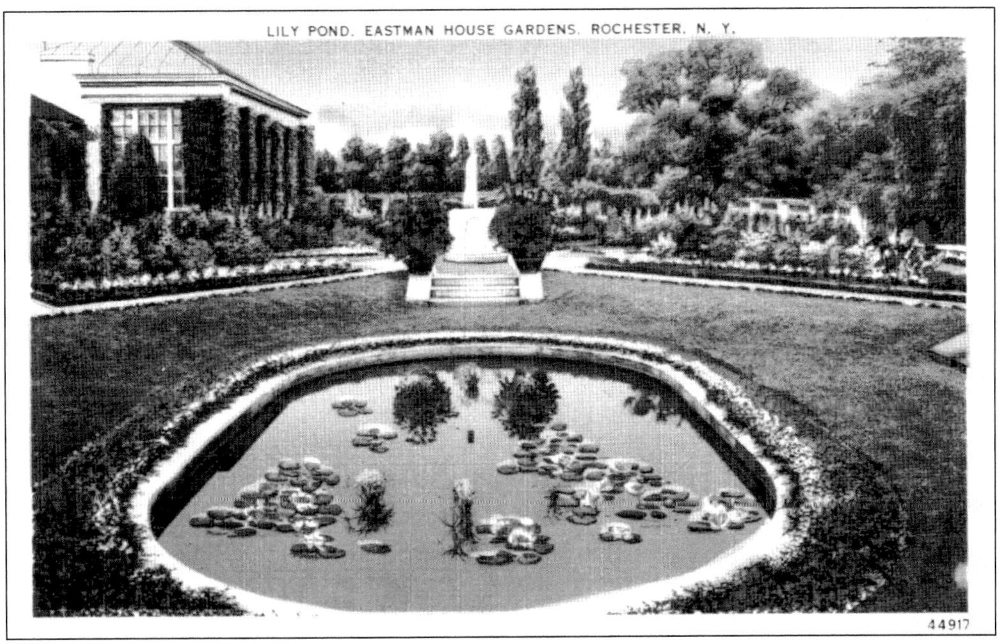

In keeping with the Flower City's tradition of excellent gardens, George Eastman made certain the terraced gardens around his mansion were as grand as any on the avenue.

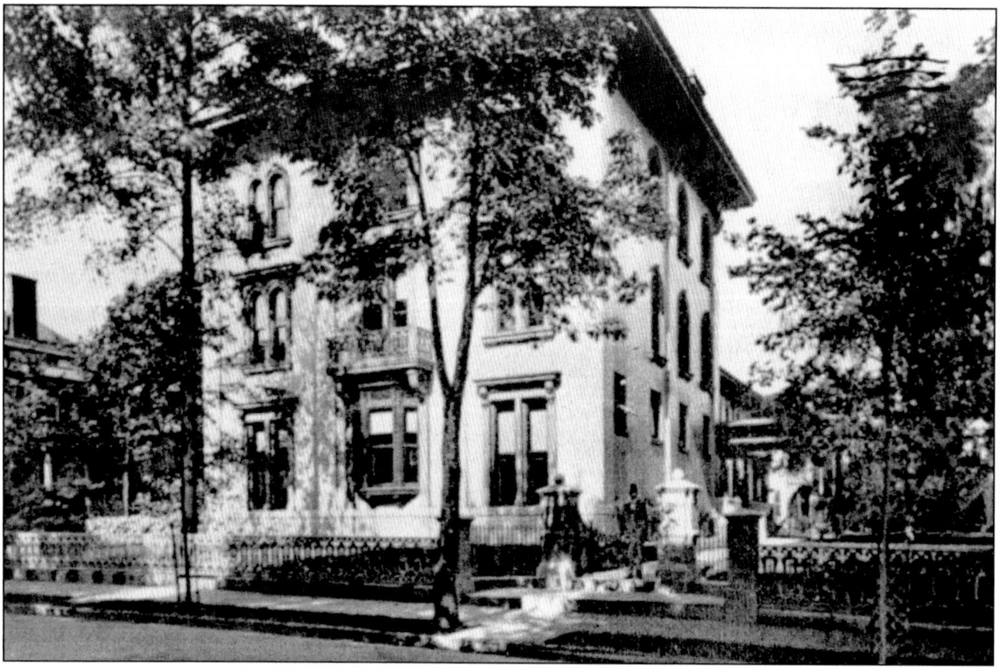

This elegant neighborhood was developed immediately beside the Erie Canal. It was the Third Ward and was variously referred to as Corn Hill and the Ruffled Shirt District because the well-dressed, upper-crust families built mansions there. The Reynolds family occupied this home on Spring Street in the ward. It became the Reynolds Library and offered over 35,000 volumes.

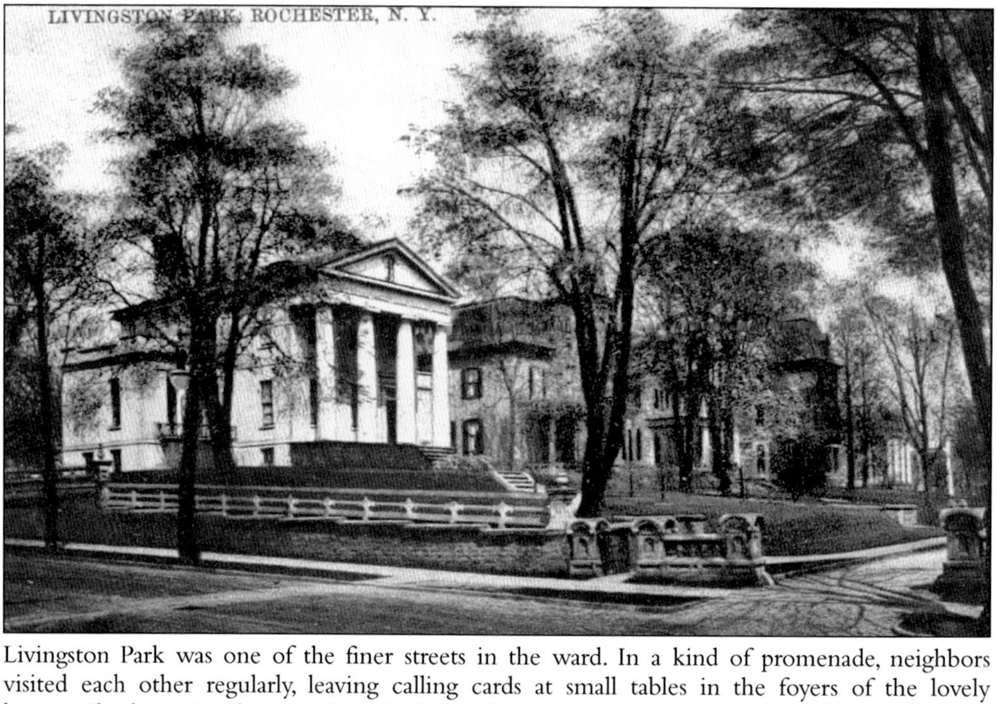

Livingston Park was one of the finer streets in the ward. In a kind of promenade, neighbors visited each other regularly, leaving calling cards at small tables in the foyers of the lovely homes. This large Greek Revival was built by Hervey Ely. It is now owned by the Daughters of the American Revolution.

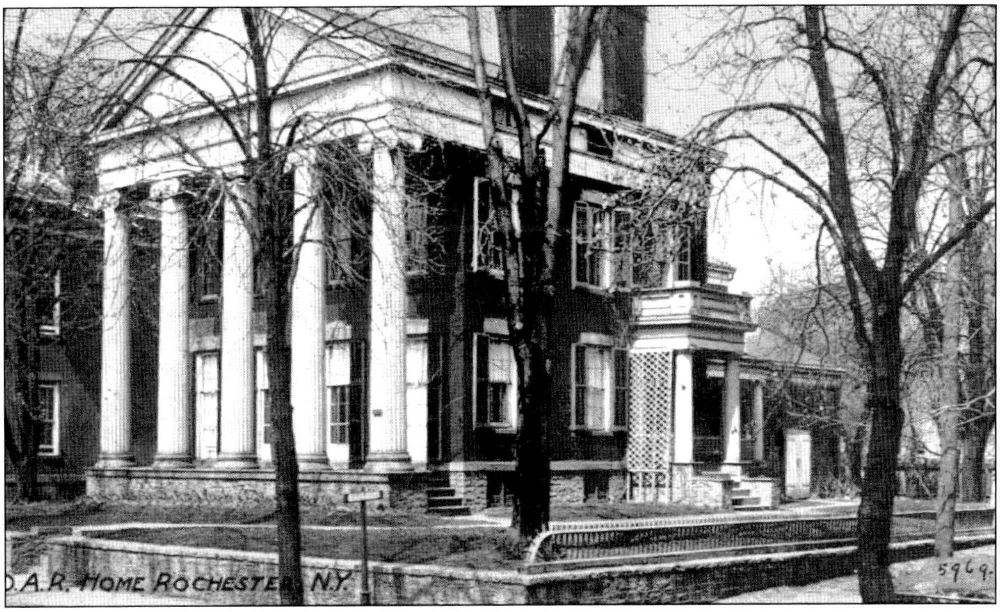

The city was recognized for having some of the most beautiful Greek Revival buildings outside of the South. The *c.* 1835 Montgomery house on Spring Street was considered one of the most appealing. A traveler once entered the city at twilight on the Genesee Valley Canal and then transferred to the Erie. Impressed by the magnificent homes of the Third Ward and the reflection of gaslights in the canals, millraces, and river, he wrote to his brother, "This is as fine a place I've seen. Its many water routes, bridges and large residences make you think you are entering Venice."

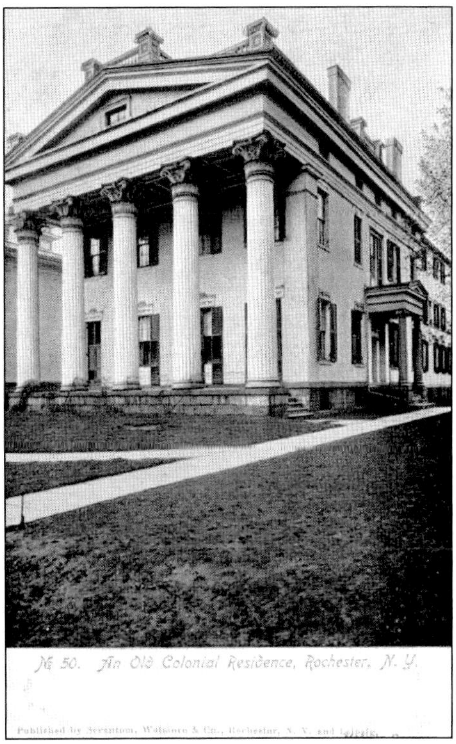

A monumental residence in the ward is the *c.* 1837 Jonathan Child house at 37 South Washington Street. It was built west of the aqueduct, near a basin, by Jonathan Child, Rochester's first mayor. A good portion of the ward was gutted for the construction of a highway, and the rest was left to decay until citizens recognizing the significance of the area resurrected it in astounding ways. This house has been put to many uses. It has served as offices and, more recently, was transformed into the beautiful Edward's Restaurant.

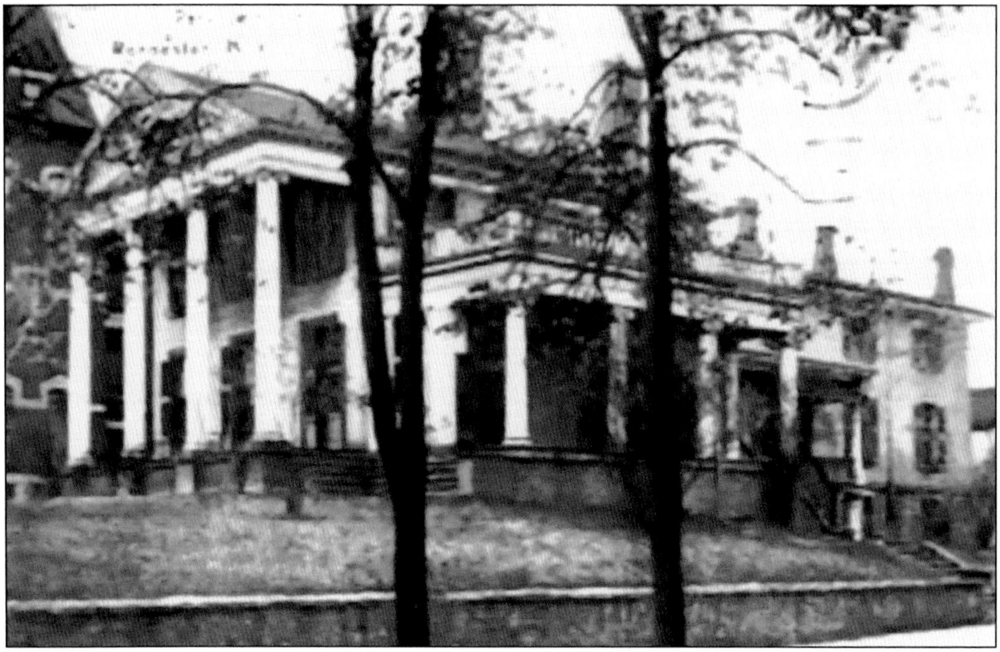

The original part of the Livingston-Backus house dates from 1827. Located in the Third Ward, it later served nearly 75 years as Livingston Park Seminary. Amazingly, it was saved from destruction in the 1950s by a benefactor who had it dismantled and stored. In 1970, he presented it to Genesee Country Museum in Mumford, where it was reconstructed.

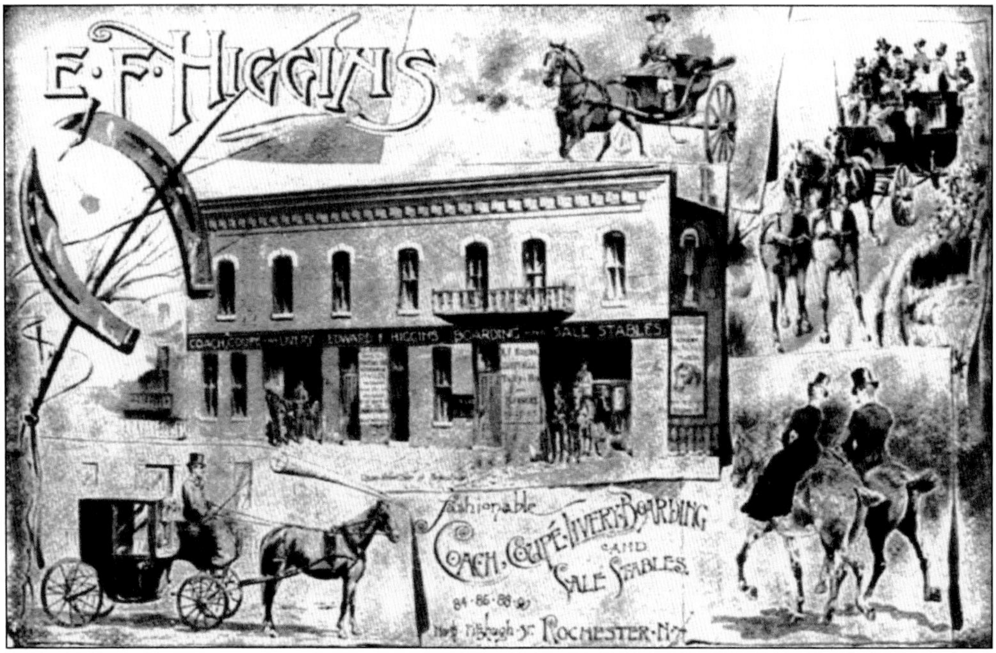

The Third Ward was serviced by E.F. Higgins on South Fitzhugh Street. The advertisement card shows that Higgins offered fashionable coach, coupe, livery, boarding, and sale stables.

A view of South Fitzhugh Street in the ward looking south from the city conveys a sense of order. There are fine residences on both sides of the narrow tree-lined street. Note the carriage blocks. There are no signs of horse-car tracks or even street lamps. This view appeared in the 1898 *Souvenir of Rochester* book, but given the absence of tracks and lamps and the fact that street is still dirt, the original image may be from the Civil War era.

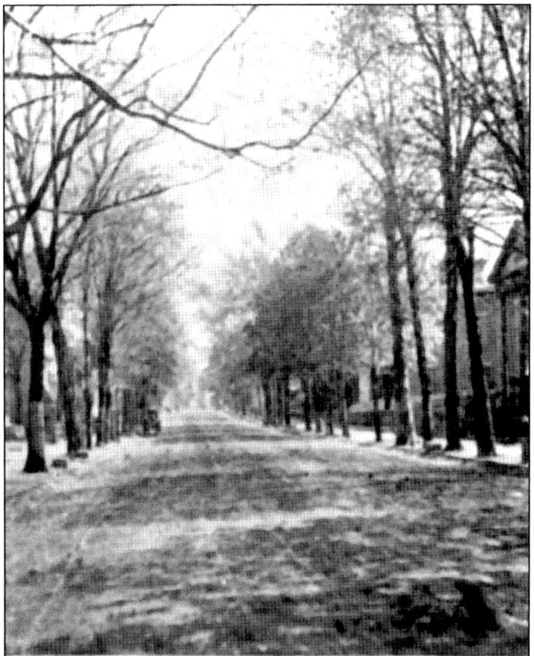

SOUTH FITZHUGH STREET.

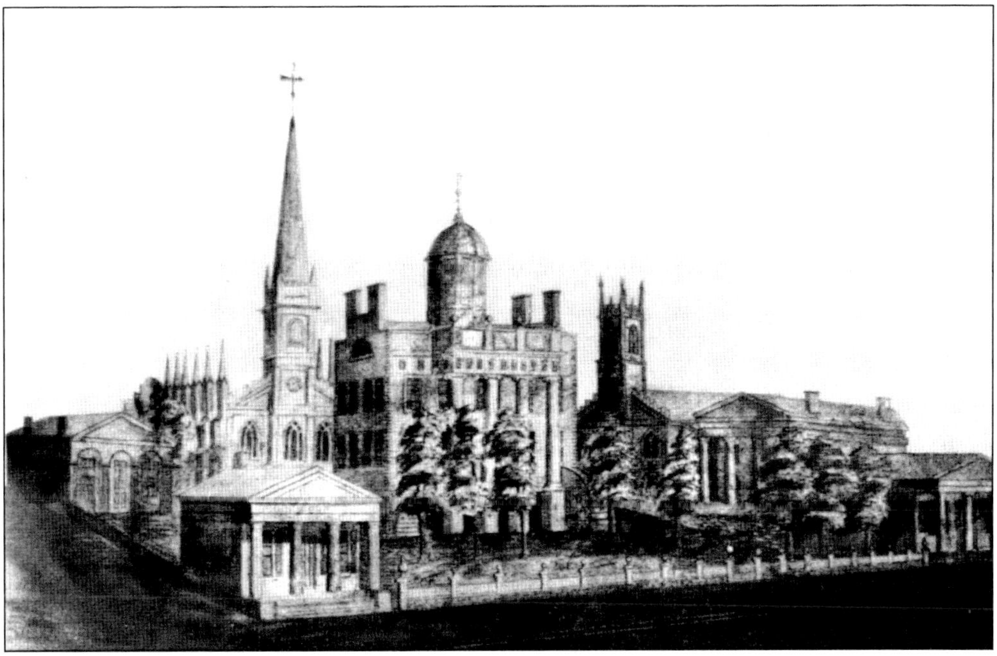

Rochesterville grew rapidly from this nucleus, where the first courthouse stands prominently in the center. Immigrants, investors, entrepreneurs, dreamers, inventers, activists, and artists all found a fertile ground here to launch enterprises and movements that affected people in all corners of the world. Even in this grouping, dating back to the 1820s, there is stateliness and a rigid determination.

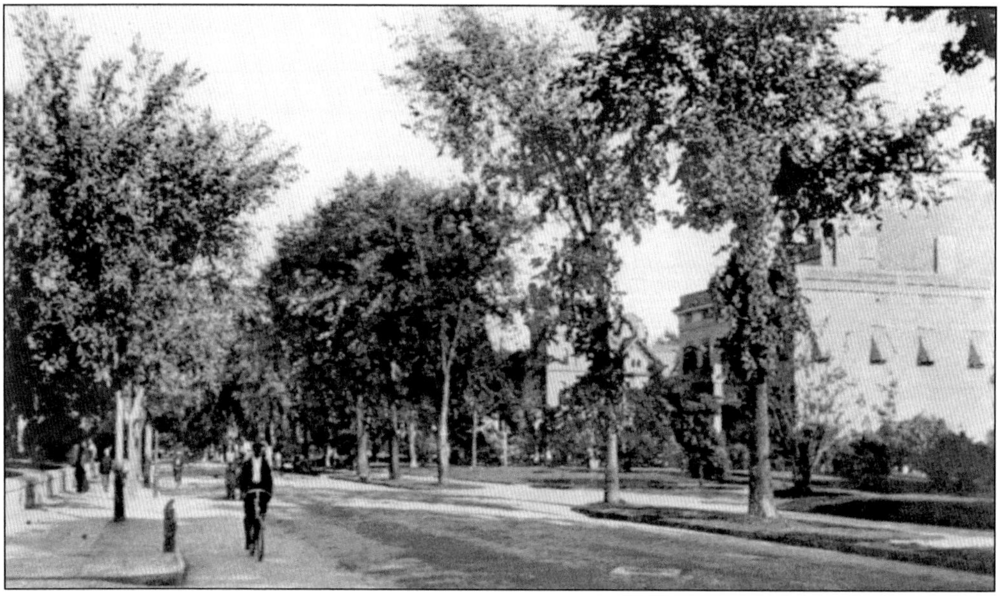

As fortunes grew so did the need for larger homes. When the Third Ward began to feel the press of an increasingly industrialized city, the wealthy responded to the rural beckoning of East Avenue. Farmlands were subdivided, and reeking swamps and fouled sewers—where the city ran drains to empty where they may—were repaired or removed. Soon, the mansions started going up. The Silas O. Smith home is on the right in this *c.* 1890 view up East Avenue.

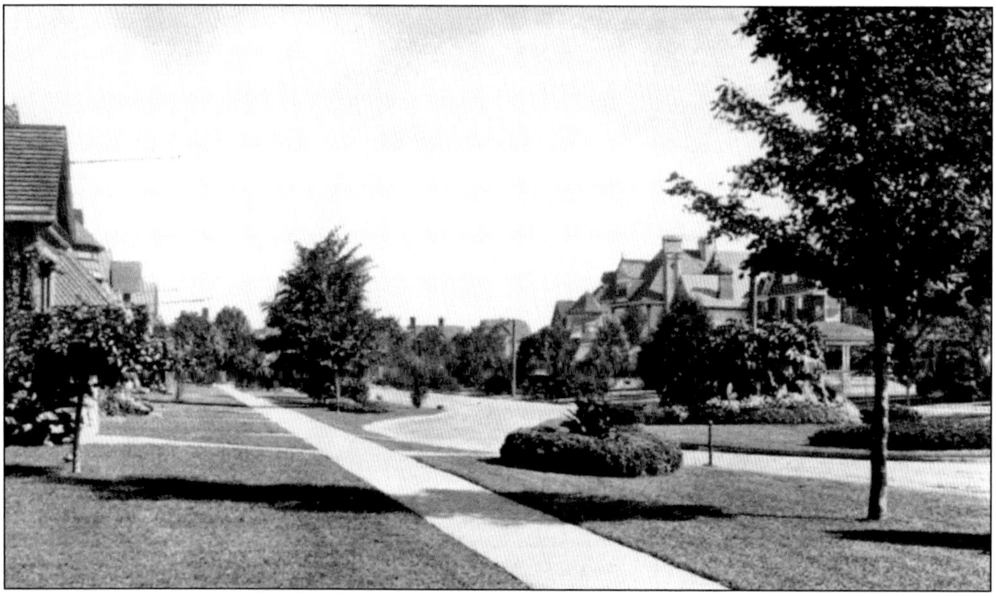

Fine side streets ran off East Avenue. Portsmouth Terrace is manicured and inviting. These were big homes with servant quarters. Many immigrants from the rougher neighborhoods around the canal and railroads sent their teenage daughters to work as maids or nannies. In the 1920s, street after street of more affordable homes appeared, usually built near a local industry and made self-sufficient with stores and services. These homes were of exceptional quality for the money, featuring stained glass, ceramic tile, and fine woods. The 19th ward and Browncroft areas were good examples of these subdivisions.

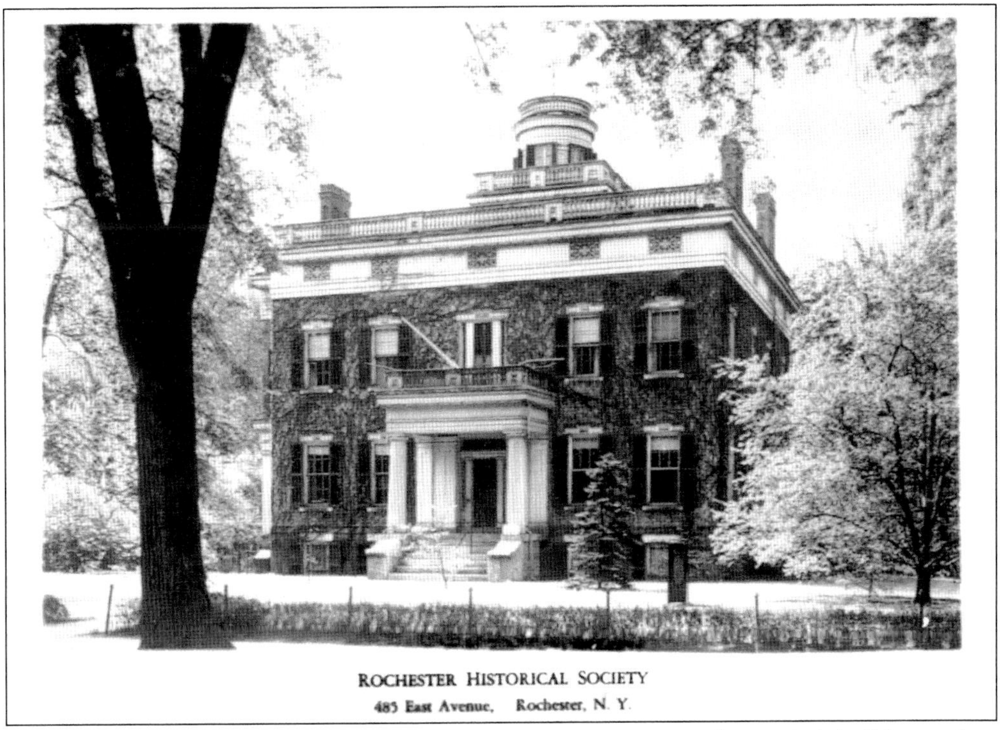

Silas O. Smith built Woodside, this impressive and inviting Greek Revival building, when East Avenue was still considered the country. The Rochester Historical Society now maintains it as their headquarters. Across the street and slightly north was Hiram Sibley's mansion, which was built in the 1860s. Sibley was president of Western Union. In the 1850s, he joined all of the nation's telegraph systems together. He invested heavily in higher learning institutions such as Cornell, the University of Rochester, and Mechanics Institute. This was not the same Sibley of department store fame.

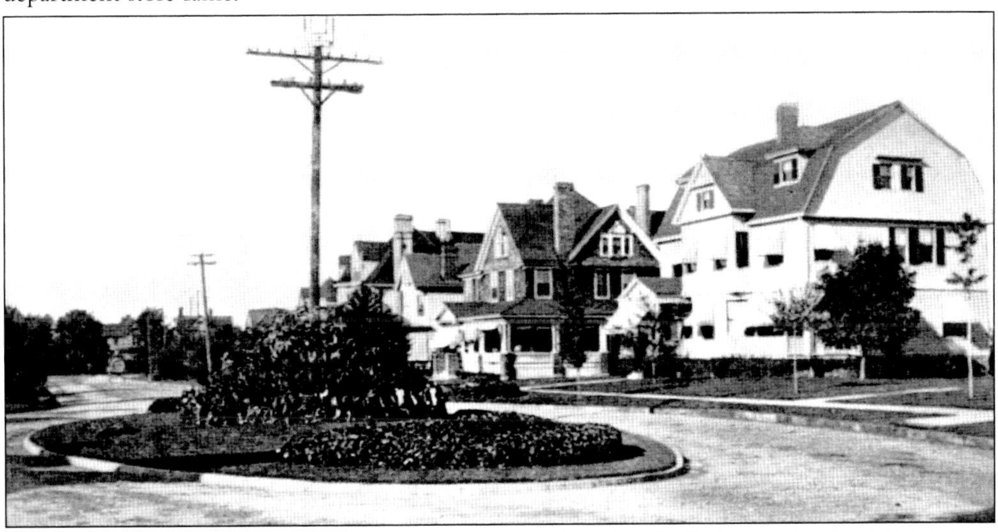

Another view of Portsmouth Terrace shows us how big they built homes in the 1890s. These homes were modest, however, compared to the elaborate stone mansions on East Avenue. That was at a time of cheap labor, high craftsmanship, and no income tax.

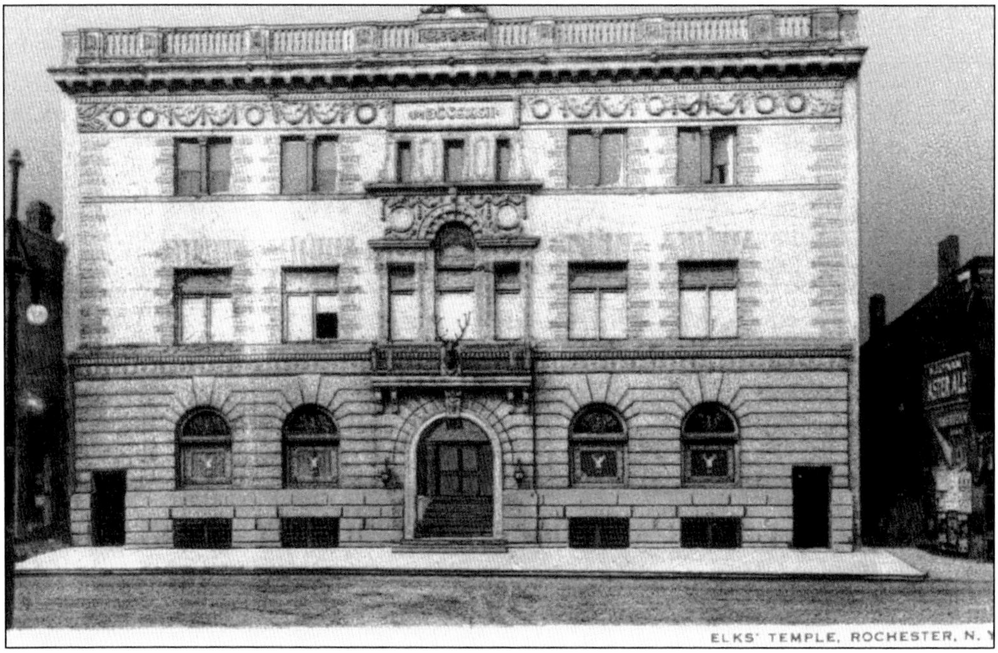

Social clubs began springing up as prosperity continued. The Elk's Temple and Eureka club was built in the Italian Renaissance–style on North Clinton. The clubhouse provided a "place of resort for members and their families to congregate for social, literary and dramatic entertainments. It [had] a library, billiards room, and ballroom, banquet hall, bowling alley, lounging room, writing rooms and reception rooms."

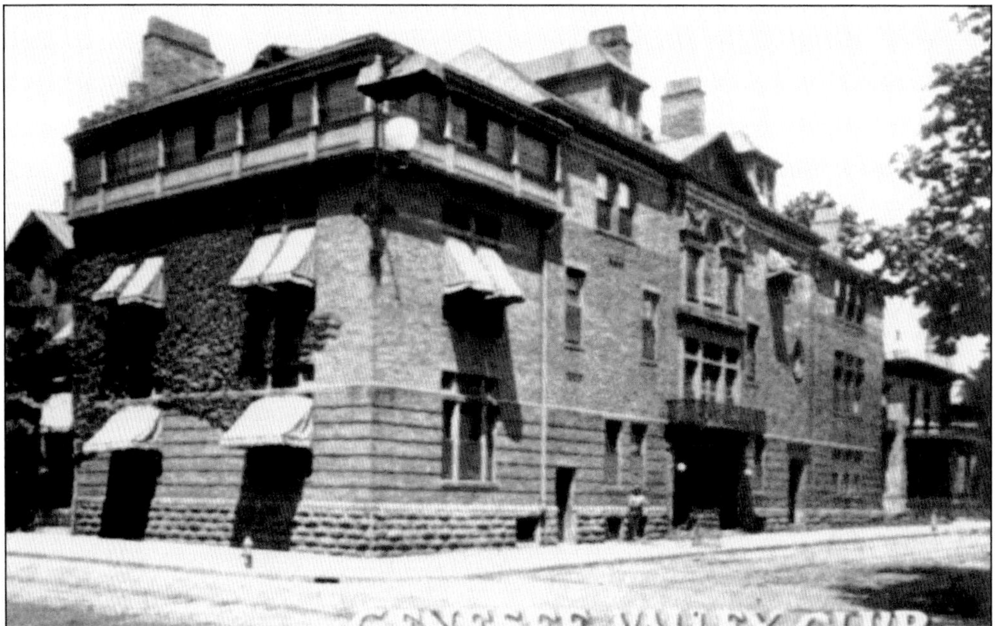

The Genesee Valley Club, seen here in an 1898 *Souvenir of Rochester* view, was located on the corner of East Avenue and Gibbs Street. Although some of these clubs were cliquish, most contributed to the community through donations to charity and underwriting worthwhile projects.

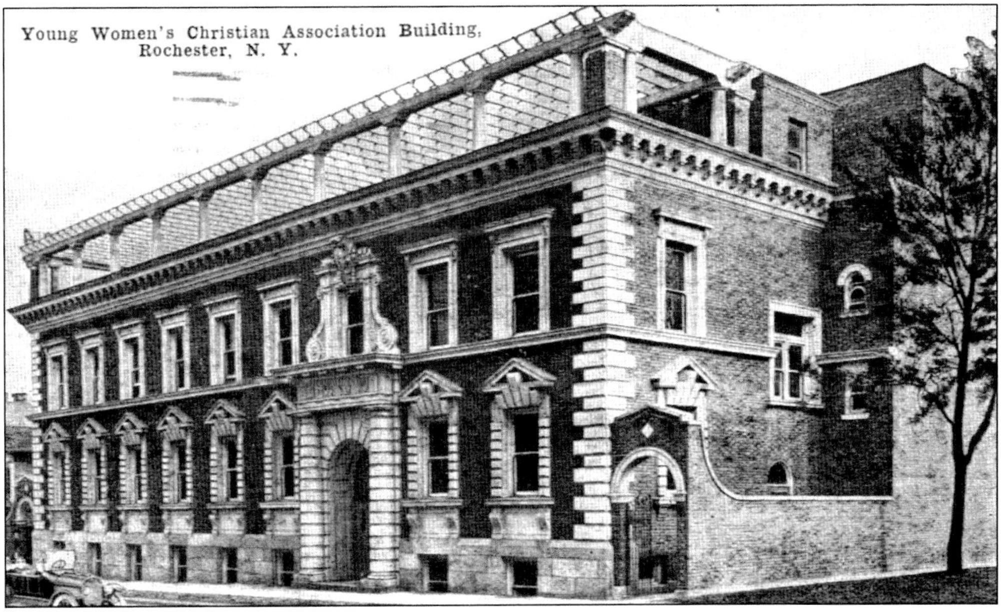

The downtown YWCA provided women at all socioeconomic levels with a facility for physical and spiritual renewal.

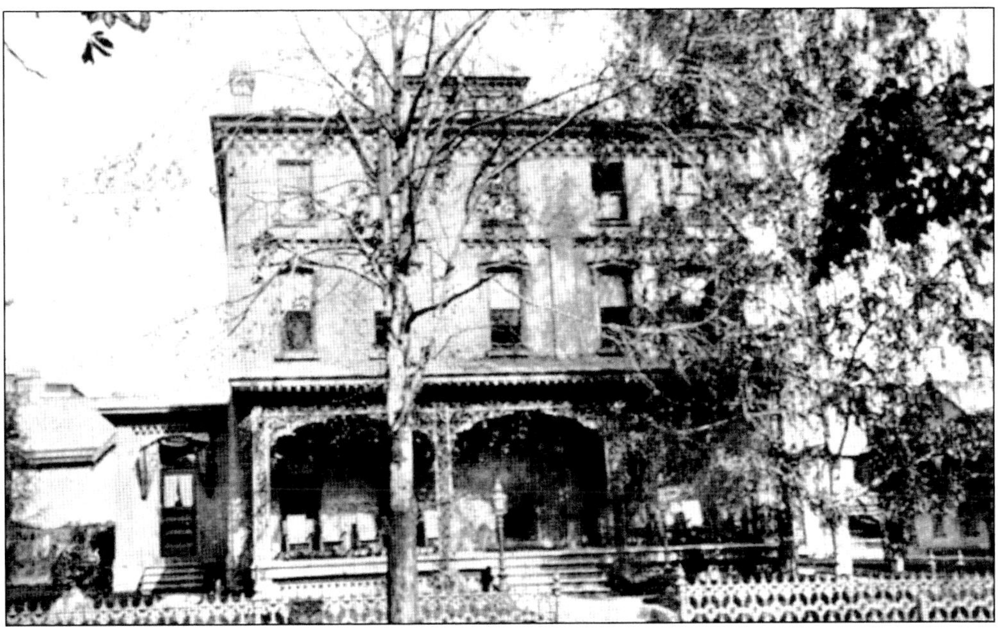

Organized in 1860, the Rochester Club provided social and recreational activities. It was located at 78 East Avenue. It had a membership of 220 in 1898 when this souvenir image was taken.

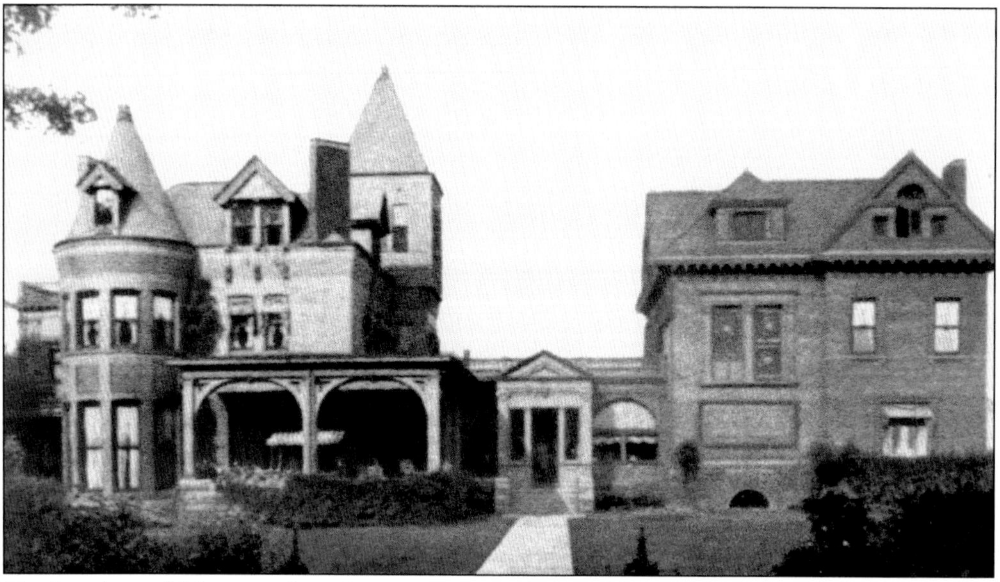

The location of this unusual residence is not certain. It appears a gallery joined two substantial homes. It may have been a doctor's residence and adjoining office.

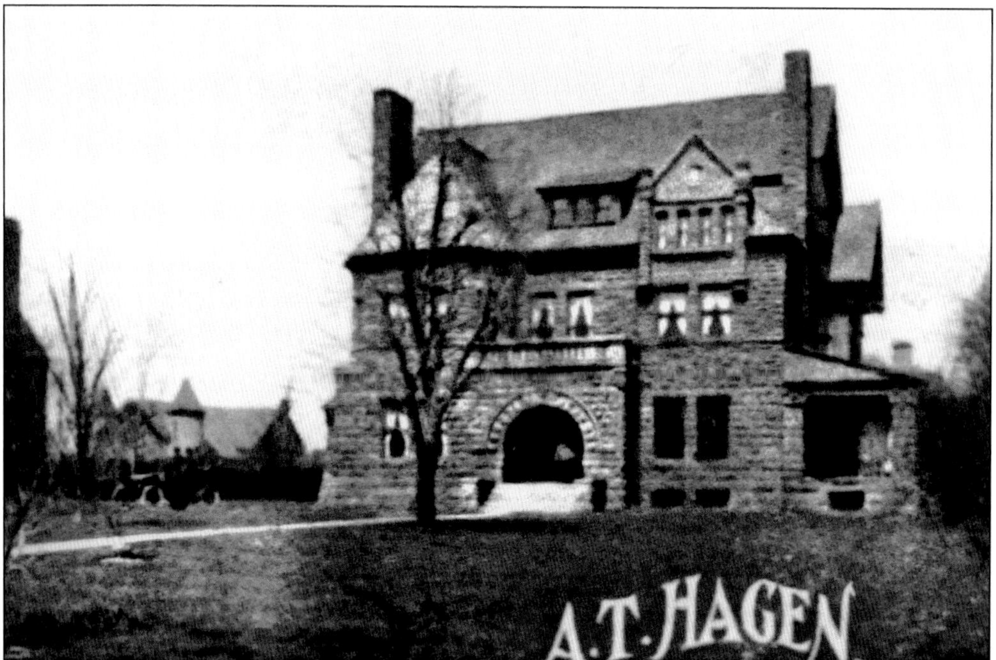

The excesses of Victorian-American architecture are certainly missing from this severe baronial east-side mansion. The Victorian era, which began with the reign of Queen Victoria, beloved champion of the middle class, dictated much of social conduct, from how children were raised to how people dressed and designed their houses.

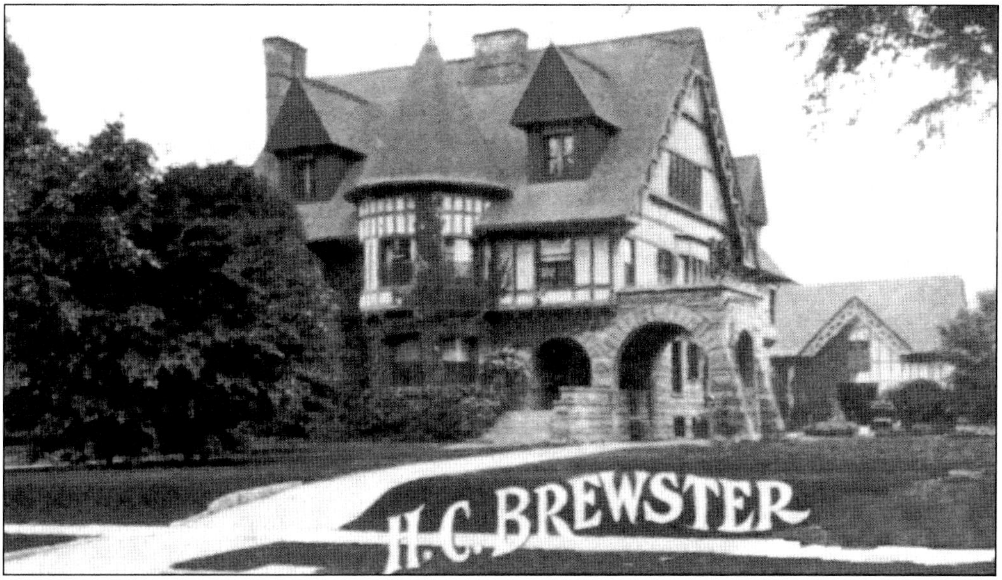

This is another east-side mansion that reflects the stunning architectural heritage of this city. Neighborhoods like Maplewood, Browncroft, Sibley Tract, Jones Park, St. Paul Boulevard, and others all had blocks of splendid residences.

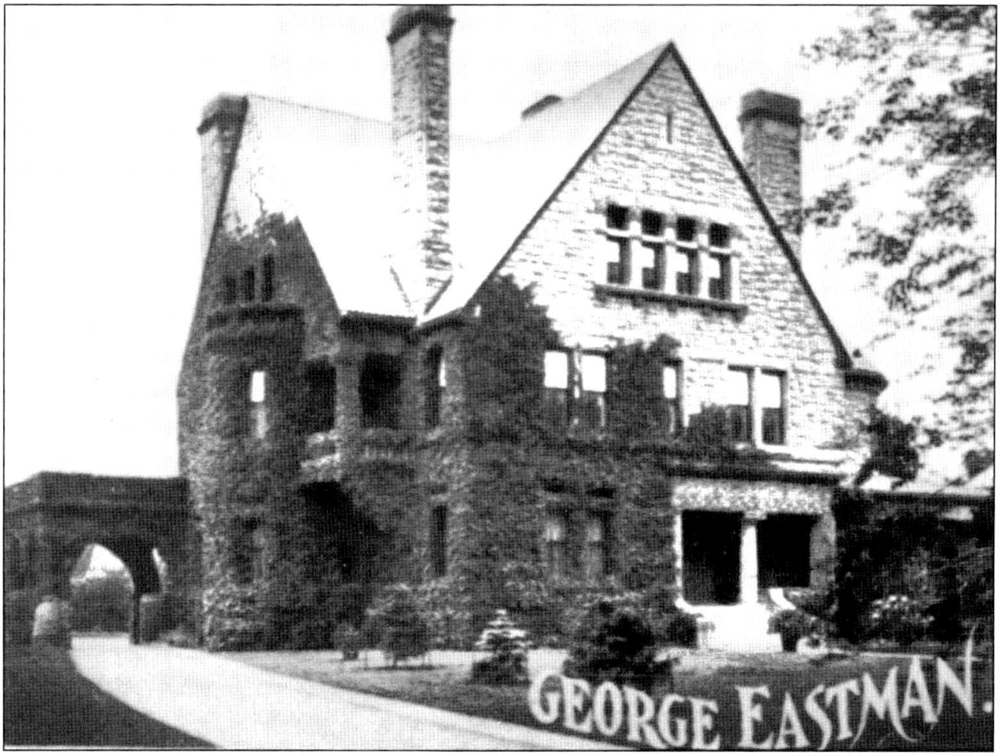

George Eastman lived here at 1050 East Avenue while his grander mansion was being built up the street. This substantial residence is actually the Wilson Soule house dating to the 1880s. It incorporated Richardsonian Romanesque elements in an attempt to develop a distinct American architectural style.

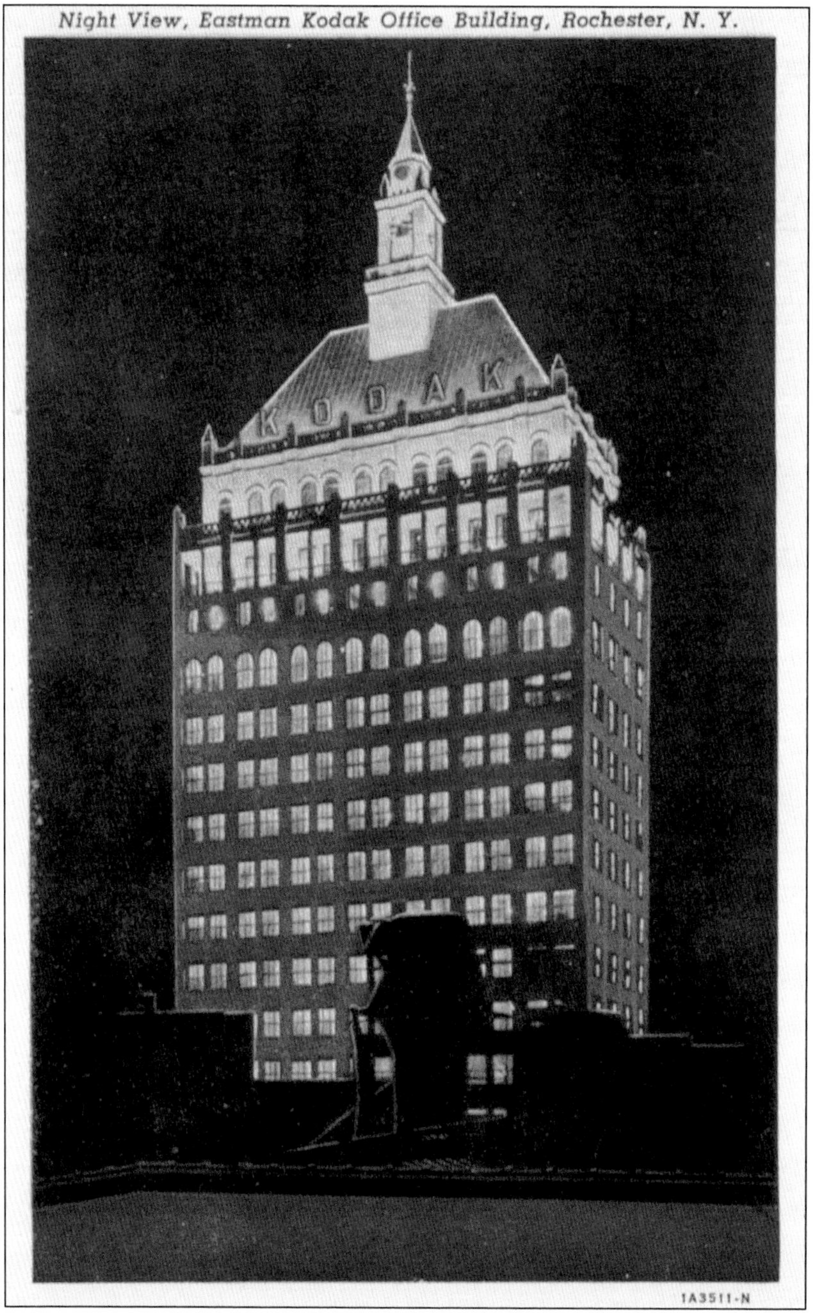

Reigning at the top of those in our midst was George Eastman who lorded, quietly, over the city for the common good. Kodak was the bedrock upon which this modern city was built. Along with him strode others like Strong, Sibley, Reynolds, Vick, Ellwanger, Barry, Susan B. Anthony, Frederick Douglass, Keating, Gannett, Lewis Henry Morgan, Henry Ward, Bragdon, Warner, Ellis, Rush Rhees, Helen Montgomery, Bausch, Lomb, Edgerton, Gleason, Seth Green, and others. From the Genesee country came Chester A. Arthur, Clara Barton, Francis Bellamy, Mary Jemison, Mary Seymour Howell, Millard Fillmore, John Young, the Wadsworths, Daniel Shays, Bishop McQuaid, Henry Jarvis Raymond, and William Pryor Letchworth, to name a few.

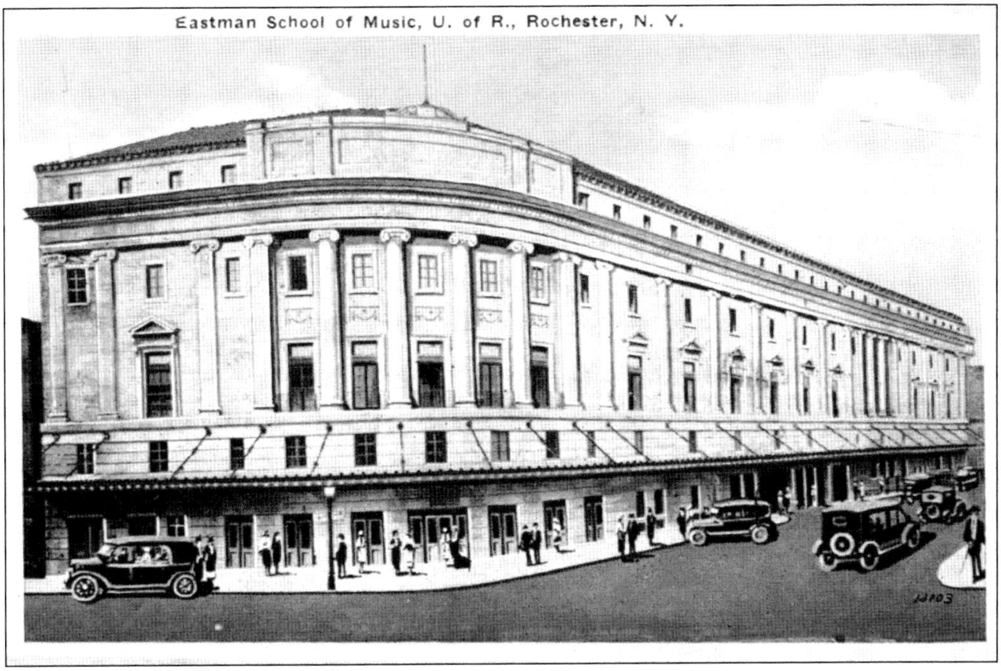

The Eastman Theater and Eastman School of Music, monumental gifts to the community, continue to attract students from around the world. Designed by McKim, Mead and White of New York, the 1922 structure is noted for its hand-painted murals and fantastic chandelier. The institution added music to the list of things Rochester is famous for. The others are photography, architecture, and flowers.

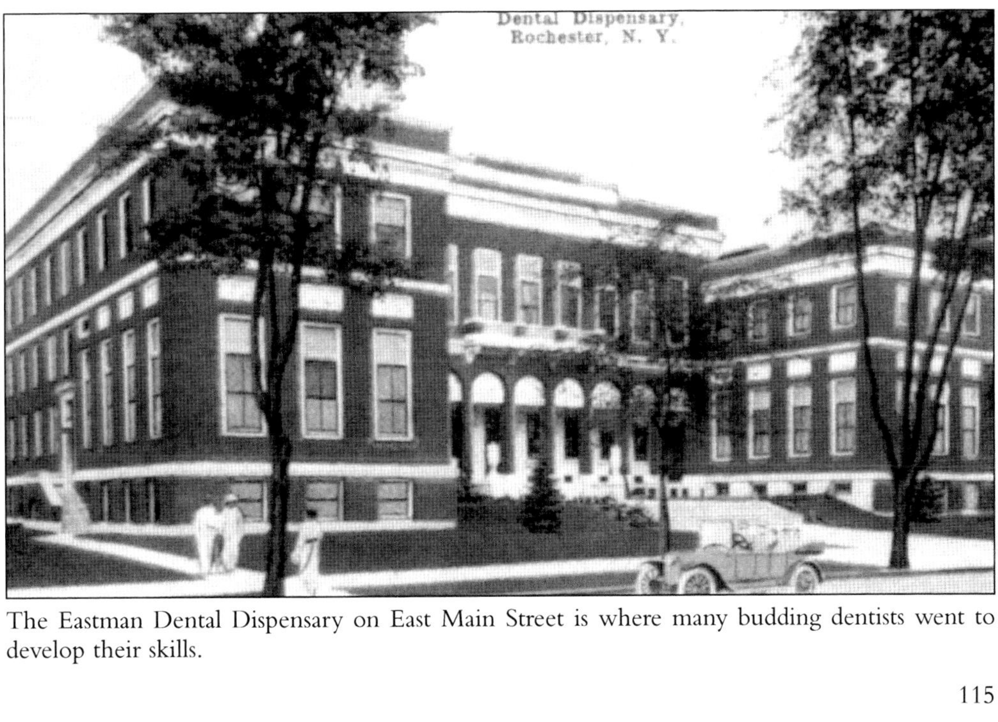

The Eastman Dental Dispensary on East Main Street is where many budding dentists went to develop their skills.

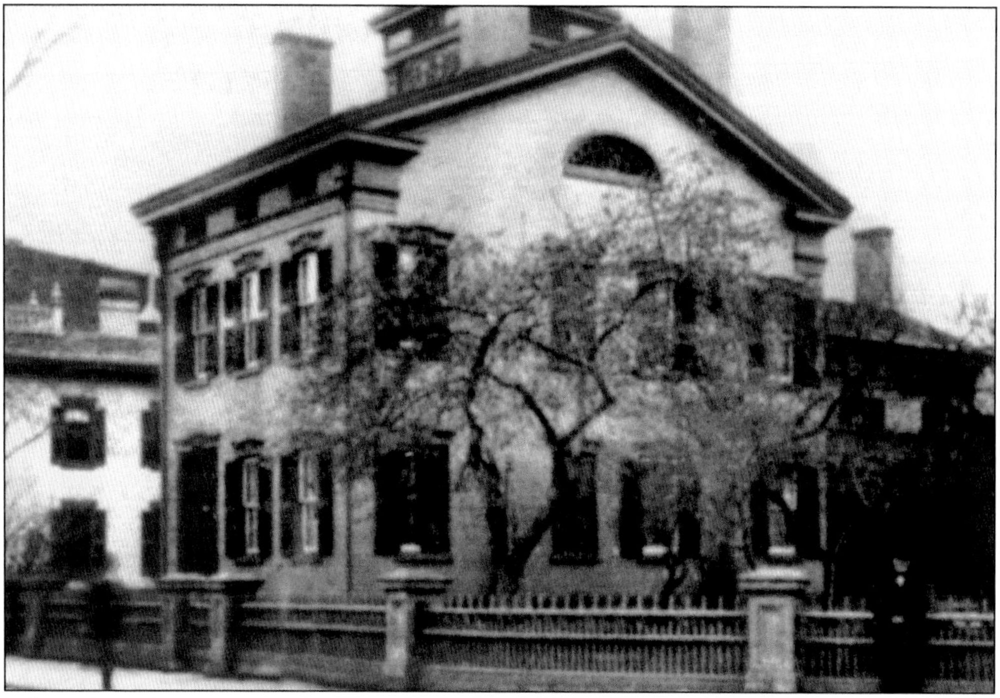

When the Osborne residence was built on the corner of East Main Street and East Avenue, this part of town was still somewhat rural. However, the commercial blocks that grew from the river and canal were not long in reaching this end of town. The house was later used as Security Trust Company's first location when it opened in 1892.

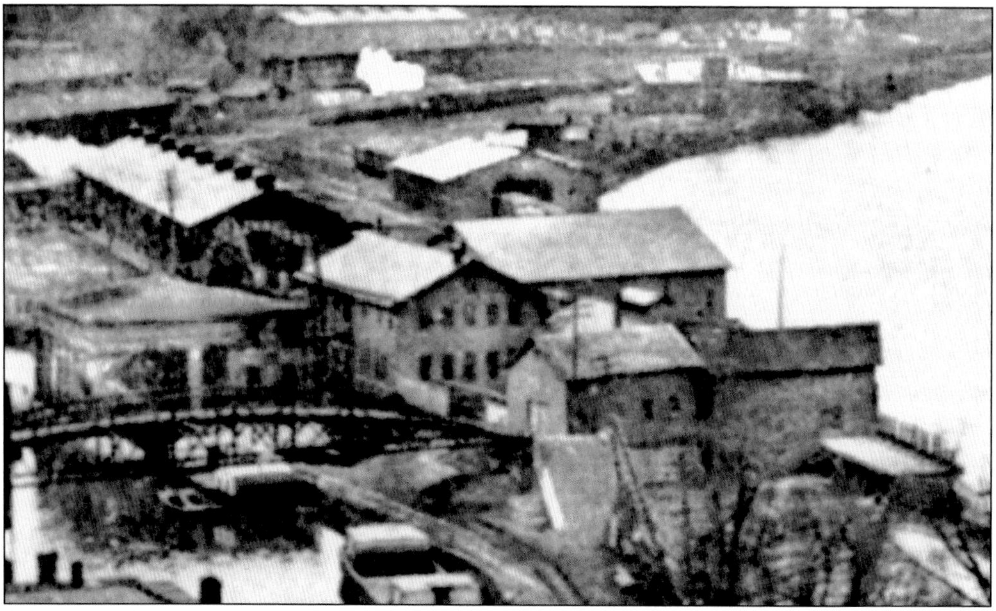

An excerpt from a souvenir image shows the intense level of development along the east bank of the river downtown, *c.* 1900. A barge is moored along the Erie Canal towpath. Beyond the iron bridge is the weight lock where boats were weighed. Further south is a sprawling railroad yard with numerous engine facilities.

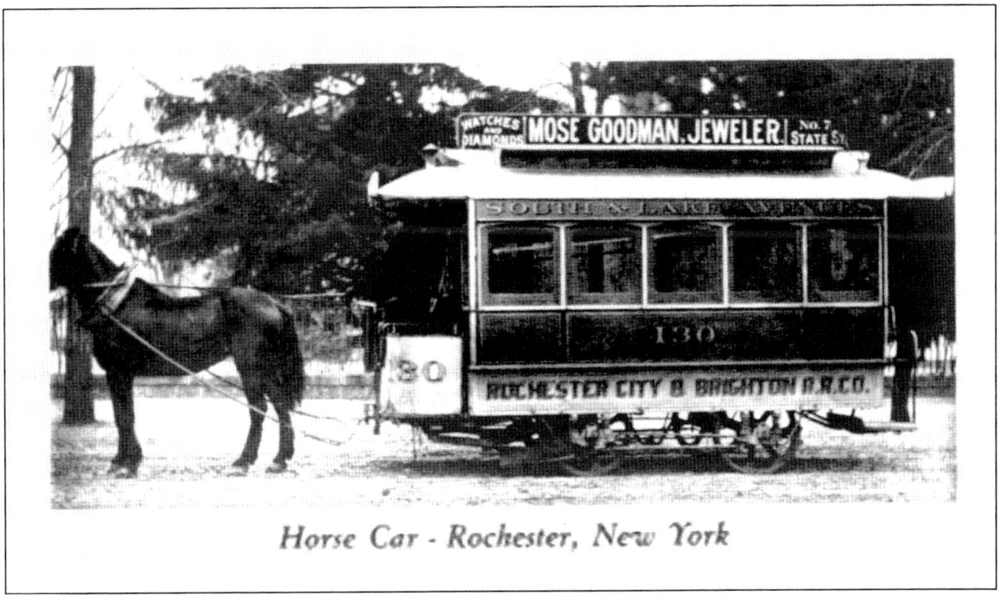

Small horse cars, like this one in a William Gordon postcard, served small neighborhoods. There is a diagonal rail visible through the windows where passengers set their nickels so they could roll to a waiting fare box. Sometimes, boys leaving the car through the rear door would jump up and down on the vestibule platform, causing the car to jump the track.

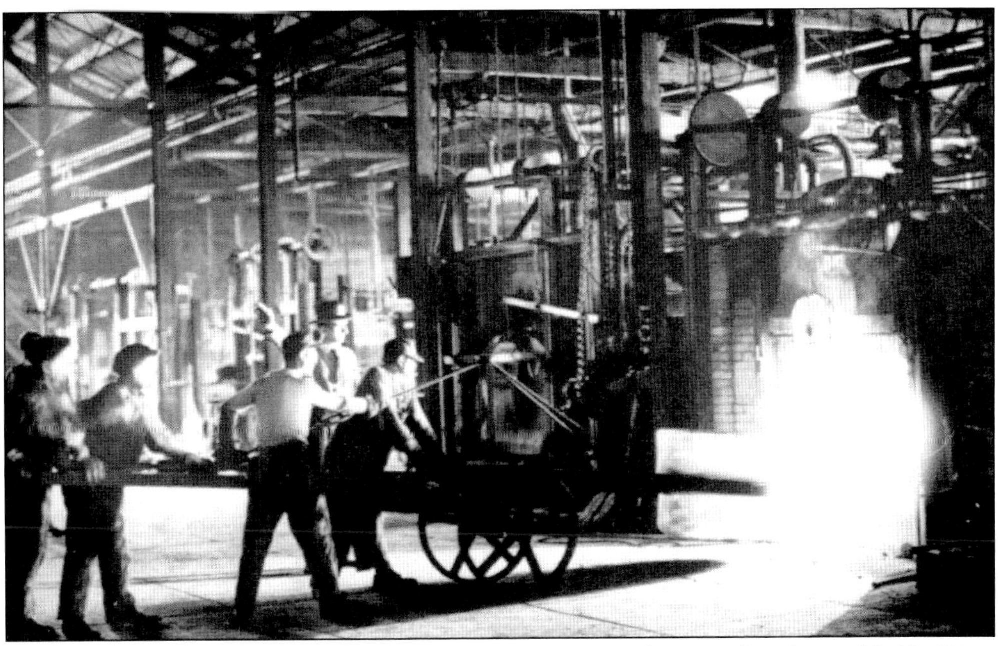

Bausch and Lomb established Rochester as the leading manufacturer of optics worldwide. Here, workers direct a gurney holding a vessel full of glass products into a blast furnace or kiln—all in a day's work.

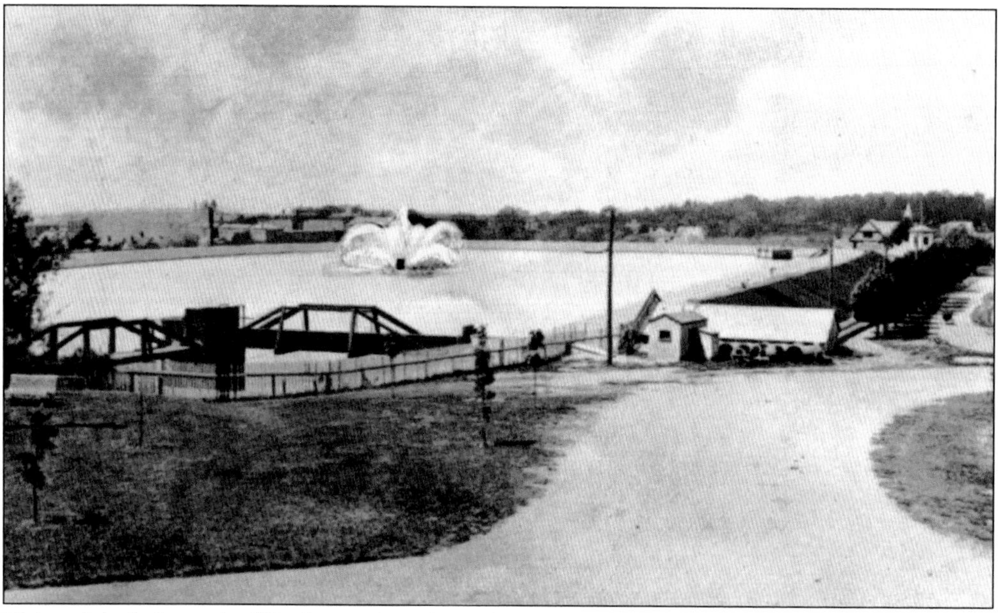

This original *Souvenir of Rochester* view from the reservoir atop Highland Park has been used in numerous postcards. Every one of them has made use of the subtle highlighting of the fountain seen here.

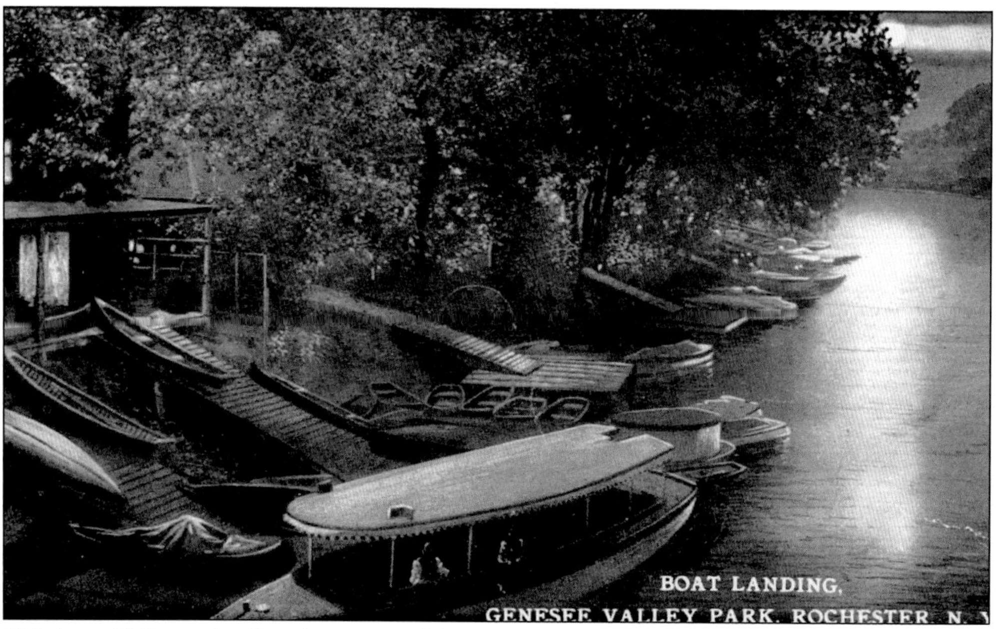

This beautifully rendered night image of the boat landing at Genesee Valley Park was certainly a daylight photograph before the artist went at it with transparent dyes and glazes. The park was a triumph for Olmstead. Genesee Park Boulevard was laid out in a graceful curve to provide an elegant residential entrance to the park.

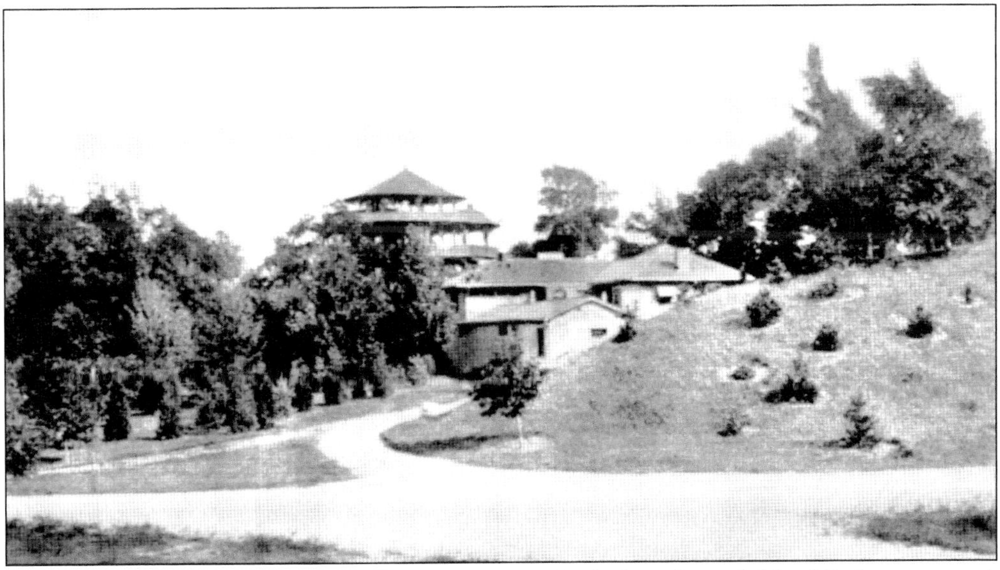

Olmstead had a special affection for the hill around which the infant Highland Park was wound. His use of imported shrubs gave the hill slopes color and visual interest, but it was his use of lilacs that won greatest public approval. Lilac Sunday evolved into the Lilac Festival. It was first just held on one spring Sunday when the lilacs were in bloom. Visitors from around the country would stroll leisurely along the walkways and then listen to band music from the children's pavilion, the circular roof of which is visible here.

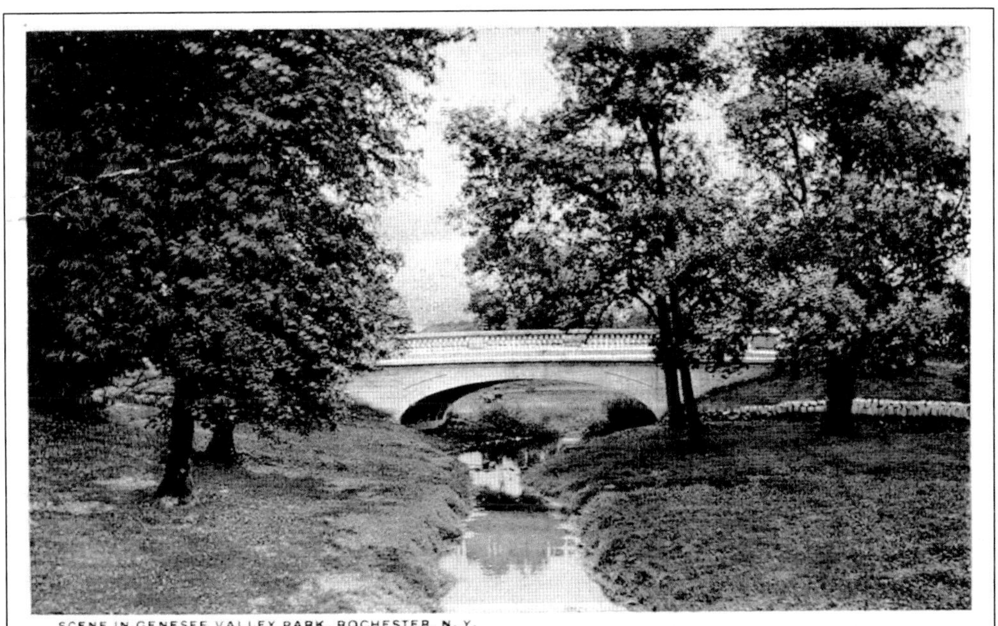

Olmstead made sure Genesee Valley Park had hidden solitudes where families could escape the grind of every day life. Picturesque little bridges like this were found throughout the park.

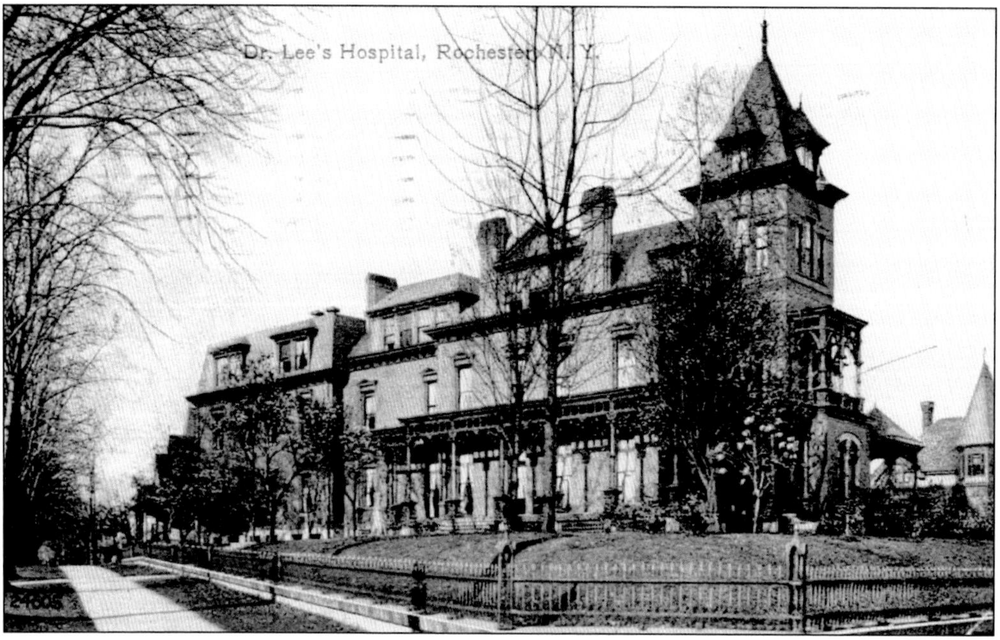

As other hospitals grew, private institutions such as Dr. Lee's Hospital in Rochester were either incorporated into the larger ones or closed. During harsh influenza outbreaks, there were sometimes not enough rooms to handle the sick. Occasionally, the wealthy would take extended vacations and make their large homes available to hospitals during those times.

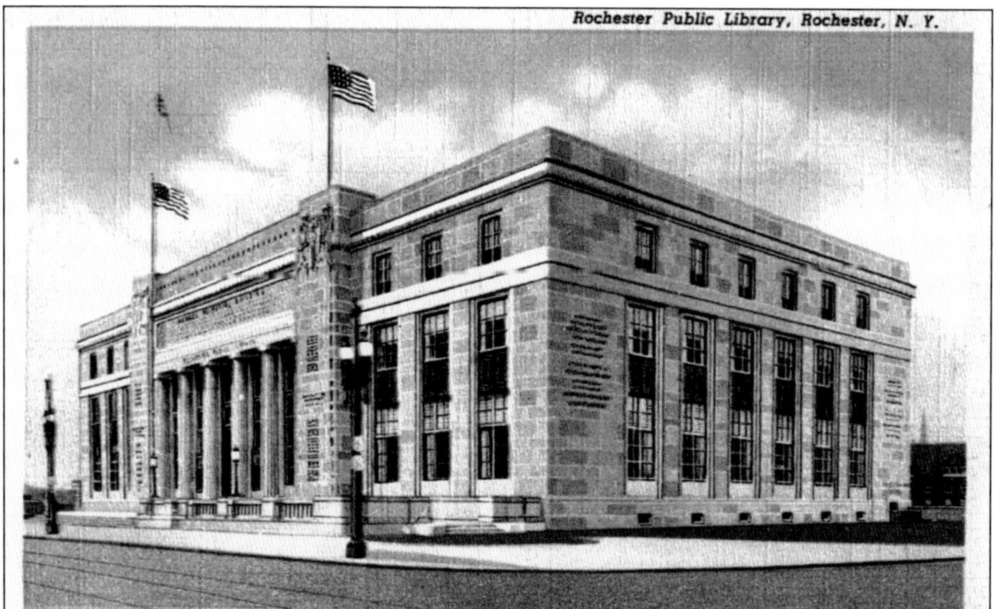

The Rundel Memorial Library was built in the 1930s. Part of the rear is built over a spillway beside the river. Substantial funding for the library was provided by Morton Rundel.

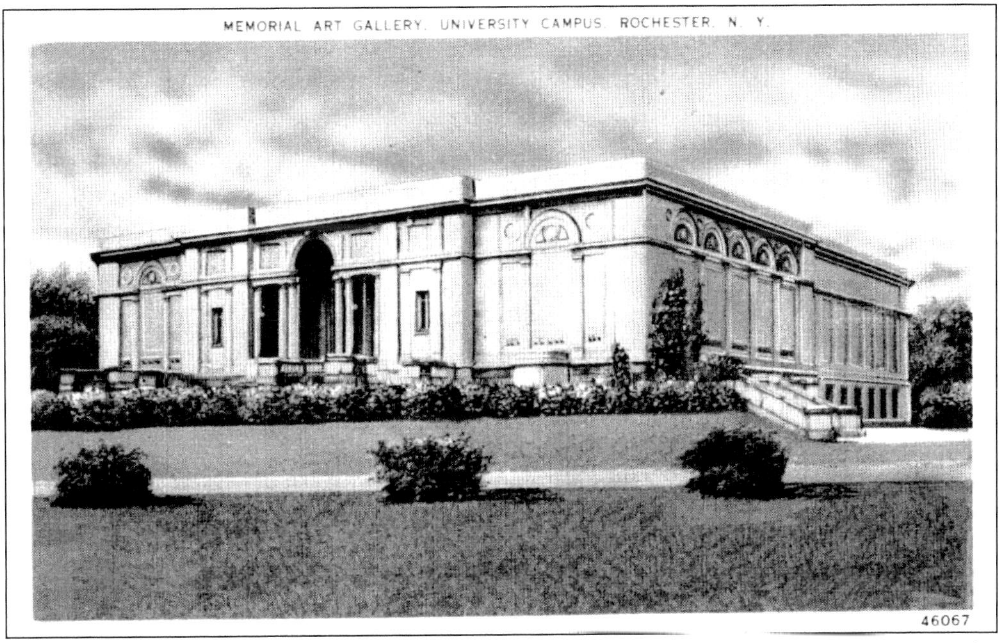

The Memorial Art Gallery on University Avenue was yet another distinguished addition to the region's cultural offerings.

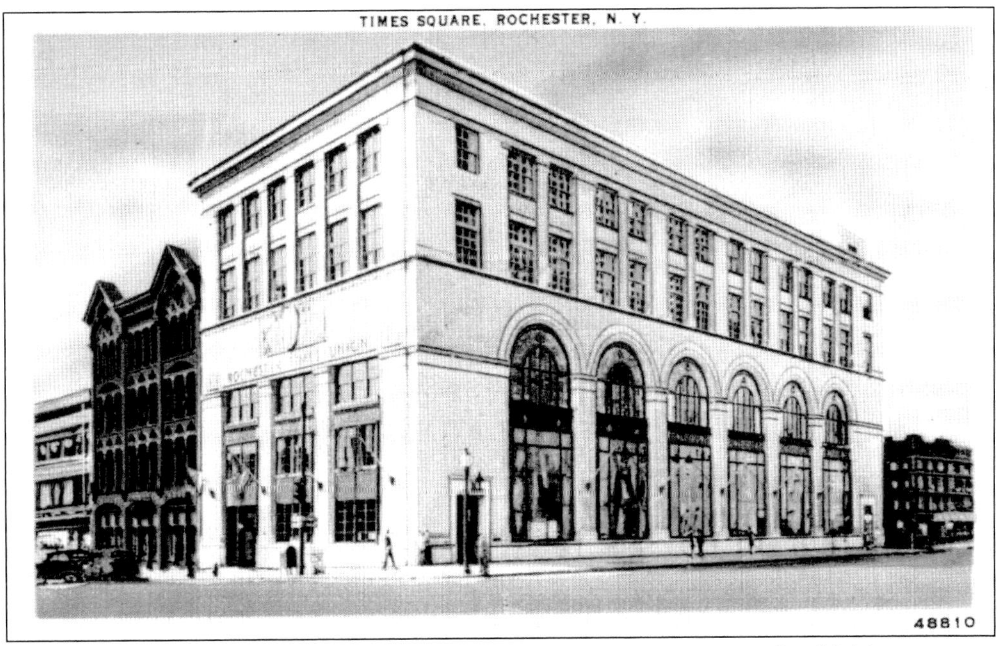

The Times Square Building located downtown housed the empire of publishing magnate Frank E. Gannett for many years. Among his newspapers was the *Times Union,* a superbly written afternoon paper. Many of its reporters went on to larger papers, like the *New York Times* and *Washington Post.* A trip to the city usually included a stop at this building to watch the gigantic presses whirl through the tall windows along the side.

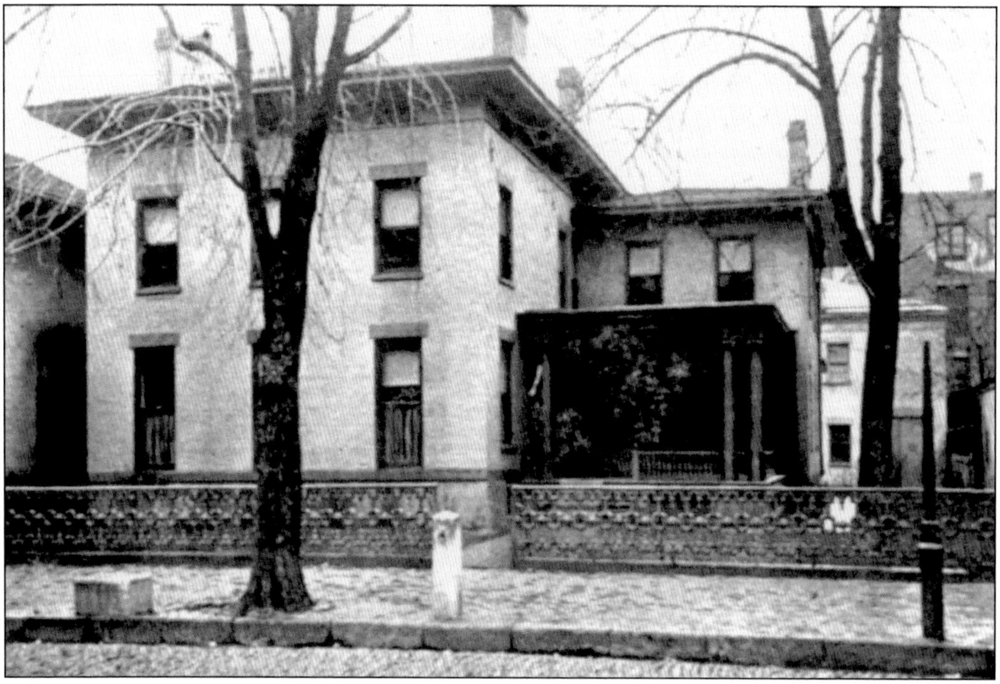

The Rochester Whist Club occupied this house, formerly owned by Dr. Dean, located on North Fitzhugh Street between the government building on Church Street and the Powers Hotel. It is clear that the expanding city quickly gobbled up fine residences like this one. Note the press of commercial buildings behind it. Homeowners left for the more clearly defined neighborhoods.

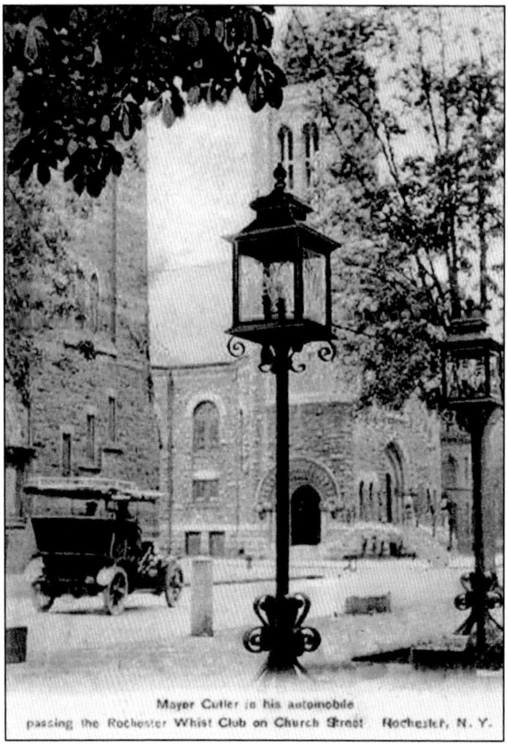

The stone streets and buildings of this government enclave echo with the clattering of Mayor Cutler's automobile as it passes the Rochester Whist Club on Church Street. Whist was a card game, a forerunner of bridge.

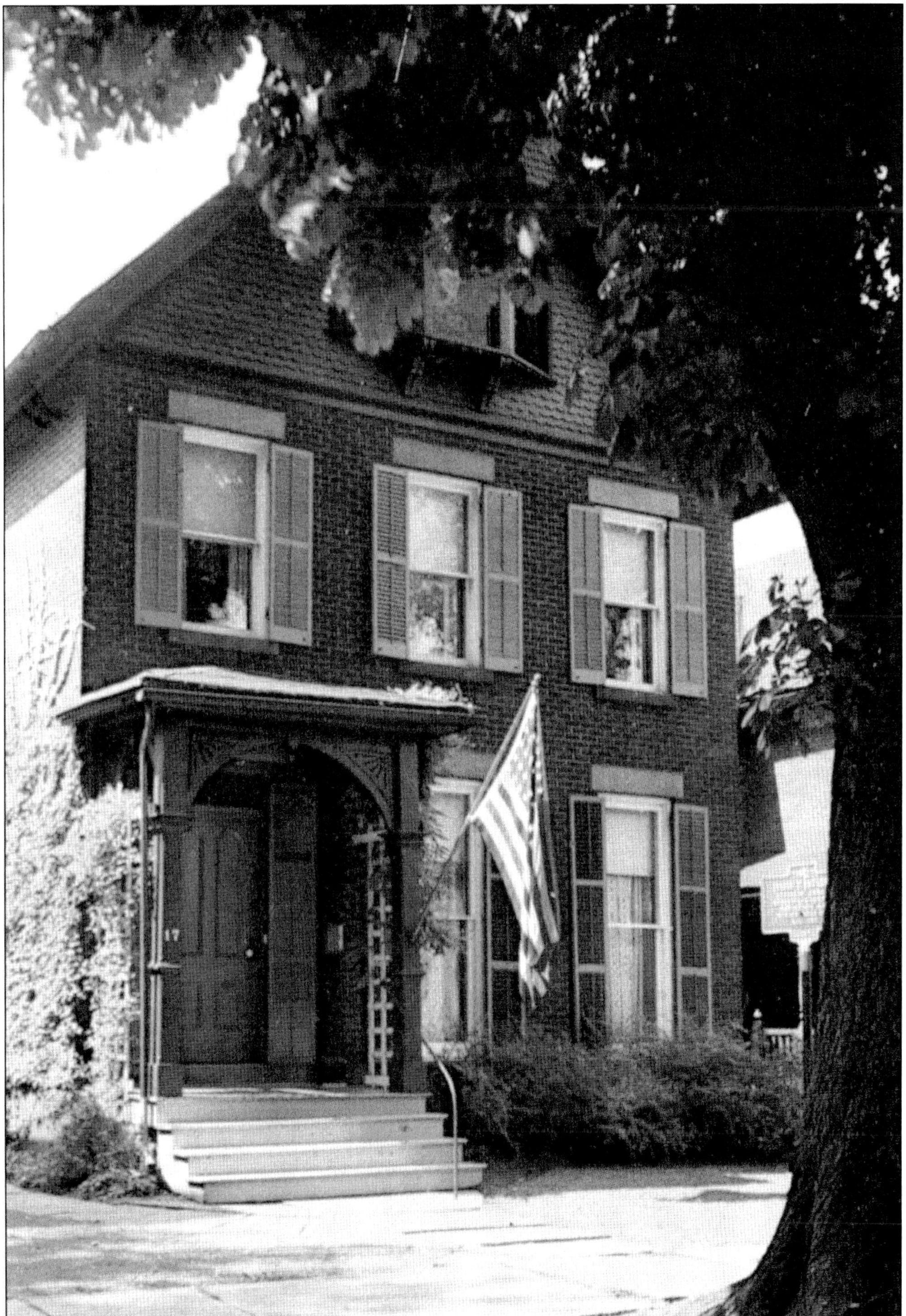

The Susan B. Anthony House is located at 17 Madison Street. It was home to the great women's suffrage leader for 40 years.

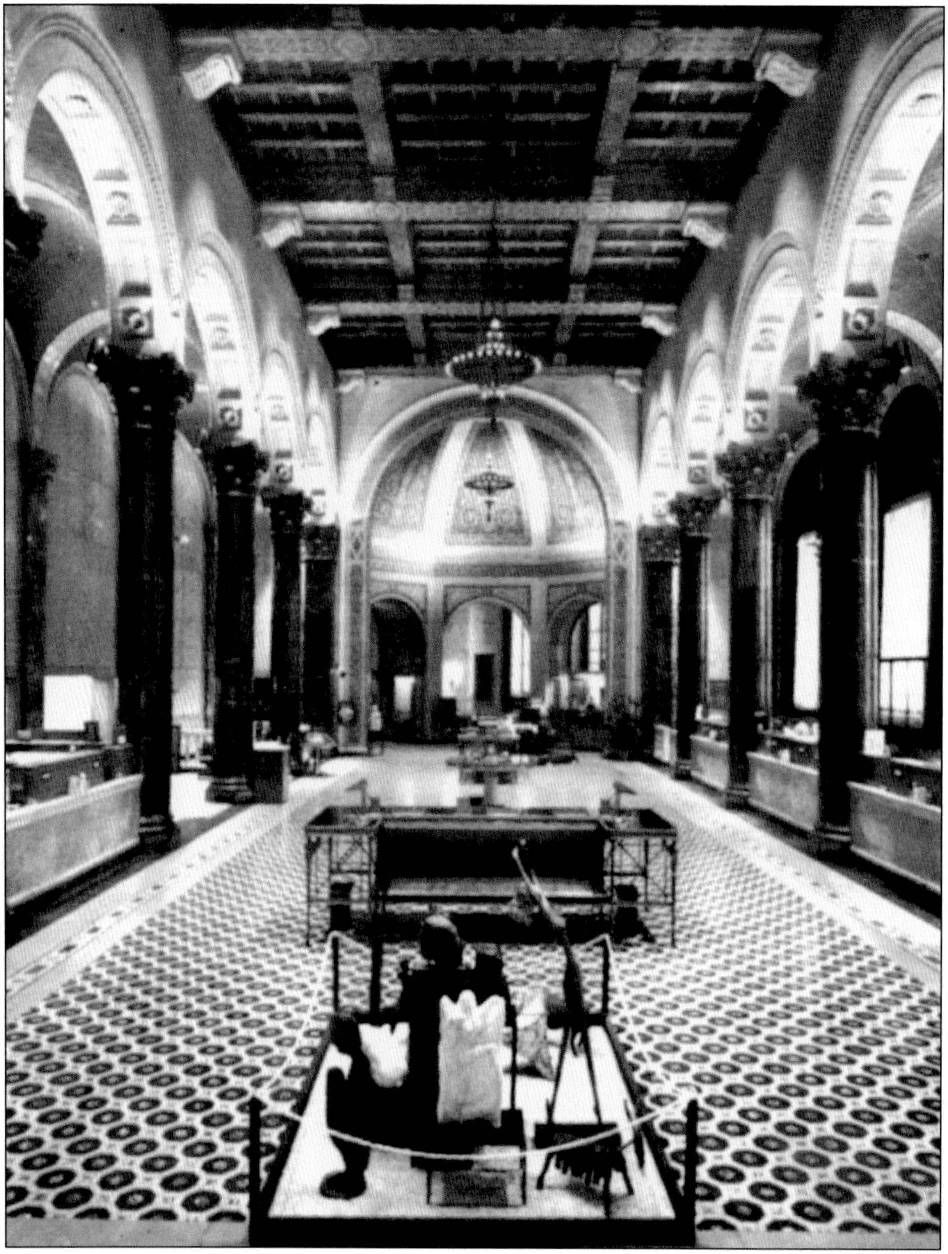

Souvenir views of Rochester Savings Bank are much prized because they picture what many consider to be the most beautiful interior in Monroe County. The building on Franklin Street opened in 1928 and was built by the same firm that built George Eastman's mansion. Eastman worked for the bank before starting his own photograph business. Every square inch of this interior, built like an ancient basilica, sparkles with mosaics, metals, and marbles. The mosaic encrusted arches supported by large rouge marble columns, together with the applications of Botticino and Sienna marbles, surround customers with a deep richness. A beautiful allegorical glass mosaic on the north wall, made at the Ravenna studios in Berlin, features an appropriate motto not just for the bank but also for the city that gave it rise; it reads, "Industry and Thrift are the Foundations of Prosperity."

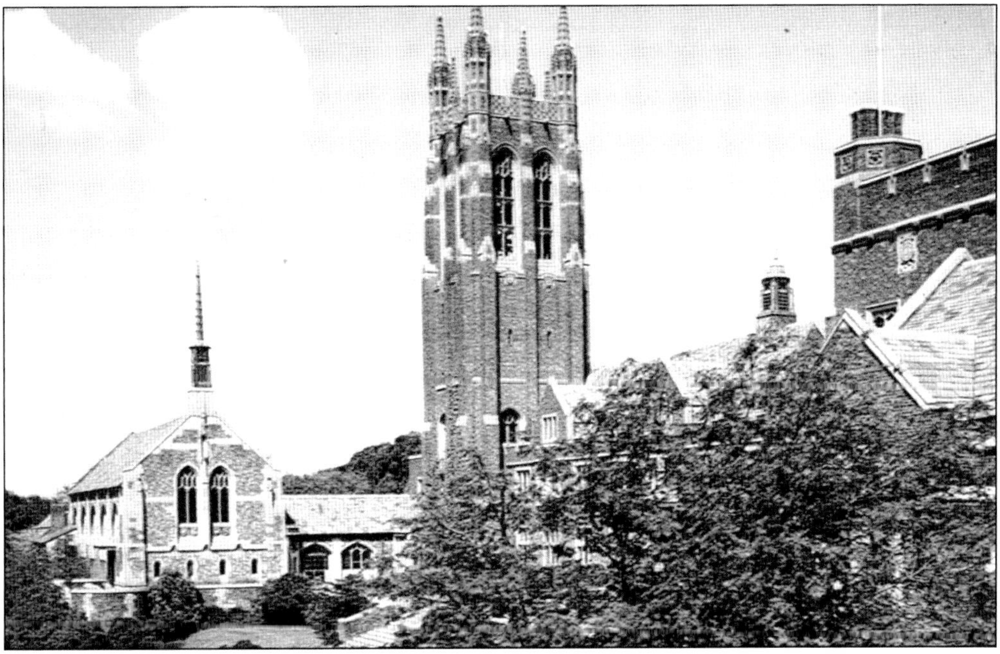

Colgate Rochester Divinity School on South Goodman Street is a graduate school of theology for the training of ministers for Baptist churches and other denominations. The bell tower, visible from Highland Park, was often called the "million-dollar view."

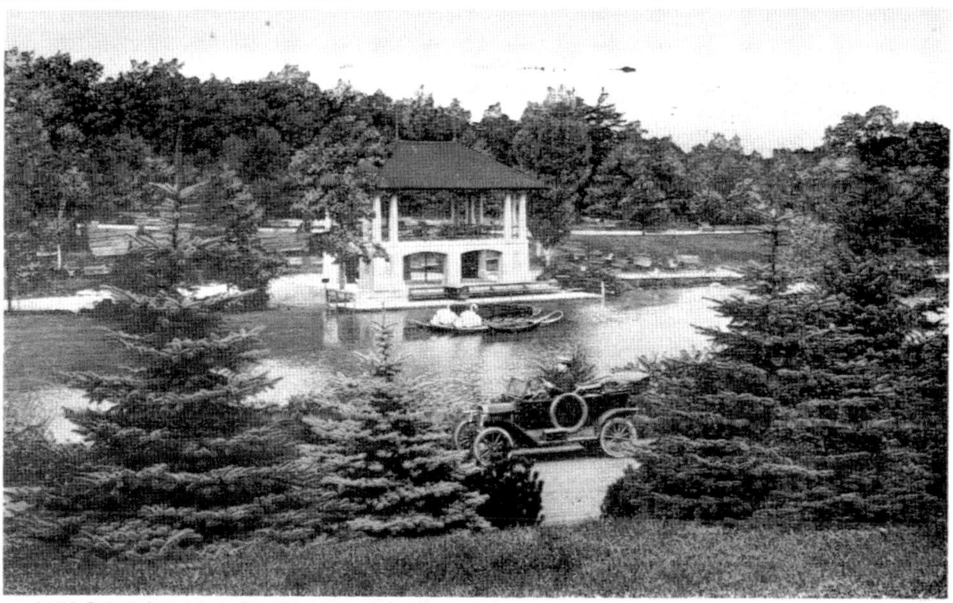

BAND STAND AND LAKE, SENECA PARK, ROCHESTER, N. Y.

This card captures the beauty of Olmstead's Seneca Park. A ride around Trout Lake on the Swan Boat was a favorite attraction. In the spring, the bandstand would fill with music while children danced around the Maypole.

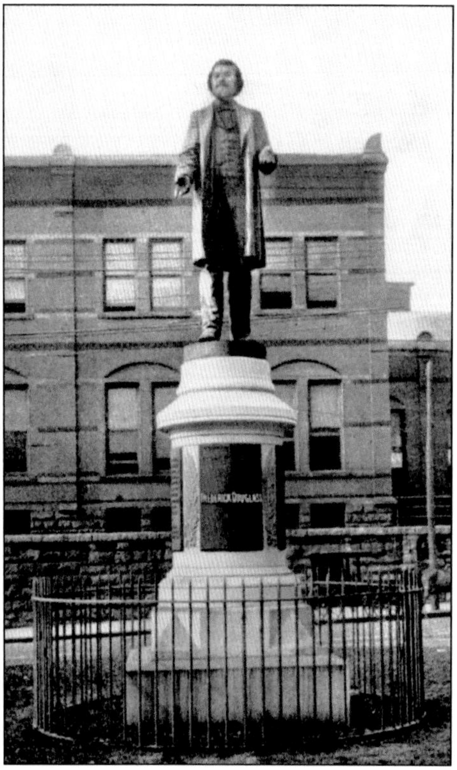

Frederick Douglass was the most famous black leader of his time, and Rochesterians memorialized his activism with this statue. He elevated Rochester's antislavery movement to a model for the rest of the nation. His newspaper, first the *North Star* and then the *Frederick Douglass' Paper,* made him our most noted figure abroad. He used his house near Highland Park as a depot on the Underground Railroad. This statue was later moved to Highland Bowl. Douglass is buried at Mount Hope Cemetery.

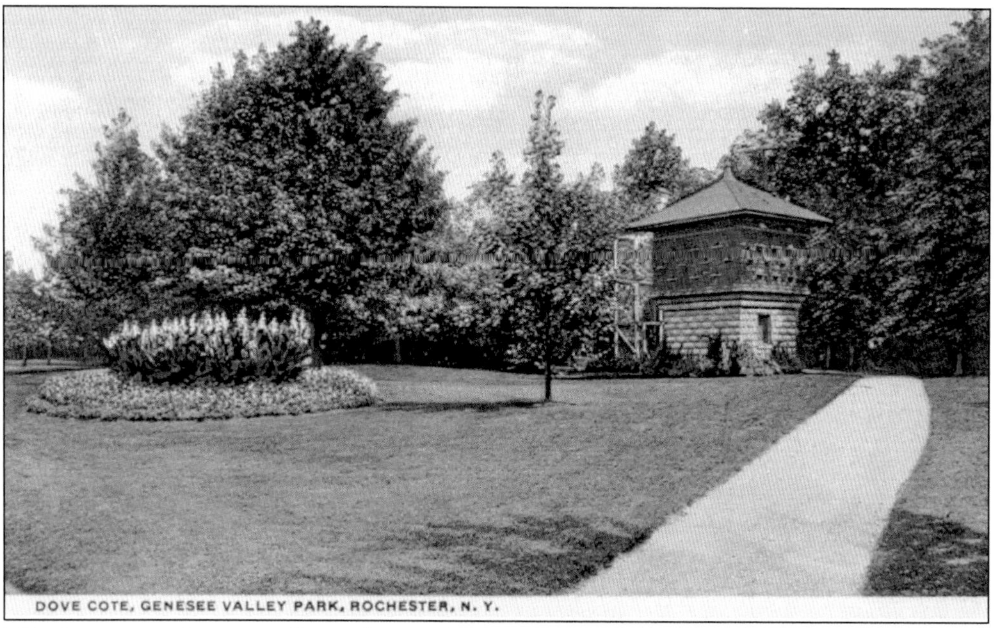

This dovecote at Genesee Valley Park is similar to the blockhouse upriver at Kelsey's Landing, the terminus of the Underground Railroad before the Civil War.

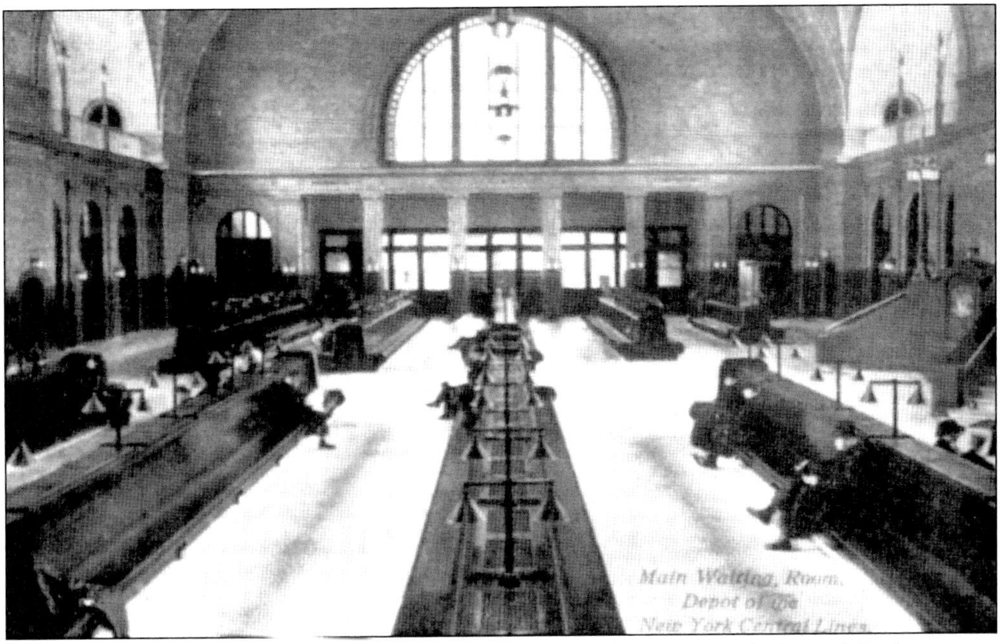

Claude Bragdon made sure that the interior of his masterpiece New York Central Station was as beautiful as its exterior. This is the main waiting room.

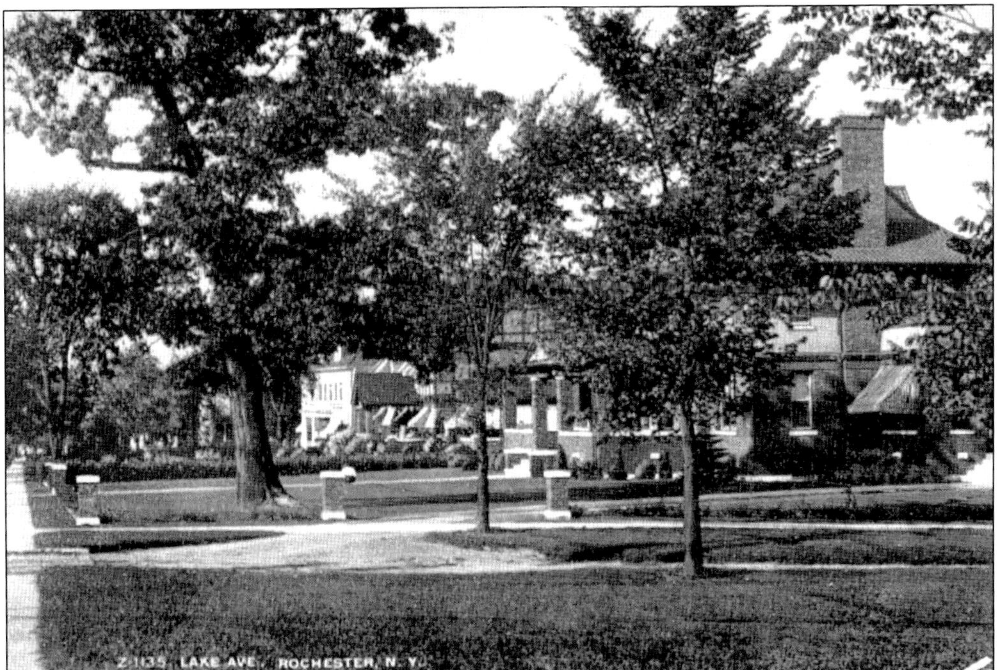

The Lake Avenue subdivisions were filled with some of the city's most impressive homes. Developers sometimes made use of the old flower nurseries when laying out neighborhoods. A lot of thought went into planning the newer avenues, and efforts were made to design them around the natural features of the area. Most older streets evolved from early Seneca trails.

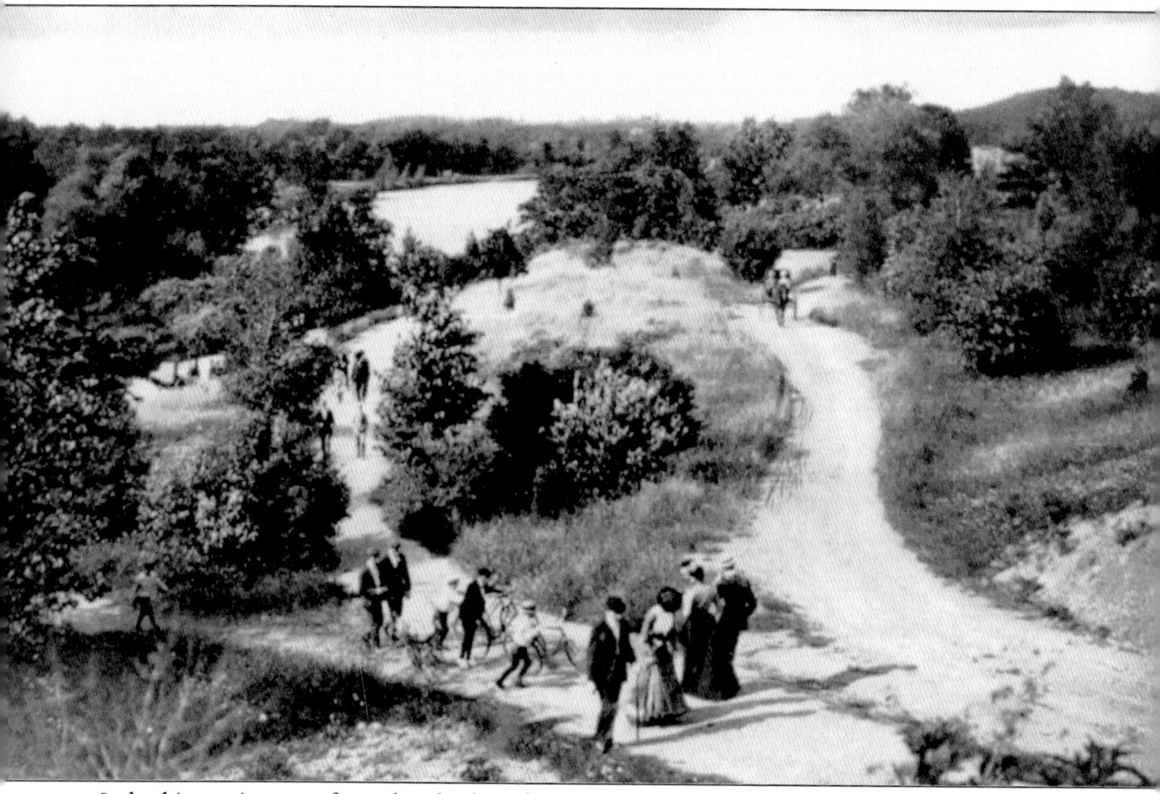

In looking at images of people who have long since gone to the sweet beyond, the inclination to think that their lives were lacking because they were without our modern technologies is natural. Yet they lived, loved, and sorrowed together. They fought for us and confronted the great social issues of our nation with intelligence and poise. When they strolled through beautiful Seneca Park this day, the sun was warm and bright, colors were vivid, birds were singing, and young folk expressed notions of love. Lives speed by like the careless flipping of pages in a forgotten photograph album. We are blessed to have this goodly heritage of photography so ingrained in us. The technology continues to amaze. Now, we can look back in time. Maybe someday we will be able to step back in time—to enter a virtual photograph and touch again the face of someone we miss or step into that sparkling postcard and see the carnival lights, at night, along the midway.